INDUSTRIAL PSYCHOLOGY

INDUSTRIAL PSYCHOLOGY

As per the New Syllabus for B.Tech. II Year of U.P. Technical University

(THIRD EDITION)

Vikram Bisen
Director
ITM School of Management
Lucknow (UP)

Priya
Assistant Professor
School of Management
Babu Banarasi Das, University
Lucknow (UP)

NEW AGE
UPTU

An Imprint of

NEW AGE INTERNATIONAL (P) LIMITED, PUBLISHERS

New Delhi • Bangalore • Chennai • Cochin • Guwahati
Hyderabad • Kolkata • Lucknow • Mumbai
Visit us at **www.newagepublishers.com**

Published by New Age International (P) Ltd., Publishers
First Edition: 2010
Third Edition: 2015

BRANCHES

- **Bangalore** 37/10, 8th Cross (Near Hanuman Temple), Azad Nagar, Chamarajpet Bangalore-560 018, Tel.: (080) 26756823, Telefax: 26756820 **E-mail: bangalore@newagepublishers.com**
- **Chennai** 26, Damodaran Street, T. Nagar, Chennai-600 017, Tel.: (044) 24353401 Telefax: 24351463, **E-mail: chennai@newagepublishers.com**
- **Cochin** CC-39/1016, Carrier Station Road, Ernakulam South, Cochin-682 016 Tel.: (0484) 2377303, Telefax: 4051303 **E-mail: cochin@newagepublishers.com**
- **Guwahati** Hemsen Complex, Mohd. Shah Road, Paltan Bazar, Near Starline Hotel Guwahati-781 008 Tel.: (0361) 2513881, Telefax: 2543669 **E-mail: guwahati@newagepublishers.com**
- **Hyderabad** 105, 1st Floor, Madhiray Kaveri Tower, 3-2-19, Azam Jahi Road, Near Kumar Theater Nimboliadda, Kachiguda, Hyderabad-500 027, Tel.: (040) 24652456 Telefax: 24652457 **E-mail: hyderabad@newagepublishers.com**
- **Kolkata** RDB Chambers (Formerly Lotus Cinema) 106A, 1st Floor, S N Banerjee Road Kolkata-700 014 Tel.: (033) 22273773, Telefax: 22275247 **E-mail: kolkata@newagepublishers.com**
- **Lucknow** 16-A, Jopling Road, Lucknow-226 001, Tel.: (0522) 2209578, 4045297 Telefax: 2204098, **E-mail:lucknow@newagepublishers.com**
- **Mumbai** 142C, Victor House, Ground Floor, N.M. Joshi Marg, Lower Parel Mumbai-400 013, Tel.: (022) 24927869, Telefax: 24915415 **E-mail: mumbai@newagepublishers.com**
- **New Delhi** 22, Golden House, Daryaganj, New Delhi-110 002 Tel.: (011) 23262368, 23262370, Telefax: 43551305 **E-mail: sales@newagepublishers.com**

ISBN: 978-81-224-3874-1

₹ 150.00

C-14-10-8018

Printed in India at R. K. Printers, Delhi.
Typeset at In House, Delhi.

PUBLISHING GLOBALLY
NEW AGE INTERNATIONAL (P) LIMITED, PUBLISHERS
7/30 A, Daryaganj, New Delhi - 110002
Visit us at **www.newagepublishers.com**

PREFACE

It is really a matter of great pleasure to bring out the present revised third edition of Industrial Psychology. Two new chapters, namely, Engineering Psychology and Interview have also been added in the present edition to make it more useful to the students pursuing various undergraduate and post-graduate course. The new edition of this book is now spread over twenty one chapters, each having a number of sections and sub-sections for the better and logical understanding of the subject by the student.

We are confident that the book will meet all your requirement and come up to your expectation.

We shall eagerly await your response. Do write back. Do communicate what you feel about it.

Authors

SYLLABUS

NHU-301/NHU-401: INDUSTRIAL PSYCHOLOGY

UNIT-I

Introduction to Industrial Psychology—Definitions and Scope. Major influences on Industrial Psychology—Scientific Management and Human relations—Hawthorne Experiments. Implications of Industrial Psychology on Modern Industries.

UNIT-II

Individual in Workplace

Motivation and job satisfaction, Stress management. Organizational culture, Leadership and Group dynamics.

UNIT-III

Work Environment and Engineering Psychology—Fatigue, Monotony, Boredom, Accidents and Safety. Job analysis, Recruitment, Selection and Interview—Reliability and Validity of recruitment tests.

UNIT-IV

Performance Management: Training and Development.

CONTENTS

CHAPTER 1

INDUSTRIAL PSYCHOLOGY

1.1 Introduction

Industrial psychology is that branch of applied psychology that is concerned with efficient management of an industrial labour force and especially with problems encountered by workers in a mechanized environment. The time was gone when the workers treated as machine and employers always think about the higher production at any cost or without taking consideration of workers'. Now, management better knows if the workers' feel ease/ comfortable then they give their maximum contribution. There are some other factors then wages which directly affect the performance of individuals. If employers provide adequate working conditions, proper distribution of work, attractive compensation, effective leader etc. then definitely organization achieve its success. In this chapter we define the industrial psychology, their characteristics, scope and historical development.

1.2 Concept and Meaning

Industrial psychology is concerned with people's work-related values, attitudes and behaviours, and how these are influenced by the conditions in which they work. The term 'Industrial Psychology' is a combination of two words 'Industrial' and 'Psychology'. Industrial is that part of social life whose function is to provide civilized man with the material goals that his condition of life demand. Psychology is the science of behaviour in relation to environment. Thus industrial psychology is the systematic study of the behaviour of the people at work. It studies how the social, industrial, economic, political and other factors affect the behaviour of the people at work.

According to **C.S. Myres**, 'The aim of industrial psychology is primarily not to obtain greater production or output but to give the worker greater ease at his work'.

According to **Thomas W. Harrell**, 'Industrial psychology may be defined as the study of people as individuals and in groups and of the relationship between individual and group'.

'Industrial psychology is simply the application or extension of psychology facts and principles to the problem concerning human beings operating within the context of business and industry', says Blum and Naylor.

According to **Tiffin and McCormick**, 'Industrial psychology is concerned with the study of human behaviour in those aspects of life that are related to production, distribution and use of goods and services of our civilization'.

'The scientific study of the relationship between man and the world at work: The study of adjustment people make to the place they go, the people they meet and the things they do in the process of making a living', says Guion.

1.3 Characteristics of Industrial Psychology

- Systematic study—Industrial psychology is the systematic study of human behaviour concerned with collecting the information regarding human behaviour at work. What are the different factors which affect the work of an individual either they are personal or related to working conditions.
- Research—Industrial psychology is not concerned with administration. They are the part of the research. Whatever information gathered from the work should be implemented and the personnel administration is the application of such research.
- Functional/Applied—It is concerned with the application of information about human behaviour to the various problems of industrial human life.
- Human engineering—It studies the varied methods of performing manual operations for the better utilization and the least waste of effort through human engineering.

1.4 Scopes of Industrial Psychology

- Scientific selection of workers'—Industrial psychology offers a whole arrangement of tests such as systematic depth interviews and psychological tests of intelligence, aptitude, skills, abilities and interest the personnel characteristic etc. By these tests candidates are measured and properly selected and placed on the job.
- Proper division of work—One of the scopes of industrial psychology is the work should be properly divided according to the abilities, skills and aptitude of the workers so they may feel comfortable and satisfied. It may also lead higher production.
- Minimizing the wastage of human efforts—Industrial psychology tries to minimize the wastage of human power. It studies psychological factors causing fatigue or accident and give feasible suggestions to prevent them. The techniques of motivation and morale are used for this purpose.

- Promoting labour welfare—It promotes the welfare of the labour by introducing adequate working environment through which job satisfaction, work efficiency increases and also state the provisions of higher incentives.
- Enhancement of human relations—Human relations are the relation among individuals in an organization and the group behaviour that emerge from their relations. Most of problems arise in the industries are connected to human relation. If workers' feel ease with the surrounding then automatically they get motivated and productivity will be higher. Industrial psychology has made significant contribution in framing the techniques of leadership, worker participation, communication etc.
- Developing industrial relations—Industrial psychology studies the attitude of the employer and employees. Individuals differ from each others in their thoughts, thinking, behaviour and other parameters. Therefore, different measures may be adopted in solving the problem relating to each individual like transfers, promotions, grievances etc. This helps in developing industrial relationship among workers' and management.
- Increase production—It helps in attaining the major objective of the organization that to get the best output from the existing resources. The production is automatically increased if proper selection is made, the work will be properly distributed, accident prevention and safety measures suggested. This will improve and promote individual as well as industrial relations.

American Psychologist Association, Division of Industrial Psychology, *The psychologist industry*, Washington, D.C., 1959 cited seven major areas which comprised the content area of industrial psychology. These were:

(1) Selection and testing.
(2) Management development.
(3) Counseling.
(4) Employee motivation.
(5) Human engineering.
(6) Marketing research.
(7) Public relations research.

1.5 Historical Development of Industrial Psychology

Bryan & Harter (1897) published a first paper describing the study and application of psychology to work activities (Morse code telegraphic) coined the term "industrial psychology" by mistake.

During the First and Second World War when various industrial organizations and plants faced a number of problems related to production, efficiency and individual employees, the help of industrial psychologist are in great demand. At this stage, industrial psychology received a special status, although it began in America in 1901, and England soon after.

The first book, "The Psychology of Industrial Efficiency", written by Hugo Munsterberg in 1913 was dealing with various problems faced by the industries and analysis of such problem from the psychological point of view. During the war years, the Fatigue Research Board was organized in Great Britain to discover the problems connected with working hours, condition of work, problems associated with fatigue and monotony/boredom, accident and safety measures and other work related matters.

In 1925, social psychology of industry entered into the arena of industrial psychology therefore, interpersonal and intrapersonal relationships, theories of motivations, importance of communication and other associated areas were investigated.

In 1917, Journal of applied psychology made its appearance and at the same time it introduced as a subject of applied psychology.

The classical studies, started in 1927 by the famous Hawthorne group, contributed to the development of industrial psychology in a major way. Their finding ultimately changed the trends and approach of industrial psychology from economic to social , from the work-oriented attitude to a workers-oriented attitude.

During the Second World War, the applied psychology research unit of the Medical Research Council of Great Britain carried out several researches and investigations to solve many industrial and organizational problems.

American Association of Applied Psychology, 1937 was the first association for industrial psychology. Major organization after the Second World War divided into two parts.

Human factor society, it was associated with the American group of applied psychology with interest in human engineering problem. **Ergonomics society**, it was British counterpart of human factor. Society occupational psychology and ergonomics are two journals.

Considerable attention was focussed on various human relations and social problems of industry during the later part of 1940's and in the 1950's. Problems related to supervision, group dynamics, leadership, employees' interaction with others, employees attitude, morale, job satisfaction, communication process and others.

In the beginning of the 1960's organizational psychology began to enter the area of industrial psychology and as such, special emphasis was given to the organizational inputs in the industrial situation.

The psychologists who have made valuable contributions to the development of industrial psychology are Walter, Dill and Scott. The industrial psychology division of American Psychological Association was established in 1945 and gave professional recognition to industrial psychology.

Though industrial psychology was a neglected branch of applied psychology in India. After the Second World War and particularly after Independence, it got special recognition from Indian psychologists. With the establishment of various universities, centre and institutes in India, research in industrial psychology has been accelerated after 1950's.

In 1970's, the division of industrial psychology was renamed as the division of industrial and organizational psychology. An eminent industrial and organizational psychologist of India Professor Durganand Sinha (1971) has made a valuable survey of the important topics of research in industrial psychology in India.

1.6 Implications of Industrial Psychology on Modern Industries

In today's competitive environment industrial psychologist play a quite important role for the betterment of employees as well as industries. They play a vital role in reducing stress, anxiety, monotony, boredom, fatigue etc. and increasing motivation, morale, job satisfaction among employees. Now a day it becomes an essential element of industrial work. By achieving these objectives an industry can grow and survive fates as compared to others. Industrial psychologists had shifted their attention and interest from physical environment of work situation to the scientific and clinical studies of individual who work in these settings. These are the following implications of industrial psychology in modern industries:

- Technological changes in workplace create division of labour and automation of work. Work has become more mechanical, uninteresting and monotonous. To overcome that problems psychologists need to analyse the causes and suggest measures to reduce them.
- Human engineering includes designing machines as per the capabilities of average individuals or workers so that they can perform their works easily and efficiently. Industrial psychologies provide an opportunity to industries how to maximize their productivity.
- As we always talk about the efficiency and capabilities of workers towards their job. One of the most important implications of industrial psychology on modern industries is recruitment and selection. Industrial psychology deals adequate process of recruitment and selection by which modern industries recruit and select employees as per their capability and industries requirement, which also helps in reducing absenteeism and employee's turnover.
- Human engineering reduces the chance of accidents under industries as this is the obligation of organization to provide safe and healthy environment to their workers. Poor working condition affects employee's performance badly and employees may find it difficult to concentrate on their work.
- In current competitive environment, there is a real need of that system which helps into increase the skills and competencies of employee so that they can improve the work performance. This can be done by training and development of employees. Industrial psychology provides ample opportunity to enhance the skills and competencies of an employee.
- The structure system of society undergone through various changes. Now, the family gets nuclear where both the parents are working. They had less time for family and friends. There is a need if work life balance which provides ease to employees at workplace as well as home.

❍❍❍

CHAPTER 2

SCIENTIFIC MANAGEMENT

2.1 INTRODUCTION

The Industrial Revolution and the ideas of Adam Smith had transformed the economies of the United States and Western Europe in the 18th Century. Technology and industry might had replaced population and agriculture as the major determinants of national strength. France, rich in population and farmland, had once been the dominant power of Europe. It was now overshadowed by its more industrial rival, Great Britain. And America was emerging as the industrial powerhouse whose factories would swing the outcomes of the century's two world wars.

The factories of the early 20th Century were beginning to look like something that could be reasonably compared to the factories of today, but appearances could be deceiving. Early mass production methods were more efficient than the cottage industry methods of several centuries earlier; but processes were chaotic by today's standards. Despite the fact that large-scale production was taking place in factories that employed hundreds or thousands of employees, worker training was minimal, and sophisticated systems of equipment maintenance, quality assurance, and production control were still decades in the future. The improvement of efficiency in industry is one of the prime objectives of industrial psychology. In every enterprise where goods are produced, increased production at a lower cost has been the main consideration for growth of the enterprise. In particular chapter first we explain the significance of scientific management and then discuss the Taylorism and lastly explain briefly time-motion study.

2.2 SCIENTIFIC MANAGEMENT SCHOOL

Frederick Winslow Taylor devised a system he called scientific management, a form of industrial engineering that established the organization of work as in Ford's assembly line. This discipline, along with the industrial psychology established by others at the Hawthorne Works of Western Electric in the 1920s, moved management theory from early time-and-motion studies to the latest total quality control ideas.

Scientific management theory arose in part from the need to increase productivity. In the United States especially, skilled labour was in short supply at the beginning of the 20th century. The only way to expand the productivity was to raise the efficiency of workers. Therefore, Frederick W. Taylor, Henry Gantt, and Frank and Lillian Gilbreth devised the body of principles known as scientific management theory.

Scientific management (also called Taylorism or the Taylor system) is a theory of management that analyzes and synthesizes workflows, with the objective of improving labour productivity. The core ideas of the theory were developed by Frederick Winslow Taylor in the 1880s and 1890s, and were first published in his monographs, *Shop Management* (1905) and *The Principles of Scientific Management* (1911). Taylor believed that decisions based upon tradition and rules of thumb should be replaced by precise procedures developed after careful study of an individual at work. Its application is contingent on a high level of managerial control over employee work practices.

Taylor was a foreman for the Midvale Steel Company in Philadelphia from 1878 to 1890. Early in his management career, Taylor observed that the workers under his supervision engaged in soldiering—the practice of deliberately working slower than one's capabilities. Because the management of Midvale Steel had little real knowledge about the jobs performed in the plant, the practice went mostly undetected.

Taylor (1986–1915) rested his philosophy on four basic principles.

1. The development of a true science of management instead of rule of thumb so that the best method for performing each task could be determined.
2. The scientific selection of workers so that each worker's would be given responsibility for the task for which he or she was best suited.
3. The scientific education and development of workers.
4. Intimate friendly cooperation between management and labour.

Taylor contended that the success of these principles require "a complete mental revolution" on the part of management and labour. Rather than quarrel over profits both side should increase production, by so doing, he believed profits would rise to such an extent that labour have to fight over them. Employers to pay more productive workers higher rate than others. Using a "scientifically correct" rate that would benefit both the company and workers. Thus the workers were urged to surpass their previous performance standards to earn more pay. Taylor called his plan the differential rate system. Taylor believed that management and labour had common interest in increasing productivity.

- Taylor based his management system on production line time studies. Instead of relying on traditional work methods, he analyzed and timed steel workers movements on a series of jobs.
- Using time study he broke each job down into its components and designed the quickest and best method of performing each component. In this way he established.

LIMITATIONS OF SCIENTIFIC MANAGEMENT THEORY

Although Taylor's method led to dramatic increase in productivity and higher pay in number of instance. Workers and unions began to oppose his approach because they feared that working harder or faster would exhaust whatever work was available causing layoffs.

Individuals are different from each other the most efficient way of working for one person may be inefficient for another.

Moreover, Taylor's system clearly meant that time was of the essence. His critics objected to the speed up condition that placed undue pressure on employees to perform at faster and faster levels.

The emphasis on productivity and by extension profitability led some managers to exploit both the workers and customers. As a result more workers joined unions and thus reinforced a pattern of suspicious and mistrust that shaded labour relations for decades.

Scientific management practices led to improvements in the consistency and efficiency of workplace processes. However, scientific management practices were also criticized for making jobs more monotonous. Attempts by management to implement scientific management practices sometimes resulted in backlashes. Workers particularly resented the use of stopwatches.

HENRY L. GANNT

Henry L. Gannt (1861–1919) worked with Taylor on several projects but when he went out on his own as a consulting industrial engineer, Gannt began to reconsider Taylor's insensitive systems. Abandoning the differential rate system as having too little motivational impact Gannt came up with new idea.

- Every worker who finished days assigned work load win 50 per cent bonus.
- Then he added a second motivation, the supervisor would earn a bonus for each worker who reached the daily standard.
- Plus an extra bonus if all the workers reached it.
- This Gantt reasoned would spur superviser to train their workers to do a better job.
- Every workers progress was rated publicly and recorded in individual bar charts. On the basis of this chart they are rewarded.

THE GILBRETHS

A time and motion study (or time-motion study) is a business efficiency technique combining the Time Study work of Frederick Winslow Taylor with the Motion Study work of Frank and Lillian. Gilbreth Frank B. and Lillian M.Gilbreth (1968–1924) and (1878–1972) made their contribution to the scientific management movement as a husband and wife team. Lillian and Franck collaborated on fatigue and motion studies and focus on ways on promoting the individual workers welfare to them. The ultimate aim of scientific management was to help workers reach their full potential as human beings. In their conception motion and fatigue were intertwined every motion that was eliminated reduced fatigue. Using motion picture cameras they tried to find out the most economical motions for each task in order to upgrade performance and reduce fatigue.

❍❍❍

CHAPTER 3

THE HAWTHORNE STUDIES

3.1 INTRODUCTION

Most of the thoughts which were come from earlier studies are shown that, organization paid more attention on the amount of production. And for this reason organization paid more wages to their workers'. But gradually it was realized that by giving high wages production will never goes high. There are some other non-material factors which influence employees to work hard and made more production. In simple words, people do not always work for money alone.

Thus the industrial psychology, according to Blum (1956), "tries for other means by which the workers can be bribed to work, some of which are excellent ideas, other merely an insult to intelligence". Now, many psychologists (industrial and social) were trying to find out the other factors which were not associated with money. In this chapter we discuss the Hawthorne experiment in detail.

3.2 HAWTHORNE STUDIES

The Hawthorne plant of the General Electric Company, Chicago, faces the problem of workers' dissatisfaction, although they provide material benefits to the workers' like pension schemes, sickness benefits and other recreation facilities which resultant into loss of production. Now, it became necessary a thorough investigation of the problem of low productivity and to find out the relationship between production and various factors of efficiency.

To find out the relationship between productivity and working conditions a number of studies were conducted by Professor Elton Mayo and his researcher team which was started in 1927. **George Elton Mayo** (26 December 1880–7 September 1949) was an Australian psychologist, sociologist and organization theorist. He lectured at the University of Queensland from 1919 to 1923 before moving to the University of Pennsylvania, but spent most of his career at Harvard Business School (1926–1947), where he was professor of industrial research.

The Hawthorne studies consist of four phases and each phase giving the answer to the question arises at the previous phase.

Phase I (1924–27)

Experiment on Illumination—Under this experiment researcher tries to find out how varying levels of illumination affect the efficiency of workers'. The hypothesis was that, with higher illumination productivity increases. They divided workers' into two groups. One was test group, which were undergo environmental changes and second was control group. The members of the control group would work under normal, constant environment condition. The researchers began by manipulating the lighting of the test group. When lighting for the test group was increased, their productivity increased but the productivity of the control group increased, as well. This result was somewhat unexpected, since the lighting at the workstations of the control group had not been altered.

The researchers then decreased the lighting at the test group's workstations. Surprisingly, both the test group and the control group continued to improve their productivity. There were no decrease in productivity until the light was reduced to the point where the workers could barely see. The researchers concluded that light did not have a significant impact on the motivation of production workers. This led General Electric, a light bulb manufacturer, to withdraw their funding.

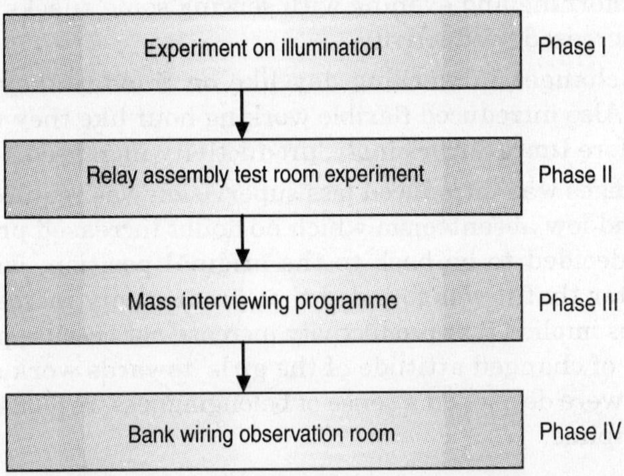

Exhibit 1: Phases of Hawthorne Studies

Phase II (1927–28)

Relay Assembly Test Room Experiment—In this experiment, researcher test the hypothesis that production would be higher if incentive system was improved, and work week become shorter with rest and lunch periods. For this purpose, the researcher set up a relay assembly test room and two experienced workers' were chosen. There experienced workers' were asked to choose four girls as coworkers'. The work related to the assembly of telephone relay, "because it is simple and highly repetitive and require no machinery and permits an accurate measure of production" (Blum and Naylor, 1968).

Each relay consisted of different part which should be assembled into finished product. The result depended on the speed, continuity and co-ordination among these workers' and they are placed under the group piece rate system. One observer was associated with girls to supervise their work and they also consulted girls before any changes. The whole experiment latest from 1927–1932, and were spread over 14 periods in all and experiment started with numerous changes in sequence. Following were the change and their outcomes:

- The incentive system was changed so that each girl's extra pay was based on the group activities of all the members of the small group irrespective of large group.
- With the increasing time of rest periods from five to ten minutes it resultant into increased productivity.
- The time of rest period was reduced to again five minutes but the frequency of rest period increased. It leads to slightly low productivity and girls complained that frequent rest periods affected their flow of work.
- Now the duration of rest periods become ten minutes and they should be only on morning and evening with serving some snacks or tea. It again shows increased productivity.
- Certain changes in working day like on Sunday they announce the holiday. Also introduced flexible working hour like they were allowed to leave before time. Surprisingly, productivity increased.

As changes was introduced less supervision was required, girls morale increased and low absenteeism which no doubt increased productivity. But researcher decided to go back to the original position, with some other benefits. After that it was founded that productivity increased as earlier. The outcomes implied that productivity increase not because positive changes but because of changed attitude of the girls' towards work and their work group. Girls were developed a sense of belongingness, responsibility, stability and self-discipline.

PHASE III (1928–30)

Mass Interviewing Programme—The objective of this experiment is to find out the employees attitudes towards supervisor, company, wages, facilities, promotion, morale etc. and this can be done by mass interview programme. These interviews were conducted by the means of direct and then after indirect questions. The major findings of the mass interview programme are:

- A worker is satisfied or dissatisfied, not in terms of any objective forms of reference but rather in terms of how he regards his social status and what he feels he is entitled to receive by way of rewards.(Brown, J.A.C., *The Social Psychology of Industry*, Pelican Books, p.79)

- In "non-directive" interviews, the interviewer pretends that whatever information they get from workers' were treated as confidential. They trained to listen more and to talk less; they are offering advice in respect of arguments.
- The complaints generally involved an employees' social position in the group in which he worked.

From the mass interview programme, it was discovered that employees' behaviour was being influenced by group behaviour. This result was not very satisfactory and researchers decided to conduct another experiment.

Phase IV (1931–32)

Bank Wiring Observation Room—The main objective of this study is to find out exact information about informal groups in plant and what are the factors or causes which influence output.

A group of three kinds of workers' were engaged in the bank wiring room: wiremen, solder men and inspector, who together constituted a group of 14 (9 wiremen, 3 solder men and two inspectors). The work involved step-by-step fixing of switches for central office equipment. The payment was based on a group performance; it would assume that for this reason they would help each other to produce more. But, workers' decided the target for themselves which was lower than the plant target. The workers' gave following reasons for restricted output (Prasad L.M., *Principles & Practice of Management*, 2002, p. 58):

- Workers' think that if they produce more per head, some of the workers' would be retrenched.
- Once they reach the target as compared to standard company raise the standard.
- Workers' form a social group so they know what are the responsibilities a workers' had for his family. If any worker not doing well he may be retrenched, by considering this reason faster workers protected them by not overproducing.

This study imposed that informal relationship are important factor in determining the human behaviour. Along with experiment workers' were counselled for developing and maintaining good human relation in the plant. The counselling emphasised on worker relationship with other workers', with the management, personal adjustment, satisfaction, motivation and many more aspects.

3.3 Implication of Hawthorne Studies

- It was now clear that factory is a social system and informal group in plant equally affect human behaviour as formal group.
- A worker is not merely an 'economic man' who is motivated only by the monetary benefits. Non-monetary incentives are sometime more

important in influencing workers' attitude to their work.

- There is a possibility of conflict between company and informal group. It may be because of incompatible objectives of the both.
- Sometime, informal leaders were more important and impressive than formal in directing group behaviour because he identifies group attitude, opinion, and objective more efficiently than formal leader.

3.4 Criticisms of Hawthorne Studies

- Behavioural scientists believe that in this series of experiment whatever the conclusion were drawn it lack scientific objectivity.
- Some feels that there was bias and preconception on the part of the Harvard researcher.
- The study has ignored the existence of trade unions.

Apart from these criticism the Hawthorne studies comes with the outcome of human relation is an important part of company. And it drew attention to the social needs as an additional source of motivation.

❍❍❍

CHAPTER 4

TIME AND MOTION STUDY

4.1 INTRODUCTION

To find of the method by which management set a standards for increase the productivity of the workers. This can be done by setting standards in which a complex task is broken into small, simple steps, the sequence of movements taken by the worker in performing those steps is carefully observed to notice and eliminate any wasteful motion and to find out the precise time taken for each correct movement is measured. From these measurements production and delivery times and prices can be computed and incentive schemes can be devised. Generally appropriate only for repetitive tasks, time and motion studies were pioneered by the US industrial engineer **Frederick Winslow Taylor** (1856–1915) and developed by the husband and wife team of **Frank Gilbreth** (1868–1924) and **Dr. Lillian Gilbreth** (1878–1972). In this chapter we discuss the time and motion study concept, their aim and objectives, also merits and demerits of these studies. And lastly state the relationship between time and motion study.

4.2 CONCEPT AND MEANING OF TIME STUDY

Time study understood as to set up the method to determine the actual time for performing a particular task. According to Kimball and Kimball, "Time study may be defined primarily as the art of observing and recording time required doing each detailed element of industrial operation".

Time study is, "the analysis and determination of the time necessary to perform a given task" says John A. Shubin.

According to Alford and Beaty time study is a, "searching scientific analysis of methods and equipment used or planned in doing a piece of work, development in practical detail of the best way of doing it and determination of the time required".

4.3 Aims and Objectives of Time Study

- To determine or fix *standards* time required for an operation under normal situation/conditions.
- To avoid unusual *idle time* and delay in the execution of the task/job.
- To use the standard time data so as to fix a fair *incentive* wage plan.
- To create *time consciousness* among the workers.
- To minimize and control the cost.
- To set a fair *hourly output* standards for a worker.
- To improve *working conditions.*

4.4 Procedure of Time Study

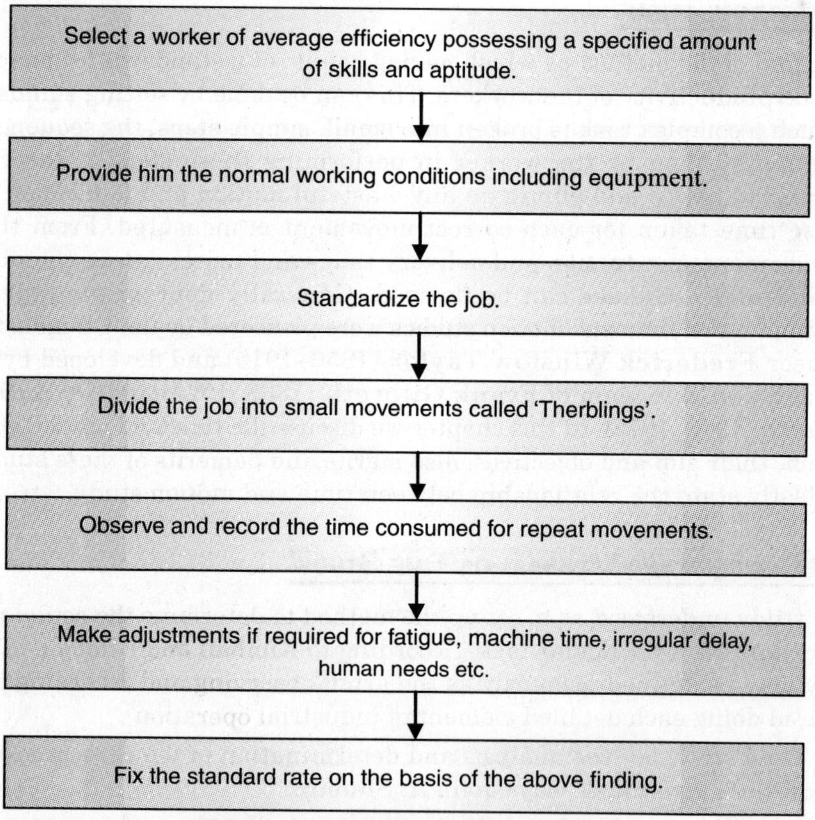

Exhibit 1: Procedure of Time Study

4.5 Advantages and Disadvantages of Time Study

Advantages

- It helps to measure the efficiency of each worker by setting standards.
- It helps in making the effective incentive plan.

- It helps in setting of production schedules for use in production, planning and control.
- It gives direction to management for formulating sound wage structure.
- It creates time consciousness in worker by this they give their effort more as compared to earlier.
- It reduces the cost also.
- It enables computation of standard costs.
- It gives an alternative methods and it helps in to find out the one best way to perform the task.
- It helps in to improve the working conditions.

Disadvantages

- It is not useful for repetitive job.
- Standardization is not possible until equipments, products, materials, working conditions and work methods all are standard.
- It is possible that standards based upon time study may affect adversely the quality of the product.
- It is difficult to impose on that kind of job which was indirectly affecting the productivity like clerical and supervisory staff.
- If worker had more skill or knowledge as compared to others they get same incentive as others which is one of the defects of time study.

4.6 Concept and Meaning of Motion Study

A motion study is a method to establish 'the one best way' to perform the task. According to Frank Gilbreth, "Motion study is the science of eliminating wastefulness resulting from using unnecessary, ill-directed and inefficient motions. The aim of motion study is to find and perpetuate the schemes of least waste methods of labours".

"Motion study consists of dividing work into the most fundamental elements possible, studying these elements separately and in relation to one another, and from these studied elements building the methods of least waste", says, Frank Gilbreth.

According to Kimball and Kimball, "Motion study may be defined as the study of movements, whether of a machine or an operator, in performing an operation for the purpose of eliminating useless motions and of arranging the sequence of useful motions in the most efficient order".

According to Marvin E. Mundel, "Motion study is a procedure for scientific analysis of work methods, considering":

- the raw materials;
- the design of the product;
- the process or order of work;

- the tools, work place and equipment for each individual step in the process; and
- the hand and body motions used in each step, in order to determine or design preferable work methods".

Therblings

Frank B. Gilbreth, the originator of motion study involves the study of the movement of operations of a worker. It aims at eliminating unnecessary, ill-directed and inefficient motions so as to perform the work in the best possible manner. Frank B. Gilbreth and his wife Dr. Lillian M. Gilbreth studied the various movements of the limbs of brick-layer and classified bodily movements into basic elements called "therblings" (a term coined by spelling Gilbreth's backwards). The therblings are listed below:

1. Search;	10. Inspect;
2. Find;	11. Disassemble;
3. Select;	12. Release Load;
4. Grasp;	13. Transport Empty;
5. Transport Loaded;	14. Rest for Overcoming Fatigue;
6. Position;	15. Unavoidable Delay;
7. Pre-position;	16. Avoidable Delay;
8. Assemble;	17. Plan; and
9. Use;	18. Hold

Exhibit 2: Therblings

Lillian M. Gilbreth summed up the ideology of motion study as, 'study your men, determine what product he can best make, give him the proper working conditions, machines and materials that are best suited to him and you may expect success'.

Tools of Motion Study

1. ***Process Charts***–Various charts are prepared to display the movements of a job so as to find out the way to improve it.
2. ***Application of Laws of Motion Economy***–The laws of motion economy suggest ways to do the work with minimum fatigue and time. According to Gilbreths, the laws of motion economy are:
   - Both hands should work and rest at the same time.
   - Both hands should begin and complete their therblings at the same instant.
   - Motion of arms should be in opposite and symmetrical directions instead of in the same direction and should be made simultaneously.
   - All materials and tools should be so located to permit proper sequence of therblings. The part required at the beginning of the cycle should be next to the point of release of the finished piece from the former.

- All materials and tools should be located within the normal grasp area, which is within the maximum working areas.
- Sequences of motion should be arranged to build rhythm and automatically in the operation.
- Hands should be relieved of all work that can be done by feet or other parts of body.
- Tools and materials should be prepositioned as much as possible to reduce the search, find and select operations.
- The paths of fast motions should be taught and learned.

3. ***Preparation of Questionnaires***–By preparing certain questionnaires and seeking the answers certain suggestive improvements may emerge. Some of the questions which may be posed are as below:
   - Who, where, why and when is the job done?
   - How many workers will be able to do the work?
   - Can we eliminate or combine certain operations?
   - Can the job be performed by machines?
   - Can it be better performed at some other time?
4. ***Analysis of Therblings***–Bodily movements called therblings are analyzed to find a better method of doing a work.
5. ***Micro-Motion Study***–It is the study of very small elements of motions and their analysis with the aid of a special camera and a timing device. It enables greater detailing than eye observation provides greater accuracy than pencil-paper and stop watch techniques.

4.7 Advantages and Disadvantages of Motion Study

Advantages

- It leads to increase the production.
- It increases the efficiency of workers by reducing fatigue and manual labour.
- It helps in to reduce the cost of the production.
- It ensures low price of goods.
- It leads to increase wage structure.
- It improves the working conditions.

Disadvantages

- It adversely affects the initiative and creativeness of workers.
- It lays down a certain pattern of motions which, if employed task become monotonous.
- It does not take into consideration the differences in the efficiency of various workers.

- It fixes standards which may not be achievable and hence disliked by workers.

4.8 Relation between Motion and Time Study

Previously, time and motion studies were used in the manufacturing industry to evolve wage structure with the thought that money was the only motivation for work. In modern era:

- time and motion studies can be effective for performance standards;
- time and motion studies can be used for planning purpose in order to predict the level of output that may be achieved;
- time and motion studies can be used to uncover problem and create solutions; and
- time and motion studies can be used for time cost analysis.

Motion and time study both are closely related. The adoption of one without the other does not give the best result. According to Frank Gilbreth time study would be misleading if it was not proceed by motion study. Both are complimentary and not competitive to each other.

Although time study can be made without motion study and vice-versa but it is not possible to fix ideal standards of work without the study of both. Motion study involves the study of the various elements of motion to work and lays down standards motions. Time study is required to measure the economic of motion study so as to find the 'one best way, of doing a job.

❍❍❍

CHAPTER 5

MOTIVATION

5.1 INTRODUCTION

At one time, employees were considered just another input into the production of goods and services. What perhaps changed this way of thinking about employees was research, referred to as the Hawthorne Studies, conducted by Elton Mayo from 1924 to 1932 (Dickson, 1973). This study found employees are not motivated solely by money and employee behaviour is linked to their attitudes (Dickson, 1973). The Hawthorne Studies began the human relations approach to management, whereby the needs and motivation of employees become the primary focus of managers (Bedeian, 1993).

Workers in any organization need something to keep them working. Most times the salary of the employee is enough to keep he or she working for an organization. However, sometimes just working for salary is not enough for employees to stay at an organization. An employee must be motivated to work for a company or organization. If no motivation is present in an employee, then that employee's quality of work or all work in general will deteriorate.

Keeping an employee working at full potential is the ultimate goal of employee motivation. Just as there are unlimited amounts of motivators, there are unlimited amounts of methods to help keep employees motivated. Some traditional ways or motivating workers are placing them in completion with each other. Friendly competition is a great way to generate motivation among employees. This gives a chance for employees to flex their working skills in a competition against their peers. This not only will motivate employees with a result of greater production. But the competition with recorded results will give the employer an idea of who is being most productive. In this chapter firstly we define the term motivation and also the types of motivation. Discuss the various motivational theories and studies conducted on motivation. And lastly listing some tips for improving motivation at workplace.

5.2 Concept and Meaning

A simple definition of *motivation* is the ability to change behaviour. It is a drive that compels one to act because human behaviour is directed toward some goal. Motivation is intrinsic (internal); it comes from within based on personal interests, desires, and need for fulfillment. However, extrinsic (external) factors such as rewards, praise, and promotions also influence motivation. Motivation is the need or desire that causes a person to act; to have initiative, spirit or be enterprising.

Motivation has been defined as: the psychological process that gives behaviour purpose and direction.[1] A predisposition to behave in a purposive manner to achieve specific, unmet needs.[2] An internal drive to satisfy an unsatisfied need.[3]

Motivation is operationally defined as the inner force that drives individuals to accomplish personal and organizational goals.[4]

The processes that account for an individual's intensity, direction and persistence of effort towards attaining a goal.[5]

People who are committed to achieving organizational objectives generally outperform those who are not committed. Those who are intrinsically rewarded by accomplishments in the workplace are satisfied with their jobs and are individuals with high self-esteem. Therefore, an important part of management is to help make work more satisfying and rewarding for employees and to keep employee motivation consistent with organizational objectives. With the diversity of contemporary workplaces, this is a complex task. Many factors, including the influences of different cultures, affect what people value and what is rewarding to them.

From a manager's perspective, it is important to understand what prompts people, what influences them, and why they persist in particular actions. Quick (1985)[6] presented these four underlying principles that are important to understanding motivation:

1. People have reasons for everything they do.
2. Whatever people choose as a goal is something they believe is good for them.
3. The goal people choose must be seen as attainable.
4. The conditions under which the work is done can affect its value to the employee and his or her perceptions of attainability or success.

5.3 Types of Motivation

Motivation

Positive Motivation

It involves the possibility of increased motive satisfaction.

Positive or incentive motivation is generally based on reward.

Negative Motivation

Negative motivation involves the possibility of decreased motive satisfaction. It is also called fear motivation, is based on force and fear. Fear causes workers to act in a certain way because they are afraid of the consequences.

Exhibit 1(a): Types of Motivation

Motivation

Extrinsic Motivation

It is concerned with external motivators which workers enjoy—pay promotion, status, fringe benefits, retirement plan, health insurance schemes, holidays and vacations etc. These motivators are associated with the financial rewards.

Intrinsic Motivation

It is concerned with the feeling of having accomplished something worthwhile, or the satisfaction one gets after doing one's work well. Praise, responsibility, recognition, esteem, competition, participation, power etc. are the examples of intrinsic motivation.

Exhibit 1(b): Types of Motivation

5.4 Motivation Theories

NEED THEORIES

Maslow's Need Hierarchy Theory

Maslow's hierarchy of needs is a theory in psychology, proposed by Abraham Maslow, (a professor at Brandeis University and a practicing psychologist) in his 1943 paper *A Theory of Human Motivation*,[7] which he subsequently extended to include his observations of humans' innate curiosity. He identified a set of needs that he prioritized into a hierarchy based on two conclusions:

1. Human needs are either of an attraction/desire nature or of an avoidance nature.
2. Because humans are "wanting" beings, when one desire is satisfied, another desire will take its place.

The five levels of needs are the following:

- ***Physiological***: These are basic physical comfort or bodily needs: food, sex, drink and sleep. In the workplace, these needs translate into a safe, ergonomically designed work environment with appropriate base salary compensation.

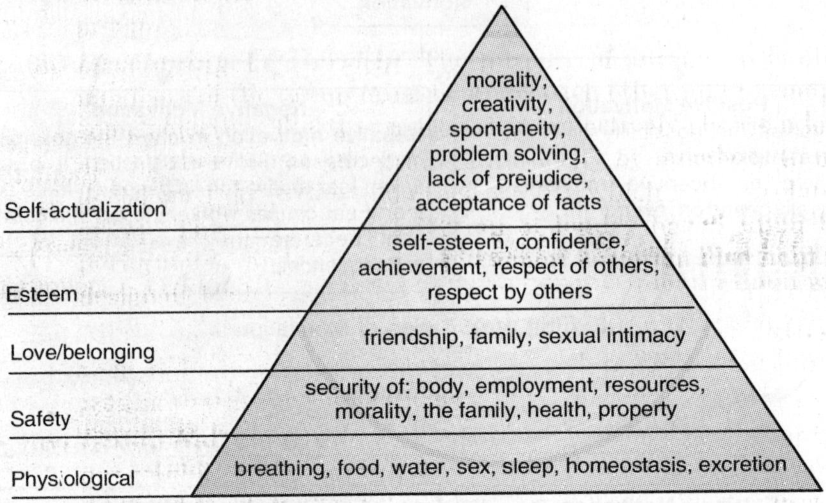

Exhibit 1(c): Maslow's Need Hieraracy

- ***Security/safety***: People want to feel safe, secure, and free from fear. They need stability, structure, and order. In the workplace, job security and fringe benefits, along with an environment free of violence, fills these needs.
- ***Belongingness and love***: This is a need for friends, family, and intimacy—for social acceptance and affection from one's peers. In the workplace, this need is satisfied by participation in work groups with good relationships among co-workers and between workers and managers.
- ***Esteem***: People want the esteem of others and they want to be regarded as useful, competent, and important. People also desire self-esteem and need a good self image. In the workplace, increased responsibility, high status, and recognition for contributions satisfy these needs.
- ***Self-actualization***: This highest motivation level involves people striving to actualize their full potential, to become more of what they are capable of being. They seek to attain self-fulfillment. In the workplace, people satisfy this need by being creative, receiving training, or accepting challenging assignments.

Focussing on the needs of retraining for growth and challenge as well as rewards and recognition is important to the quality of work life. Managers can affect the physical, social, and psychological environment in the workplace, and they have a responsibility to help employees fulfill their needs.

ERG Theory

ERG Theory In his work, Clayton Alderfer expanded on Maslow's hierarchical theory. He proposed three need categories and suggested that movement between the need levels is not necessarily straightforward. Failure to meet a higher-order need could cause an individual to regress to a lower-order need. These *ERG theory* categories are:

- *Existence needs*: Needs for physical well-being
- *Relatedness needs*: Needs for satisfactory relationships with others
- *Growth needs*: The development of human potential and the desire for personal growth and increased competence (Daft, 1997)[8].

Motivation-Hygiene Theory

Frederick Herzberg, a professor of psychology at Case Western Reserve University, studied the attitudes of workers toward their jobs. Herzberg proposed that an individual will be moved to action based on the desire to avoid deprivation. However, this motivation does not provide positive satisfaction because it does not provide a sense of growth. Herzberg's research found that positive job attitudes were associated with a feeling of psychological growth. He thought that people work for two reasons: for financial reasons to avoid physical deprivation and for achievement because of the happiness and meaning it provides. Herzberg also identified the concept of job enrichment, whereby the responsibilities of a job are changed to provide greater growth and challenge (1985). His *motivation-hygiene* theory includes two types of factors:

1. ***Motivation*** is based on the positive satisfaction that psychological growth provides. The presence of factors such as responsibility, achievement, recognition, and possibility for growth or advancement will motivate and satisfy people. The absence of these factors will not necessarily de-motivate or cause dissatisfaction.
2. ***Hygiene*** is based on an individual's desire to avoid deprivation and the resulting physical and emotional discomfort. Hygiene factors include willingness to supervise; positive working conditions; interpersonal relations with peers, subordinates, and superiors; status; job security; and salary. These factors do not motivate, nor will their presence cause job satisfaction. Their absence, however, will cause dissatisfaction.

Although salary is considered a hygiene factor, it plays an indirect part in motivation as a measure of growth and advancement or as a symbol of recognition of achievement.

Theory X and Theory Y

Douglas McGregor, a professor at the Massachusetts Institute of Technology and a social psychologist, was greatly influenced by the work of Maslow.

McGregor recognized that people have needs and that those needs are satisfied at work. He described two sets of assumptions about people that he labelled *Theory X* and *Theory Y*:

- The assumptions of *Theory X* are that most people will avoid work because they don't like it and must be threatened or persuaded to put forth adequate effort. People have little ambition and don't want responsibility. They want to be directed and are most interested in job security.
- The assumptions of *Theory Y* are that work is very natural to people and that most people are self-directed to achieve objectives to which they are committed. People are ambitious and creative. They desire responsibility and derive a sense of satisfaction from the work itself.

These assumptions were, at one time, applied to management styles, with autocratic managers labelled as adhering to Theory X and democratic managers to Theory Y. Unfortunately, this fostered a tendency to see people as members of a group rather than as individuals. The important contribution of McGregor's theory was to recognize these two perspectives and to recognize that people can achieve personal objectives through helping organizations achieve their objectives. Their work can be a motivator.

Acquired Needs Theory

David McClelland developed the acquired needs theory because he felt that different needs are acquired throughout an individual's lifetime. He proposed three needs:

1. ***Need for achievement***: The desire to accomplish something difficult, attain a high standard of success, master complex tasks, and surpass others.
2. ***Need for affiliation***: The desire to form close personal relationships, avoid conflict, and establish warm friendships.
3. ***Need for power***: The desire to influence or control others, be responsible for others, and have authority over others.

McClelland found through his research that early life experiences determine whether people acquire these needs. The need to achieve as an adult is influenced by the reinforcement of behaviour received as a child when a child is encouraged to do things independently. If a child is reinforced for warm, human relationships, then the need for affiliation as an adult develops. If a child gains satisfaction from controlling others, then the need for power will be evident as an adult (Daft, 1997)[8].

PROCESS THEORIES

Process theories help to explain how individuals select particular behaviours and how individuals determine if these behaviours meet their needs. Because these theories involve rational selection, concepts of cognition are employed. Cognition, according to Petri (1996)[9], "is generally used to describe those intellectual or perceptual processes occurring within us when we analyze and interpret both the world around us and our own thoughts and actions.

Expectancy Theory

Victor Vroom developed the *expectancy theory*, which suggests that individuals' expectations about their ability to accomplish something will affect their success in accomplishing it. Therefore, this theory is based on cognition—on thought processes that individuals use.

The expectancy theory is based on an individual's effort and performance, as well as the desirability of outcomes associated with high performance. The value of or preference for a particular outcome is called valence. To determine valence, people will ask themselves whether or not they can accomplish a goal, how important is the goal to them (in the immediate as well as the long term), and what course of action will provide the greatest reward. An individual's expectation of actually achieving the outcome is crucial to success, and many factors influence this.

The expectancy theory can be applied through incentive systems that identify desired outcomes and give all workers the same opportunities to achieve rewards, such as stock ownership or other recognition for achievement.

Equity Theory

The *equity theory* focuses on individuals' perceptions of how fairly they are treated in comparison to others. It was developed by J. Stacy Adams, who found that equity exists when people consider their compensation equal to the compensation of others who perform similar work. People judge equity by comparing inputs (such as education, experience, effort, and ability) to outputs (such as pay, recognition, benefits, and promotion).

When the ratio is out of balance, inequity occurs. And inequitable pay can create an impossible situation when implementing salary and incentive systems. According to Daft (1997)[8], Individuals will work to reduce perceived inequity by doing the following:

- *Change inputs*: Examples include increasing or reducing effort.
- *Change outcomes*: Examples include requesting a salary increase or improved working conditions.
- *Distort perceptions*: This occurs when individuals cannot change their inputs or outcomes; one example is artificially increasing the importance of awards.
- *Leave the job*: Individuals might do this rather than experience what they perceive to be continued inequity.

When administering compensation and incentive programs, managers must be careful to assure that the rewards are equitable; if programs are not perceived as equitable, then they will not contribute to employee motivation.

REINFORCEMENT THEORIES

Theories of reinforcement are based not on need but on the relationship between behaviour and its consequences. In the workplace, these theories can be applied to change or modify on-the-job behaviour through rewards and punishments.

B.F. Skinner, a professor at Harvard, was a highly controversial behavioural psychologist known for his work in operant conditioning and behaviour modification. His *reinforcement theories* take into consideration both motivation and the environment, focusing on stimulus and response relationships. Through his research, Skinner noted that a stimulus will initiate behaviour; thus, the stimulus is an antecedent to behaviour. The behaviour will generate a result; therefore, results are consequences of behaviour.

According to McCoy (1992)[10], "The quality of the results will be directly related to the quality and timeliness of the antecedent. The more specific the antecedent is and the closer in time it is to the behaviour, the greater will be its effect on the behaviour. The consequences provide feedback to the individual".

If the results are considered positive, then the behaviour is positively reinforced. When the behaviour is positively reinforced, the individual is more likely to repeat the behaviour. People tend to have an intrinsic (internal) need for positive reinforcement. And when a behaviour is ignored, the behaviour tends to go away or become extinct. The four types of reinforcement are the following (Daft, 1997)[8]:

	Pleasant or Desirable Event	Unpleasant or Undesirable Event
Event is applied	**Positive Reinforcement** Behaviour becomes more likely to occur again	**Punishment** Behaviour becomes less likely to occur again
Event is withdrawn	**Extinction** Behaviour becomes less likely to occur again	**Negative Reinforcement** Behaviour becomes more likely to occur again

Exhibit 1(d): Types of Reinforcement

- *Positive reinforcement:* The application of a pleasant and rewarding consequence following a desired behavior or after a desired behaviour we can motivate individual by rewarding them or provide positive outcomes like praise, pay, bonus, recognition etc.
- *Negative reinforcement:* The removal of an unpleasant consequence following a desired behaviour, such as a manager may continuous reprimand (warning) and harass an employee until the employee being performing a job correctly.

- *Extinction:* It is an effective method of controlling undesirable behaviour. It is based on the principle that if a response is not reinforced, it will eventually disappear. Like if a teacher ignore a noisy student, the student may drop the attention towards their behaviour and might change his/her behaviour in classroom.
- *Punishment*:It is control device employed in organization to discourage and reduce annoying behaviour of other.The application of an unpleasant outcome when an undesirable behaviour occurs to reduce the likelihood of that behaviour happening again. This form of reinforcement does not indicate a correct behaviour, so its use in business is not usually appropriate

Continuous reinforcement can be effective in the early stages of behaviour modification, but partial reinforcement is more commonly used. Reinforcement is most powerful when it is administered immediately.

The appropriateness of a reward depends on the situation. But for managers to apply rewards appropriate for work performance, it is necessary to understand what constitutes a reward. And no single reward will be perceived as positive by all employees. Rewards, however, are important in behaviour-based incentive plans because they reward employee behaviour that is desirable for the company. According to McCoy (1992)[10], both incentives and recognition provide a reward; however, incentives drive performance while recognition is an after-the-fact display of appreciation for a contribution.

Financial rewards are certainly important in compensation programs. Social recognition provides employees with a sense of self-worth by acknowledging the contributions they have made. This recognition could be given in the form of a ceremony that helps to validate and is an important compensation—and one that probably costs a company very little in relationship to the benefit to employees (McCoy, 1992)[10].

5.5 Implication of Motivation Theories in Workplace

At lower levels of Maslow's hierarchy of needs, such as Physiological needs, money is a motivator, however it tends to have a motivating effect on staff that lasts only for a short period (in accordance with Herzberg's two-factor model of motivation). At higher levels of the hierarchy, praise, respect, recognition, empowerment and a sense of belonging are far more powerful motivators than money, as both Abraham Maslow's theory of motivation and Douglas McGregor's Theory X and theory Y (pertaining to the theory of leadership) demonstrate.

Maslow's has money at the lowest level of the hierarchy and shows other needs are better motivators to staff. McGregor places money in his Theory X category and feels it is a poor motivator. Praise and recognition are placed in the Theory Y category and are considered stronger motivators than money.

- Motivated employees always look for better ways to do a job.
- Motivated employees are more quality oriented.
- Motivated workers are more productive.

The average workplace is about midway between the extremes of high threat and high opportunity. Motivation by threat is a dead-end strategy, and naturally staffs are more attracted to the opportunity side of the motivation curve than the threat side. Motivation is a powerful tool in the work environment that can lead to employees working at their most efficient levels of production.[11]

Nonetheless, Steinmertz also discusses three common character types of subordinates: ascendant, indifferent, and ambivalent that all react and interact uniquely, and must be treated, managed, and motivated accordingly. An effective leader must understand how to manage all characters, and more importantly the manager must utilize avenues that allow room for employees to work, grow, and find answers independently.[12]

The assumptions of Maslow and Herzberg were challenged by a classic study[13] at Vauxhall Motors' UK manufacturing plant. This introduced the concept of orientation to work and distinguished three main orientations: instrumental (where work is a means to an end), bureaucratic (where work is a source of status, security and immediate reward) and solidarity (which prioritizes group loyalty).

Other theories which expanded and extended those of Maslow and Herzberg included Kurt Lewin's Force Field Theory, Edwin Locke's Goal Theory and Victor Vroom's Expectancy Theory. These tend to stress cultural differences and the fact that individuals tend to be motivated by different factors at different times.[14]

According to the system of scientific management developed by Frederick Winslow Taylor, a worker's motivation is solely determined by pay, and therefore management need not consider psychological or social aspects of work. In essence, scientific management bases human motivation wholly on extrinsic rewards and discards the idea of intrinsic rewards.

In contrast, David McClelland believed that workers could not be motivated by the mere need for money — in fact, extrinsic motivation (e.g., money) could extinguish intrinsic motivation such as achievement motivation, though money could be used as an indicator of success for various motives, e.g., keeping score. In keeping with this view, his consulting firm, McBer & Company, had as its first motto "To make everyone productive, happy, and free." For McClelland, satisfaction lay in aligning a person's life with their fundamental motivations.

Elton Mayo found out that the social contacts a worker has at the workplace are very important and that boredom and repetitiveness of tasks lead to reduced motivation. Mayo believed that workers could be motivated by acknowledging their social needs and making them feel important. As a result, employees were given freedom to make decisions on the job and greater attention was paid to informal work groups. Mayo named the model the Hawthorne effect. His model has been judged as placing undue reliance on social contacts at work situations for motivating employees.[15]

In *Essentials of Organizational Behaviour*, Robbins and Judge examine recognition programs as motivators, and identify five principles that contribute to the success of an employee incentive program.[16]

Recognition of employees' individual differences and clear identification of behaviour deemed worthy of recognition:

- Allowing employees to participate
- Linking rewards to performance
- Rewarding of nominators
- Visibility of the recognition process

5.6 Studies on Motivation

In one of the most elaborate studies conducted on employee motivation, the Minneapolis Gas Company sought to determine what their potential employees desired most from a job. This twenty-year in-depth study (carried out from 1945–1965) involved 31,000 men and 13,000 women. Contrary to common belief the number one motivator of both men and women was job security, with advancement rating 2nd, type of work 3rd and company (proud to work for) rating 4th. Factors such as money, benefits and working conditions were given a low rating by both men and women.[17]

The purpose of research conducted by James Lindner (1998)[18] Research and Extension Associate at The Ohio State University Piketon Research and Extension Center was to describe the importance of certain factors in motivating employees at the Piketon Research and Extension Center and Enterprise Center. Specifically, the study sought to determine the ranked importance of ten motivating factors. The final ranked order of these factors was:

- Interesting work
- Good wages
- Full appreciation of work done
- Job security
- Good working conditions
- Promotions and growth in the organization
- Feelings of being in on things
- Personal loyalty to employees
- Tactful discipline
- Sympathetic help with personal problems

Two further studies cited by Lindner returned the following results:

A study of industrial employees conducted by Kovach (1987) yielded the following ranked order of motivational factors (a) interesting work, (b) full appreciation of work done and (c) a feeling of being in on things.

The second study, also on employees and conducted by Harpaz (1990) found the following rankings of motivational factors:

- interesting work
- good wages
- job security

The final conclusions that Lindner draws from his own and others research is that "The discrepancies in these research findings supports the idea that what motivates employees differs given the context in which the employee works. What is clear, however, is that employees rank interesting work as the most important motivational factor".

A study of employee attitudes undertaken by the Gallup Organization with more than 100,00 employees in 12 industries using 12 statements, shows employees who have a positive attitude toward their work are 50% more likely to achieve customer loyalty and 44% more likely to produce above-average profitability. Companies whose support of the 12 statements ranked in the top 25% averaged 24% higher profitability, 29% higher revenues and 10% lower employee turnover. The statements included:

- I know what is expected of me at work
- At work, I have the opportunity to do what I do best every day
- In the past seven days I have received recognition or praise for doing good work
- My supervisor, or someone at work, seems to care about me as a person
- There is someone at work who encourages my development

A study by John Throop (cited in IOMA's Pay for Performance Report 1998)[19] conducted using computer programmers, asked participants to identify the top 10 factors that provided the highest degree of motivation in their jobs. The programmers top three were:

- Full appreciation for work done
- Feeling that they were in on things
- Sympathetic help with personnel problems

When asked what the top motivators would be, the managers of these programmers predicted rather different priorities with the three top ranking items being:

- Wages
- Working conditions
- Fair discipline

The report also revealed research conducted by Greg Smith (2002)[20], President of Chart Your Course International, into the main causes of employee dissatisfaction at work. The factors that de-motivated staff were:

Lack of appreciation	33%
Too much paperwork	27%
Problems with supervisors	23%
Poor pay and benefits	22%
Lack of training	20%
Lack of opportunity	20%
Fairness	18%
Problems with coworkers	16%
Commute	15%
Boring job	9%

The factors that workers thought were the most effective actions a firm could take to improve retention were:

Train managers better	32%
Listen more	28%
Try something new	24%
Pay more	23%
Select managers better	22%
Set the example	22%
Hire better people	18%
Improve benefits	13%

Regardless of which theory of employee motivation is followed, the outcomes of research conclude that interesting work, appreciation, pay, good working conditions, and job security are important factors in helping to motivate. Phil Kerslake (2002)[21], General Manager of DTZ, New Zealand found in his 2001 surveys of Australasian employee attitudes that "most people were shown to have ambitions and be prepared to put some job and income security at risk if there is the opportunity to nourish their self-esteem and achieve a degree of self fulfillment".

To ensure that strategies used to enhance motivation within your organization obtain the most effective results they should based be on:

- An analysis of the factors that individual staff members believe are motivators for them
- The performance objectives of the individual
- The strategic goals of the organization
- The values and culture of the organization

Lindner highlights the importance of considering individual staff in his comment, "The key to motivating (centre) employees is to know what motivates them and designing a motivation program based on those needs—employees must be willing to let managers know what motivates them, and managers must be willing to design reward systems that motivate employees".

Jim Clemmer (2004)[22], a writer and motivational speaker states, "When confronting morale problems, managers will often succumb to the victims virus and blame the declining work ethic, attitudes of entitlement, softening values, the welfare state, or any number of societal factors. But these factors—which are mostly about doing the least work for the most money - are more imagined than real". He further states, "Studies show that people's real needs are much less mercenary than most managers believe. People want to take pride in their work, belong to a winning team and be part of an organization they can believe in. In fact, the morale crisis so prevalent in organizations today is primarily the result of disappointment in these needs not being met".

Paul Falcone (2002)[23], Director of Employment and Development at Paramount Pictures in Hollywood writes that "As a supervisor, it always will be your toughest job to turn around people who have lost the motivation to make a positive contribution to the team. But contrary to popular perception, your job as a manager is not to motivate your staff. Motivation is internal. Instead, you are responsible for creating an environment in which people can motivate themselves. And this can be done without relying on merit increases, incentives and bonuses". He suggests that managers need to focus on the top non-monetary motivating factors of (a) open communication, (b) recognition, (c) career development plans, and (d) the ability to make a difference at work.

5.7 Tips for Improving Employee Motivation

- *Create a positive environment*—Promote a workplace atmosphere that makes all workers' feel worthwhile and important. Don't play favourites with your staff. Keep office doors open and let folks know they can always approach you with questions or concerns. A happy workplace is a productive workplace.
- *Put people on the right path*—Most workers' are looking for advancement opportunities within their own factory. Work with each of them to develop a career growth plan that takes into consideration both their current skills and future goals. If workers' become excited about what's down the road, they will become more engaged in their present work.
- *Educate the masses*—Help workers' to improve their skills by providing on-the-job training or in-house career development. Allow them to attend workshops and seminars related to the industry. Encourage them to attend adult education classes paid for by the company. Workers' will

feel you are investing in them, and this will translate into an improved job performance.

- *Provide incentives*—Offer people incentives to perform well, either with something small like a gift certificate or something more substantial such as a performance-based bonus or salary increase. Give out "Employee of the Month" awards. Such tokens of appreciation will go far in motivating employees.
- *Acknowledge contributions*—You can make a huge difference in employee morale simply by taking the time to recognize each worker's contributions and accomplishments, large or small. Be generous with praise.
- *Honour your promises*—Getting people to give their all requires following through on promises. If you tell an employee that he or she will be considered for a bonus if numbers improve or productivity increases, you'd better put your money where your mouth is. Failure to follow through on promises will result in a loss of trust not only that person's trust, but the trust of every employee that hears the story.
- *Provide career coaching*—Help workers' reach the next level professionally by providing on-site coaching. Bring in professionals to provide one-on-one counselling, which can help people learn how to overcome personal or professional obstacles on their career paths.
- *Match tasks to talents*—You can improve employee motivation by improving employee confidence. Assign individuals with tasks you know they will enjoy or will be particularly good at. An employee who is successful at one thing will have the self-confidence to tackle other projects with renewed energy and excitement.

REFERENCES

1. Kreitner, R. (1995). *Management* (6th ed.). Houghton Mifflin, Boston. Company.
2. Buford, J.A., Jr., Bedeian, A.G., & Lindner, J.R. (1995). *Management in Extension* (3rd ed.). Columbus, Ohio: Ohio State University Extension.
3. Higgins, J.M. (1994). *The Management Challenges* (2nd ed.). Macmillan, New York.
4. James R. Lindner, *Understanding Employee Motivation*; The Ohio State University.
5. Robbins, et al., *Organizational Behavior*, Prentice Hall, New Delhi, 2008, p. 215.
6. Quick, Thomas L. (1985). *The Manager's Motivation Desk Book*. Wiley, New York.
7. A.H. Maslow, *A Theory of Human Motivation*, Psychological Review 50(4) (1943):370–96.
8. Daft, Richard L. (1997). *Management*, (4th ed.) Harcourt Brace, Orlando, Fl.

9. Petri, Herbert L. (1996). *Motivation: Theory, Research, and Applications*, (4th ed.) Pacific Grove, CA: Brooks/Cole., p.236.
10. McCoy, Thomas J. (1992). *Compensation and Motivation: Maximizing Employee Performance with Behaviour-Based Incentive Plans*. AMACOM, a division of American Management Association, New York, p. 34.
11. Steinmetz, L. (1983) *Nice Guys Finish Last: Management Myths and Reality*. Boulder, Horizon Publications Inc. Colorado.
12. Steinmetz, L.L. (1983) *Nice Guys Finish Last: Management Myths and Reality*. Boulder, Horizon Publications Inc. Colorado, (p. 43–44)
13. Goldthorpe, J.H., Lockwood, D., Bechhofer, F. and Platt, J. (1968) *The Affluent Worker: Attitudes and Behaviour*, Cambridge University Press, Cambridge.
14. Weightman, J. (2008) *The Employee Motivation Audit*: Cambridge Strategy Publications.
15. *Human Resources Management*, HT Graham and R Bennett M+E Handbooks (1993) ISBN 0-7121-0844-0.
16. Robbins, Stephen P.; Judge, Timothy A. (2007), *Essentials of Organizational Behavior* (9 ed.), Upper Saddle River, NJ: Prentice Hall, http://wps.prenhall.com/bp_robbins_eob_9/64/16396/4197506.cw/index.html
17. Accel-Team.com (2004), *Employee motivation , the organizational environment* and *productivity*.
18. Lindner, J.R., (1998) *Understanding Employee Motivation*, Journal of Extension, June 1998, Vol. 36, Number 3.
19. Anonymous, (1998), *Beware the six dangerous myths about compensation*, IOMA's Pay for Performance Report. New York: Dec. 1998. Vol. 98, Iss. 12; p. 1–4.
20. Smith, G.P.(2004), *Provide a Positive Working Environment for Productivity and Retention*, The Navigator Newsletter, Vol. 72, 19 March 2004, p. 1, Chart Your Course International, Atlanta, Georgia, USA.
21. Kerslake, P., (2002), *How to Create the Productive Office*, New Zealand Management, Vol. 49, Iss 6, pp. 41–43, Profile Publishing Limited, Auckland.
22. Clemmer, J., (2004) *Beyond Manipulating and Motivating to Leading and Inspiring*, QNews, May 2004, p. 4.
23. Falcone, P., (2002), *Motivating Staff without Money*, HR Magazine, Vol. 47, Iss 8, pp. 105–108, Society for Human Resource Management, Alexandria.

CHAPTER 6

JOB SATISFACTION

6.1 INTRODUCTION

Worker with high level of satisfaction has positive feeling about their job and worker with low satisfaction have negative feeling about their job. Job satisfaction helps to improve the performance of worker on both criterias whether it is qualitative or quantitative, satisfied worker are easily motivated and having interest in their work. They also make their surrounding more productive with their positive thinking. When the work become interesting worker, get pleasure from work and definitely if worker do the job as per their interest they get psychological satisfaction. Job satisfaction is in regard to one's feelings or state-of-mind regarding the nature of their work. Job satisfaction can be influenced by a variety of factors, e.g., the quality of one's relationship with their supervisor, the quality of the physical environment in which they work, degree of fulfillment in their work etc.

6.2 CONCEPT AND MEANING

A happy worker is a productive worker'. The Hawthorne studies conducted at an electrical plant in Chicago from 1924–1932 revealed that employee morale and satisfaction increase productivity. Since then, management has taken consideration about the topic of job satisfaction, as it is believed to enhance performance, reduce absenteeism, retain qualified workers and establish smooth employment relations.

Workers having a sense of inner fulfillment and pride achieved when performing a particular job. Job satisfaction occurs when an employee feels he has accomplished something having importance and value worthy of recognition; sense of joy. Satisfaction creates confidence, loyalty and ultimately improved quality in the performance of the workers. Job satisfaction describes how content an individual is with his or her job. According to Robbins, job satisfaction is "a positive feeling about one's job resulting from an evaluation of its characteristics". Job satisfaction has been defined as a pleasurable emotional state resulting from the appraisal of one's job. (Locke, 1976 cited in Brief, A.P., & Weiss, H.M. (2001). Organizational behaviour: affect in the workplace. Annual Review of Psychology, 53, 279–307, p. 282.)

According to Tiffin and McCormick (1971), the satisfaction which people experience in their jobs is in large part the consequence of the extent of which the various aspects of their work situations tend to be relevant to their job related value system. It is important to realize that these attitudes vary according to individual experiences and expectations and hence there is no single unitary concept of job satisfaction.

According to Business Dictionary.com, "Contentment (or lack of it) arising out of interplay of employee's positive and negative feelings toward his or her work.

Hackman and Oldham (1975) suggested that jobs differ in the extent to which they involve five core dimensions:

1. Skill variety.
2. Task identity.
3. Task significance.
4. Autonomy.
5. Task feedback.

They suggest that if jobs are designed in a way that increases the presence of these core characteristics three critical psychological states can occur in employees:

- Experienced meaningfulness of work.
- Experienced responsibility for work outcomes.
- Knowledge of results of work activities.

According to Hackman and Oldham, when these critical psychological states are experienced, work motivation and job satisfaction will be high.

6.3 History of Job Satisfaction

One of the major contributions to the study of job satisfaction was the Hawthorne studies. These studies (1924–1933), primarily credited to Elton Mayo of the Harvard Business School, he find out the reasons that affect the productivity in Hawthrone Plant, Chicago. The study shown that there are not only the physical changes but also social factor which influence the working of an individual. This finding provided strong evidence that people work for purposes other than pay, which paved the way for researchers to investigate other factors in job satisfaction.

Scientific management (Taylorism) also had a significant impact on the study of job satisfaction. Frederick Winslow Taylor's 1911 book, 'Principles of Scientific Management', argued that there was a single best way to perform any given work task. Taylor believed that decisions based upon tradition and rules of thumb should be replaced by precise procedures developed after careful study of an individual at work. Its application is contingent on a high level of managerial control over employee work practices.

The preliminary use of scientific management by industries greatly increased productivity because workers were forced to work at a faster pace. However, workers became fatigued and dissatisfied, thus leaving researchers with new questions to answer regarding job satisfaction. It should also be noted that the work of W.L. Bryan, Walter Dill Scott, and Hugo Munsterberg set the tone for Taylor's work.

Maslow's hierarchy of needs theory, a motivation theory, laid the foundation for job satisfaction theory. This theory explains that individuals want to satisfy five specific needs in life—physiological needs, safety needs, social needs, self-esteem needs, and self-actualization. This model served as a good basis from which early researchers could develop job satisfaction theories.

6.4 Factors Influencing Job Satisfaction

There are a variety of factors that can influence an employees' level of job satisfaction. They may be the level of pay and benefits, the perceived fairness of the promotion system within a company, the quality of the working conditions, leadership and social relationships, and the job itself. There are three major factors which influence the job satisfaction are:

1. Factors related to workers.

- **Age**—Worker in high age group is more satisfied than younger workers. Because they have now stagnant live, their personal life was well settled and they get approximately all what they want as compared to younger workers.
- **Sex**—Generally female have relatively lower aspiration and expectation level than male. Therefore, they are satisfied with their job easily. One of the reason for satisfaction is they have less economic burden as compared to male.
- **Length of service**—This is also a determinant factor which influences the individual satisfaction level. Workers at preliminary stage have experienced more job satisfaction but when they reaches the age of 45 to 55 than job satisfaction level will go down and it will again high after this stage.
- **Personality**—The worker who are cope with their superior, colleagues, family and also with employer or management experienced more satisfied as compared to individual who are not like this.
- **Dependents**—As the dependents in the family are in large number like 5 dependents on a single earner than it will lead dissatisfaction from the present job as compared to single earner having 2 dependents.

- **Ambitious**—When the performance and the ambition of the worker not fulfill from the concerned job than it will resultant into dissatisfaction.
- **Mental ability**—If worker have high mental ability as compared to requirement for the particular job than definitely it lead dissatisfaction. They feel they are not getting according to their ability.

	Higher Level of Job Satisfaction	Lower Level of Job Satisfaction
Age	Higher Age	Younger
Sex	Female	Male
Length of Service	Preliminary Stage	Mid of 45–55
Personality	Adjustable	Non-adjustable
Dependents	Less Number of Dependents	Large Number of Dependents
Ambitious	Less Ambitious	More Ambitious
Mental Ability	Compatible to Task	Different to Task

Exhibit 1: Individuals Factors Influencing Job Satisfaction

2. **Factors related to employers.**

- **Salary**—Salary influence the income group satisfaction level. Higher and lower income groups are more satisfied as compared to middle income group. Among all, the lower income group had the highest job satisfaction. The reason behind this lower income group had the mental ability and the living standard as low as compared to other. Therefore, they have least desire from the salary.
- **Promotions**—If workers are not getting promotions as per their performance and capability it will lead unfavourable attitude towards management which lead frustration and finally dissatisfaction. And also if promotion not in time than workers get dissatisfied.
- **Security**—If workers had social, economical and psychological security from their job then it will lead maximum satisfaction among the workers.
- **Supervisor**—If supervisor is supportive, fair and knowledgeable than it will lead job satisfaction among the workers. Workers show loyalty and sincerity toward their supervisors. The whole attitude towards work will change if supervisor is good.

	Higher Level of Job Satisfaction	Lower Level of Job Satisfaction
Salary	Higher & Lower Income Group	Middle Income Group
Promotions	On Time & Fair	Not in Time & Biased
Security	More Job Security	Less Job Security
Supervisor	Supportive & Fair	Biased

Exhibit 2: Employers Factors Influencing Job Satisfaction

3. **Factors related to work.**

- **Working conditions**—Worker love their job and give their maximum efforts when working conditions are adequate. Proper light, ventilation, humidity, temperature, cleaning, location and many more are positively related to job satisfaction.
- **Location of factory**—If factory is located in such a place where school, market, medical facilities, transportation facilities, entertainment facilities and many more are easily approachable then worker get satisfied from their job.
- **Skill**—Skilled jobs bring strong feelings of satisfaction among the workers. The nature, status and responsibility are influenced by the skill of the job. More the worker perform skilled job more he/she get satisfied.
- **Relationship with co-workers**—More the worker is connected to their co-workers, they develop strong personal and social relationship contributes the feeling of satisfaction at work.
- **Job itself**—If jobs are rotational, workers have variety of task to perform or simply if changes are introduced at the work then it will lead satisfaction against the routine job.

	Higher Level of Job Satisfaction	Lower Level of Job Satisfaction
Working Conditions	Adequate	Insufficient
Location of Factory	On Time & Fair	Not in Time & Biased
Skill	More Skilled	Less Skilled
Relationship with co-workers	Congenial	Not Friendly
Job Itself	Diversity	Uniformity

Exhibit 3: Work Related Factors Influencing Job Satisfaction

6.5 Consequences of Job Satisfaction/ Dissatisfaction

- **Work performance**–Work environment, relationship with co-workers, superior and management help in to make workers more efficient and by this they get satisfied more easily as compared to others. All their satisfaction is reflected in their better work performance.
- **Absenteeism/Turnover**—There is a positive relation between the absenteeism/turnover and satisfaction. If workers are satisfied than the rate of absenteeism/turnover is reduced.
- **Motivation**—If workers are satisfied from their job than he/she easily motivated to do the job.
- **Conflicts**—Worker who is psychologically satisfied reduces the chance of conflicts with management, co-workers and their own intra conflicts/ inner conflicts.

- **Attitude**—Satisfied workers had positive attitude towards work. They are more committed to management and their own work. They help in to maintain healthy environment in the workplace.
- **Health problem**—It includes not only physical but mental health also. Dissatisfied workers have the problem of anxiety, headache, muscular pain, low concentration, sleeping disorder and many more problems.
- **Accident proneness**—Dissatisfied workers are more accident proneness as compared to satisfied workers. There are many reasons which increased the frequency of accidents like lack of concentration, poor health, stress etc.

6.6 Tips for Reducing Dissatisfaction

- Provide adequate working environment.
- Promotion as per the capability and efficiency of individual.
- Salary should be equal and justice.
- Provide guidance or counselling for dissatisfied workers.
- Workers view are taken into consideration in decision making. (Workers participation in management).
- Provide safety measures to reduce accidents.
- Unbiased behaviour of superior should be avoided.
- Proper grievance handling machinery to reduce conflicts.
- Impose flexible work system/work hour.
- Increased autonomy.
- Emphasis on team work by which if team was not accomplished their objective within prescribed time than it will not lead dissatisfaction for individual.
- Job rotation reduces the monotony.
- Proper communication system between co-workers and management.
- Equal chance of training and development to required workers.

6.7 Experimental Studies

Richard J. Harmer, School of Psychology Australian Catholic University, St. Patrick's Campus and **Bruce M. Findlay** Faculty of Life and Social Sciences, Swinburne University of Technology, study on "The effect of workplace relationships on employee job satisfaction for 25 to 35 year olds", The aim of the study was to determine the role an employee's co-worker and direct supervisor relationships had in predicting their level of job satisfaction.

Sixty-nine individuals participated in the study, 35 males (Age: M = 31.8, SD = 6.0) and 34 females (Age: M = 29.5, SD = 5.0). Fifty-three participants indicated that they were employed full time; twelve indicated that they were employed part time; and the remaining participants indicated that they were employed part time; and the remaining participants indicated that they were employed casual or 'other'. Work and job satisfaction was measured using the Job Descriptive Index (JDI) and Job in General (JIG) scales. Results indicate that 52.1% of an employee's job satisfaction can be predicted by the quality of their workplace relationships, with an individual's relationship with their co-workers the strongest predictor. Results indicate that the quality of an employee's co-worker and immediate supervisor relationships does not significantly predict their level of well-being. Implications of the study's finding with respect to workforce planning are discussed and suggestions for further research are made.

Using individual data from the European Survey on Working Conditions (ESWC) covering all EU member states, this study aimed at contributing to our understanding of the effects of High Performance Workplace Organizations (HPWOs) on worker's job satisfaction. The estimation results show that a higher involvement of workers in HPWOs is associated with higher job satisfaction. This positive effect is dominated by the involvement of workers in flexible work systems, indicating that workers particularly value the opportunities associated with these systems, such as an increased autonomy over how to perform their tasks, and increased communication with co-workers. Being involved in team work and job rotations as well as supporting human resource practices appear to contribute relatively little to the increased job satisfaction from being involved in HPWOs.

Having a good laugh at the workplace contributes to high levels of job satisfaction, according to a latest study. Swinburne University of Technology psychologist Maren Rawlings found that individuals who use, and are surrounded by, positive humour in the workplace had higher levels of job satisfaction than those who don't.

In recent years the National Health Service (NHS) in Britain has experienced an acute shortage of qualified nurses. This has placed issues of recruitment and retention in the profession high on the political agenda. In this paper we investigate the determinants of job satisfaction for nurses, and establish the importance of job satisfaction in determining nurses' intentions to quit the NHS. We find that nurses who report overall dissatisfaction with their jobs have a 65% higher probability of intending to quit than those reporting to be satisfied. However, dissatisfaction with promotion and training opportunities are found to have a stronger impact than workload or pay. Recent policies, which focus heavily on improving the pay of all NHS nurses will only have limited success unless they are accompanied by, improved promotion and training opportunities. Better retention will, in turn, lead to reduced workload. Study done by Shields, Michael A. University of Leicester, England on "*Improving Nurse Retention in the British National Health Service: The Impact of Job Satisfaction on Intentions to Quit*".

❍❍❍

CHAPTER 7

STRESS

7.1 Introduction

Stress is an unavoidable part of most jobs roles in an organization. Stress is created for many organization members by the conflicts they feel between their independence and their commitment to the organization, organization pressure for conformity, day-to-day of the workplace and various forms of the role conflict. Young managers may be particularly at risk, some evidence indicates that young people in general are more vulnerable to stress than older employees. In this chapter first we discuss the definitions, dynamics, types and causes of stress. Along with work related stress and how to manage this stress in the workplace.

7.2 Defining Stress

The word 'stress' is defined by the Oxford Dictionary as "a state of affair involving demand of physical or mental energy". A condition or circumstances which can distribute the normal physical and mental health of an individual. Stress is the tension and pressure that result when an individual views situations which present a demand that threatens to exceed his or her capabilities or resources. Stress is a dynamic condition in which an individual confronted with an opportunity, constraint or demand related to what he or she desire and for which the outcomes is perceived to be both uncertain and important.

According to McGrath, "A person experiences stress when a situation is perceived as presenting a demand which threatens to exceed the person's capabilities and resources for meeting it."

According to Lazaraus, 'Stress denotes a general class of problems which deal with demands taxing psychological, social and psychological systems response of these systems."

Stress is a condition of strain on one's emotions, thought processes and physical conditions that seem to threaten one's ability to cope with the environment. It is particularly harmful, when stress is sustained for the long time and human does not get the opportunity to rebuild its ability to cope with the stress.

Stress is associated with constraint and demand. The former prevents you from doing what you desire. The later refers to the loss of something desired, so when you undergo your annual performance reviews at work, you feel stress because you confront opportunities, constraints and demand. A good performance review may lead to a promotion, greater responsibilities and higher salary. But a poor review may prevent you from getting the promotion. An extremely poor review might even result in your being terminated.

Two conditions are necessary for potential stress to become actual stress. There must be uncertainty over the outcomes and outcomes must be important. If keeping your jobs or earning a promotion doesn't hold any importance to you, you have no reason to fell stress while undergoing performance review.

7.3 The Dynamics of Stress

In a challenging situation the brain prepare the body for defensive action the fight or flight response by releasing stress hormones, namely, cortisone and adrenaline. These hormones raise the blood pressure and the body prepares to react to the situation. With a concrete defensive action (fight response) the stress hormones in the blood get used up, entailing reduced stress effect and symptoms of anxiety.

When we fail to counter a stress situation (flight response) the hormones and chemical unreleased in the blood stream for a long period of time. It results in stress related physical symptoms such as tense muscles, unforced anxiety, dizziness and rapid heartbeats. We all encounter various stressors (cause of stress) in everyday life, which can accumulate, if not released. Subsequently, it compels the mind and body to be in an almost constant alarm-state in preparation to fight or flee. This state of accumulated stress can increase the risk of both acute and chronic psychosomatic illnesses and weaken the immune system of the human body.

Stress management is an important part of daily living for everyone. We all need stress in order to survive. Teams need it to perform well, and in the right doses, it can be very healthy, or even enjoyable. However, when stress becomes excessive it can be very damaging. It can harm:

- health
- happiness
- work performance
- team spirit and co-operation
- relationships
- personal development

Stress management involves, at the simplest level:

(i) recognizing the symptoms of stress

(ii) identifying the causes

(iii) taking action to address the cause and thereby reduce the symptoms.

7.4 Types of Stress

Some form of stress can be good for us, but other types of stress disorders can cause major health problems and even be life threatening. It can be broke-down into four different categories:-

Types of Stress			
Eustress	**Distress**	**Hyper Stress**	**Hypo Stress**
It is one of the helpful type of stress	It is one of the negative stresses.	It is a negative type of stress that comes when a person is forced to undertake more than he/she can take.	It is just opposite to hyper stress.
It is a positive stress that leads to achievement and excellence.	It occurs when the feelings of insecurity, helplessness and depression are felt due to pressure and tension.	A stressful job that overcomes an individual will cause that individual to face hyper stress.	It is positive type of stress experienced by a person who is constantly bored.
It is that type of stress you experience right before you have that need to exert physical force.	**Acute Stress** Its comes immediately with a change of routine. It passes quickly.	**Chronic Stress** It occurs if there is a constant change of routine for week after week.	A worker performing same task over and over, will often experience hypo stress and he/she will need some more challenging task.
Stress disappears when the need is fulfilled. e.g. Playing big game/competition.		Chronic stresses affect the body for a long period of time. e.g. Financial issues, death of a family member, other problems etc.	

Exhibit 1: Types of Stress

Eustress

Eustress is one of the helpful type of stress. It is that type of stress you experience right before you have that need to exert physical force. Eustress prepare the muscles, heart and mind for the strength needed for whatever is about to occur.

Eustress can also apply to creative endeavours. When a person needs to have some extra energy or creativity, Eustress kicks in to bring them inspiration they need. An athlete will experience the strength that comes from Eustress right before they play a big game or enter a big competition. Because of the Eustress, they immediately receive the strength that they need to perform.

When the body enters the fight or flight response, it will experience Eustress. The Eustress prepare the body to fight with or flee from an imposing danger. This type of stress will cause the blood to pump to the major muscles groups, and will increase the heart rate and blood pressure. If the event or danger passes, the body will eventually returns to its normal state.

Distress

Distress is one of the negative type of stress. This is the stress that the mind and body undergoes when the normal routine is constantly adjusted and altered. The mind is not comfortable with this routine, and craves the familiarity of a common routine. There are actually two types of distress: acute stress and chronic stress.

(i) *Acute Stress*—Acute stress is the type of stress that comes immediately with a change of routine. It is an intense type of stress, but it passes quickly. Acute stress is the body's way of getting a person to stand up and take inventory of what is going on, to make sure that everything is OK.

(ii) *Chronic Stress*—It will occur if there is a constant change of routine for week after week. Chronic stress affects the body for a long period of time. This is the type of stress experienced by someone who constantly faces moves or job changes.

Hyperstress

Hyperstress is the type of negative stress that comes when a person is forced to undertake more than he/she can take. A stressful job that overworks an individual will cause that individual to face hyperstress. A person who is experiencing hyperstress will often responds to even little stressors with huge emotional outbreaks. It is important for a person who thinks they might be experiencing hyperstress to take measure to reduce the stress in their lives, because hyperstress can lead to serious emotional and physical repercussion.

Hypostress

The final of the four types of stress is hypostress. Hypostress stands in direct opposite to hyperstress. That is because hypostress is the right type of stress experienced by a person who is constantly bored. Someone in an unchallenging job, such as a factory worker performing the same tasks over and over, will often experience hypostress. The effect of hypostress is feelings of restlessness and a lack of inspiration.

7.5 The Signs of Stress

The symptoms of stress are many and varied, such as:

- irritability
- headaches
- illness
- insomnia
- tiredness/lethargy
- and many more....

Recognizing Stress Symptoms		
Physical Symptoms	Emotional Symptoms	Behavioural Symptoms
• headaches • neck pain • backaches • weakness • indigestion • high BP • accident proneness • chronic fatigue • rapid/difficult breathing • excessive sleeping	• depression • nightmares • irritability • anger • anxiety • neurotic behaviour • thoughts of suicide • frustration • helplessness • restlessness • frequent episodes of crying	• grinding teeth • nail biting • compulsive eating • increased smoking • finger tapping • chronic tardiness • loss of interest in physical appearance • increased alcohol • increased use or prescribed medication

Exhibit 1: Recognizing Stress Symptoms

Sometimes, you can be experiencing stress but your mind and body are so good at hiding it from you that you are unaware of it. In such cases the symptoms might be more subtle and therefore difficult to recognize, such as:

- working endlessly without tiring
- having little feeling or emotion (except the occasional outburst of anger)
- increased use of alcohol, caffeine, cigarettes or other drugs (which may suppress feeling of stress)
- behaviour that is 'out of character'
- an inability to relax

If you are under a lots of stress for a prolonged period of time, but do not feel stressed, eventually it may catch up with you and cause more serious symptoms, such as:

- stomach ulcers
- heart problems
- minor illness (allergies, skin disorders, migraine)
- serious illness (arthritis, cancer, diabetes)
- mental problems (depression)

Most people experience a significant period of stress or depression during their lives. To feel stresses at various times is to be normal. If you think the stress may be excessive and you need help, then consult a suitably qualified professional (such as your doctor or a counsellor).

The impact of excessive stress on teamwork is also harmful, and it can damage:

- individual work performance
- team performance
- working relationship
- co-operation between team members
- team spirit.

The more effort team members have to expend in managing their own stress, the less they have to contribute to teamwork and mutual support.

7.6 Causes of Stress

The factors that contribute to the experience of stress are many and varied. A useful overview of these causes can be gained by using the 'analysis wheel', to view them. Using this wheel, you can take six different perspectives on the causes of stress. Each of the lists below contains a sample of ideas only- there are many more causes of stress than those listed.

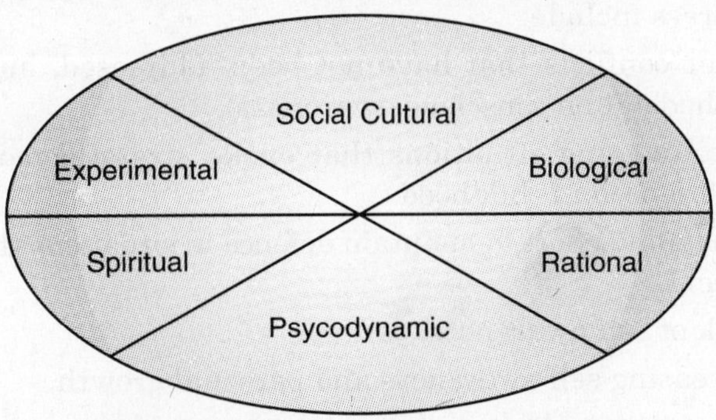

Exhibit 2: Stress Analysis Wheel

Biological

The causes of some stress lie in the biological make up of your body or the interaction of your body with the food you eat or the environment you live in. Some examples of biological causes of stress include:

- lack of fitness
- poor diet (e.g. deficiency of vitamins; too much caffeine)
- allergic reaction to chemical in food
- genetic disorder resulting in chemical imbalances in the body
- change in bodily function, such as pregnancy, puberty, menopause.

SOCIAL/CULTURAL

Stress can be caused by a whole range of social and cultural pressures, such as:

- Change of social circumstance (e.g. bereavement of spouse, moving job, marriage, holidays)
- Pressure to conform to social or employment patterns of behaviour, especially where these behaviour are not the preferred behaviours of the individuals (e.g. demands on an introvert to behave in an extrovert manner).
- Conflict in relationships, or an absence of praise and being valued by others.
- Lack of support, time to be listened.
- Having a high-pressure jobs, being unemployed, or only having a small range of social circumstances (e.g. rarely leaving the house, few hobbies).

PSYCHODYNAMIC

The term 'psychodynamic' refers to subconscious thoughts and feelings, which often arise from childhood experience. The way in which you learned to cope in childhood is by using defences mechanisms that involved a degree of self deception. You still use those defences today. Examples of psychodynamic causes of stress include:

- Inner conflicts that have not been addressed, but repressed (i.e. pushed out on conscious awareness).
- Encountering situations that evoke stressful feelings that were experienced in childhood.
- Expending effort to maintain defence in situations that threaten self-esteem.
- Lack of self awareness.
- Increasing self awareness and personal growth.

RATIONAL

The rational process in our minds constantly interprets and evaluates the world around. Events can be interpreted in many ways, and the way which is done can influence the level of stress that is felt. Some examples of rational causes of stress include:

- Perceiving the consequences of action as being dangerous or threatening. These perceptions may or may not be accurate.
- Having an inaccurate perception of self.
- Believing one is capable of achieving far too much-setting standards and expectation too high.

- Misinterpreting the action of others so as to discount (i.e. not accept) the love and support that is given.
- Not having the skill and knowledge to cope with certain situations, such as not having a rational approach to problem-solving or conflict resolution, and therefore being unable to cope with problem as they arise.

EXPERIENTIAL

The way in which the individual experiences each snapshot in time, even in very similar situations, is very different. One person may find a situation highly stressful, while another may find it stimulating or enjoyable-every reaction is unique. There may be many instant pressures that cause an individual to experience stress, such as:

- Too many simultaneous demands from different people.
- Environmental stresses, such as noise, cramped conditions, or cluttered surroundings.
- Needs that are being unmet or frustrated.
- The appearance of a threat to survival, self-esteem, or identity.
- Change in pattern of eating, sleeping, time zone, relationships etc.

SPIRITUAL

The need for individual spiritual development has long been recognized by religion. It is only during the last 30 years that psychology has acknowledged the existence of spiritual side to the individuals. Some spiritual causes of stress include:

- Violation of personal or religious moral code, contravention of accepted group practice, or violation of laws.
- Lack of spiritual development.
- An absence of truth (e.g. self-deception and deception of others).
- The lack of sense of personal agency i.e. that one can influence events or the failure to recognize and exercise choice.
- Absence of a relationship with God, and lack of forgiveness.

7.7 ADDRESSING THE CAUSES OF STRESS

Once you have identified the causes of your stress, you can then make plan to address them. For example:

Causes of stress	Action that can be taken to reduce stress
Need for time of privacy and solitude not being met	Find a place and a time of day when you can be on your own, or go on a retreat
Lack of fitness	Engage in some sport or fitness activity (may need to consult your doctor)
Unexplained inner feelings of stress	Consult a doctor, and perhaps get referral to an appropriate specialist (e.g. a counsellor or dietician)
Stressful job circumstances	Negotiate different working schedules with your boss
Lack of skill to resolve conflict or manage demanding workload	Attend training courses in assertiveness, conflict resolution or time management.

Exhibit 3: Addressing the Causes of Stress

7.8 Workplace Stress

Different jobs vary greatly in the amount of stress they generate. Physicians, office managers, supervisors, for example, must endure a good deal of stress. When most of us imagine a stressful environment, we envision a harried office worker, the in-box overflowing with work to be done, trying simultaneously to answer the phone, explain to the boss why everything is late, and write a report. This picture is not inaccurate—role overload is a major cause of stress at work. There are two kinds of overload. **Quantitative overloading** occurs when a person has more work than he or she can complete in a given time. **Qualitative overloading** occurs when the employees lack the skills or abilities needed to complete the job satisfactorily. **Under loading** can also be problem—a person who does not have enough to do face boredom and monopoly, which are also quit stressful.

Stress at work impairs the job activities and also causes physical problems like headache, backache and later on heart problem. At the extreme, chance of death is also there due to stressful work. Japanese even have a term for it—**karoushi**.

Work related stress results in decreased productivity, increased management problems and increased incidence of illness among employees. Stress related problems are the most common causes of sickness and absenteeism all over the world. Job stress can be defined as the harmful physical and emotional response that occur when the requirements of the job do not match the capabilities, resources or need of the worker. Job stress can lead to poor health and even injury.

Work related stress

The common causes of work place stress are:

- The fear of losing one's job.
- Unreasonable demands for performance.

- Lack of interpersonal relationship among the employees.
- Lack of interpersonal communication between the employer and the employees.
- Long working hours.
- Less time to spend with the family.
- Under utilization of skills.
- Underpaid jobs.
- A promotion that did not materialize.

Unlike stress in general, the work related stress affects men and women equally. Older employees are affected more than their younger counterparts. Stress at workplace could be due to:

- External causes like dangerous working condition or poor interpersonal relationship with the colleague.
- Internal causes like physical or psychological illness.
- Acute causes.
- Long term causes.

The below mentioned model identifies three sets of factors—environment, organizational, individuals that act as potential sources of stress. Whether they become actual stress depends on individual difference such as job experience and personality.

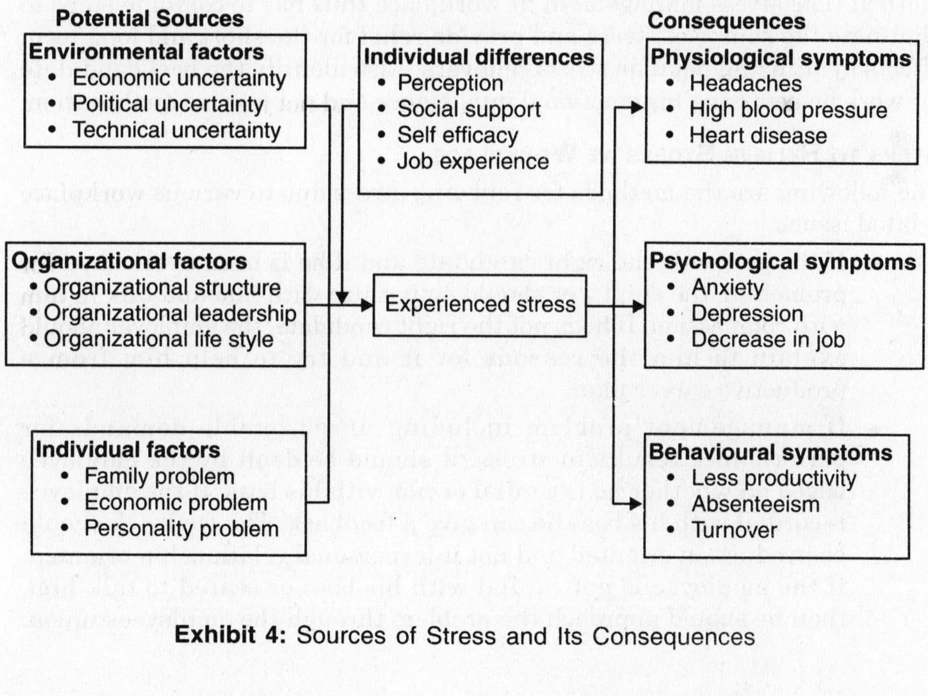

Exhibit 4: Sources of Stress and Its Consequences

Negative Stress in Workplace

Under normal circumstances people should be able to find new balances and responses in their reaction to new situations. Stress is not necessarily a negative phenomenon and it would therefore be a mistake to concentrate only on its pathological effects. A moderate level of stress can be an important motivational factor and can be instrumental in achieving a dynamic adaptation to new situations.

If health is considered as a dynamic equilibrium, stress is part of it. There is no health without interaction with other people and with the environment. Only excesses of stress are pathological.

Some stress is therefore normal and necessary, at work and outside it. But if stress is intense, continuous or repeated, if a person is unable to cope, or if support is lacking, stress than become a negative phenomenon which can lead to physical illness and psychological disorders. In a work context, it often results in inadequate adaptation to situations and people and failure to perform at an optimal level.

7.9 Managing Stress at Workplace

If an employer finds that his staff is under stress, he should not ignore them. He should take steps to help them. If he finds it difficult to provide a solution for it, he should get the help of another capable person. If the employee is suffering from non work related stress, even then it should be looked into as it may later lead on to work related stress. There is no single stress relief method. The stress management at workplace thus has to combine steps to eliminate the source of stress and provide relief for the short and long term effects by utilizing popular stress relievers. Also identify the best candidate for work by assessing his emotional intelligence and not just his qualification.

Steps to Relieve Stress at Workplace

The following are the methods for relieving stress due to various workplace related issues:

- If the person is the right candidate and if he is been overlooked for promotion, the employer should empathize with him and talk to him with compassion. If he is not the right candidate, the employer should explain to him the reasons for it and try to help him from a productive career plan.
- If management problem including unreasonable demands for performance results in stress, it should be dealt by the employee based on whether he is cordial or not with his boss. If the employee is cordial with his boss he can give a feedback. The feedback should be production oriented and not interpersonal relationship oriented. If the employee is not cordial with his boss or scared to talk him, then he should approach the problem through the employees union.

- If inappropriate or monotonous job are the causes of stress, then the employer should intervene. He should keep assessing the skills of the employee and change it accordingly. He should make the environment employee friendly and fun filled.
- If job insecurity and retirement are the causes of stress, again the employer has to intervene. He should try to find new opportunities for the stressed employee. Even after retirement he should try to involve them as mentors.
- If poor interpersonal relationship results in stress, then the employee should try to develop a cordial relationship with colleagues and the boss. During free time he should talk to them about their families, friends and other personal issues.
- Workplace conflict is a double edged sword. It may result in new ideas and researches being formed or may result in decrease in communication and a drop in the production. Based on which of these two occurs measures are taken for stress relief. 'Personal Office' concept can be used for relieving stress due to workplace conflict.

'The Personal Office' in most companies helps to resolve conflicts with other employees and to resolve problems associated with job responsibilities. If discussing the situation with the employer does not resolve the situation or if the employee finds it very uncomfortable to discuss it with the management, then Personal Office may be approached to solve the problem.

The above mentioned methods are for stress relieving methods which act by correcting the stress inducing problems. In addition work stress can also be relived by other stress relief methods like:

- Consuming a healthy, balanced nutritious diet
- Do deep breathing exercise
- Squeeze stress balls
- Listen to music
- Practice yoga, meditation
- Go for a walk
- Talk to a close friend and try to find his view of the problem
- Play games
- Play with kids
- Play with pets

Managing Stress at Workplace

Coping Strategies at the Organizational Level
- Stress reduction and stress management programmes.
- Job redesign
- Counselling
- Meditation
- Collateral programmes

Coping Strategies at the Individual Level
- Time management
- Relaxation training
- Support/ peer group
- Self-management

Coping Strategies at the Organizational Level

1. *Stress reduction and stress management programmes*: It aims to identify relevant organization stressors and to reduce their effect by improving supervisory skills, reallocating workloads or job variety.
2. *Job redesign*: Properly designed jobs and work schedules can help to reduce the stress.
3. *Counselling*: It is needed when a supervisor becomes aware that an employee is disturbed by a problem or irritated by a situation.
4. *Meditation*: It is an effective anti-anxiety treatment, lifting mood, increasing energy and relaxing mind and body. It helps to relieve from a stressful world.
5. *Collateral prcgrammes*: It is an organizational progamme specifically created to help employee deal with stress.

Coping Strategies at the Individual Level

1. *Time management*: This strategy helps people to get more of the important things done every day. It helps in reducing stress by proper balanced schedule and plan regular breaks.
2. *Relaxation training*: How to cope with your stress? What are the stressors? And many questions have to be answered by providing relaxation training.
3. *Support/ peer group*: It is a group of friends or family members with whom a person can share his feelings. They can help the people cope with routine types of stress on an ongoing basis.
4. *Self-management*: To reduce the stress caused by role ambiguity, managers should tell subordinates clearly what is expected of them and what their job responsibities are.

Some Approaches to Reduce Work Stress

- Clearly defines the role and responsibilities of the employees.
- Improve communications and reduce uncertainty about career development and future employment prospects.

- Design jobs to provide meanings, stimulation and opportunities for workers to use their skills.
- Establish work schedules that ensure availability of time for workers to fulfill their personal responsibilities outside the workers.
- Provide opportunities for social interaction among workers.
- Ensure that the workload is in line with works capabilities and resources.

There are different techniques used by Indian organization for reduction of stress which are as follows:

Peer Support Group

Workplace peer support is not a new idea. Informally, workers have offered assistance to colleagues during traumatic and stressful times. Unfortunately, in some cases, the support provided caused more problems than it solved. The concept of formal peer support is new and exciting. Peer support utilizes the experiences and skills of fellow workers to provide support and reassurance in times of distress. Psychological support for staff is provided, that is both reactive to staff distress and proactive in promoting psychological health and early detection of problems. Support is provided by fellow workers who have the same or similar experiences.

Peer support programs provide worker with the opportunity to confidentially 'talk out' any problems with specially trained coworkers. As a society-oriented people, we need other people to relate to and to communicate with. Without this part of our existence, most of us would be unable to deal with the mounting stresses we are subjected to at work and at home.

Peer support also promotes cohesiveness, by placing emphasis on staff providing support and solving their own problems. The introduction of peer support programs has been reported to increase staff morale, reduce sick leave and increase satisfaction with management.

In-house Support

Companies believe in a flat organization, where all employees are treated equal even with different designation. Communication channels need to be open at all times. If employees have any doubt about the future of the company and his own future, he should be able to approach the right authority and voice his concerns.

The standard uniform code (gray) also prevails, which makes the employees equal and which is the first, external symbol of a flat organization. The lower you are in an organization, the higher the sense of satisfaction about commonality. At the regular morning meetings, the supervisor and the group leader also leads the group for a few minutes of exercise. External faculty is regularly called in to conduct stress management programs. On the first Wednesday of every month, the plant is stopped for one hour in every shift for small group activity. A total of 600 groups meet to discuss change, improvements and solutions, in their work.

Psychological problems among employees are among the major concerns of organizations, including issues like data security and attrition. There is multiple options available in the industry today. Therefore, in the race to be the 'preferred employer' companies are adopting multiple strategies. Emotional support is one of the important roles in employee retention. It is a corporate responsibility to allow the employee to learn and enjoy work while making contribution to get the best out of them along with respect for each other within the organization. Psychological support is the most important way to sustain employee retention within the organization, when employees are helped to overcome stress, depression, health disorders and absenteeism is lowered, thus increasing the productivity.

Employees Assistance Program

It provides easily accessible, confidential and professional support to employees and their immediate family members. The objective of an EAP is to help employees develop the skills necessary to more successfully resolve personal issues that may causes concern and adversely affect their job performance. Whether issues are work-related or otherwise, most of the public and private companies running EAP.

Meditation Facility

Himachal Futuristic Communication Ltd. are in growth phase, not just because of volume of team service business it has bagged. As the company grew rapidly, so did the quantum of employee stress. Three years ago, Vinay Maloo, a promoter of HFCL, introduced the meditative technique of *preksha dhyan*, devised by the Jain Guru Acharya Tulsi in the company.

In the DCM Shriram organized a series of workshops on meditation, beginning with a common session for employees, followed up with individual sessions that taught techniques of stress management. The response was tremendous. In Mumbai, employees of Benzer have taking a 10-days break to learn Vipassana Meditation Company.

Tata Tea and Tata Chemicals have got the full treatment from MIM (Maharishi Institute of Management). Visiting professors from the Maharishi Vedic University in Holland, conducted sessions at Tata Tea headquaters in Kolkata, and then visited the company's tea gardens in Tamil Nadu and Kerala, two Southern Indian states, for a repeat. ACC, the Oriental Bank, Indian Petrochemicals Corporation and Reckitt and Colman are some other companies that have called in MIM.

TCS (Tata Consultancy Services) also in the process of setting up a gym and meditation facility, which will help employees, take a break from their stressful work environment.

HCL Infosystems is also planning to start stress management lectures for employees. "Health is key concern for our HR department. We encourage people to do exercise and also conduct stress management lectures for them," says ML Taneja, vice-president HRD, HCL Infosystems.

A recent study by the TISS (Tata Institute of Social Sciences) on 1,000 senior executives in 25 companies who had done the Art of Living programme has some interesting results. Around 88% of the respondents said they could handle stress better and deal with negative emotions. About 51% also felt that it enhanced their performance.

REFERENCES

1. Goliszek, A., *Stress Management*, 1st edition, 1993, Bantam Books, Great Britain.
2. McGrath, J.E., *Stress and Behaviour in Organization.* In M.D. Dunnette (Ed.), 1976, Handbook of Industrial and Organizational Psychology.
3. Lawler, E.E., *Pay and Organizational Effectiveness*, 1971, McGraw-Hill, New York.
4. Occupational Stress and Job Satisfaction Among Manager; Indian Journal of Occupational and Medicine, Vol. 7, No.2, May-Aug 2003.
5. Sapre, A., *Organizational Behaviour*, 1st edition, 2002, Symbiosis Centre for Distance Learning, Pune.

❍❍❍

CHAPTER 8

ORGANIZATIONAL CULTURE

8.1 INTRODUCTION

Matching individuals to organizations is a crucial part of success for any company. The match between people and the companies for which they work is determined by the kind of organizational culture that exists. The degree to which an organization's values match the values of an individual who works for the company determines whether a person is a good match for a particular organization. The success of any company depends in part on the match between individuals and the culture of the organization. Organizational culture is the set of operating principles that determine how people behave within the context of the company. Underlying the observable behaviours of people are the beliefs, values, and assumptions that dictate their actions.

8.2 CONCEPT AND MEANING

The collective rules by which an organization operates define its culture. These rules are formed by shared behaviours, values and beliefs. Culture forms the basis for how individuals operate within the context of the organization. The way a group or individual behaves, defines what is "normal" and sanctions what is not normal is determined by his or her culture. Culture can be defined either by a set of observable behaviours or by the underlying values that drive behaviour. In large organizations, vision statements, mission statements and statements of values are often formalized to describe the company's culture.

According to Denison (1984), organizational culture refers to the set of values, beliefs and behaviour patterns that form the core identity of an organization. As individuals come into contact with organizations, they come into contact with dress norms, stories people tell about what goes on, the organization's formal rules and procedures, its formal code behaviour, rituals, tasks, pay systems, jargon and jokes only understood by insiders, and so on. These elements are some of the manifestations of organizational culture.[1]

A general constellation of beliefs, morals, value systems, behavioural norms and ways of doing business that are unique to each corporation.[2]

Organizational culture is an idea in the field of organizational studies and management which describes the psychology, attitudes, experiences, beliefs and values (personal and cultural values) of an organization. It has been defined as "the specific collection of values and norms that are shared by people and groups in an organization and that control the way they interact with each other and with stakeholders outside the organization."[3]

Gareth Morgan describes culture as "an active living phenomenon through which people jointly creates and recreates the world in which they live."[4] Elements of organizational culture may include:

- Stated and unstated values.
- Overt and implicit expectations for member behaviour.
- Customs and rituals.
- Stories and myths about the history of the group.
- Shop talk—typical language used in and about the group.
- Climate—the feelings evoked by the way members interact with each other, with outsiders, and with their environment, including the physical space they occupy.
- Metaphors and symbols—may be unconscious but can be found embodied in other cultural elements.

Morgan proposes four essential strengths of the organizational culture approach:

- It focuses attention on the human side of organizational life, and finds significance and learning in even its most mundane aspects (for example, the setup in an empty meeting room).
- It makes clear the importance of creating appropriate systems of shared meaning to help people work together toward desired outcomes.
- It requires members—especially leaders—to acknowledge the impact of their behaviour on the organization's culture. Morgan proposes that people should ask themselves: "What impact am I having on the social construction of reality in my organization?" "What can I do to have a different and more positive impact?"
- It encourages the view that the perceived relationship between an organization and its environment is also affected by the organization's basic assumptions.

Supervisors need an accurate understanding of the organization's culture in order to direct activities in a productive way and to avoid the destructive influence of having workers' who are not committed to the company's goals. A shared sense of purpose starts with the hiring process and continues with careful attention to how workers' are motivated and rewarded for their efforts. Supervisor need to continually transmit the values of the culture through efforts such as story telling, rituals and firm-sponsored social events, as well as consistent positive feedback that gives each member of the organization a sense of importance.

In simple words, culture is *the way we do things round us* (Deal & Kennedy, 1982). Organizational culture provides ease to worker when they match with their own culture. It resultant into high efficiency at work place. Organizational culture is an important component of industrial psychology, if organization develops good culture at factory it will definitely leads high production.

8.3 Types of Organizational Culture

- **Strong Culture** is said to exist where staff respond to stimulus because of their association to organizational values. In such environments, strong cultures help firms operate like well-oiled machines, cruising along with outstanding execution and perhaps minor tweaking of existing procedures here and there.

  Conversely, there is **weak culture** where there is little association with organizational values and control must be exercised through extensive procedures and bureaucracy.
- **Leader-centered Culture** where all the power is concentrated on the leader. They stressed to workers' to obey his order and work in discipline. Punishments are imposed if disobedience or indiscipline occurs.

  People are more committed to decision when they participate in the decision making process. **Participative cultures** tend to emerge where most organizational members are professionals or they presume themselves as equals.
- Where core values share by majority of organizational members are termed as **dominant culture**.

  Subculture marked by a set of values that shared by the members of division or department.
- **Mechanistic Culture** exhibits the values of bureaucracy and feudalism. Direction of authority flowing from top to the lower level and communication flows in a prescribed channel.

  In the **organic culture** formal hierarchies, formal rules and regulation, communication through prescribed channel and others are not taken into consideration. Here, much more focus on task accomplishment, team work, and free flow of communication.

  Some other types of culture defined by **Cameron & Quinn**[5] are listed below:
- The **Clan Culture**—A very friendly place to work where people share a lot of themselves. It is like an extended family.
- The **Hierarchy Culture**—A much formalizes structured place to work. Procedures govern what people do.

- The **Adhocracy Culture**—A dynamic entrepreneurial and creative place to work. People stick their neck out and take risks.
- The **Market Culture**—A result oriented organization whose major concern is with getting the job done. People are competitive and goal-oriented.

8.4 Importance of Organizational Culture

- It focuses attention on the human side of organizational life, and finds significance and learning in even its most ordinary aspects.
- It clarifies the importance of creating appropriate systems of shared meaning to help people work together toward desired outcomes.
- It requires members especially leaders, to acknowledge the impact of their behaviour on the organization's culture.
- It encourages the view that the perceived relationship between an organization and its environment is also affected by the organization's basic assumptions.
- Organizational culture creates energy and momentum. The energy will permeate the organization and create a new momentum for success.

8.5 Changing Organizational Culture

Organization cannot change the culture without knowing where the organization wants to be or what elements of the current organizational culture need to change. It is more difficult to change the culture of an existing organization than to create a culture in a brand new organization. When an organizational culture is already established, people must unlearn the old values, assumptions, and behaviours before they can learn the new ones.

The two most important elements for creating organizational cultural change are workers' support and training.

- **Workers' support:** Workers' in the organization must support the cultural change, and in ways beyond verbal support. They must show behavioural support for the cultural change. Workers' must lead the change by changing their own behaviours. It is extremely important for worker to consistently support the change.
- **Training:** Cultural change depends on behaviour change. Members of the organization must clearly understand what is expected of them, and must know how to actually do the new behaviours, once they have been defined. Training can be very useful in both communicating expectations and teaching new behaviours.

Some other components are important in changing the culture of an organization is:

- **Assessment of organizational structure**: Changing the physical structure of the company to align it with the desired organizational culture may be necessary. As an example, in a small company, four distinct business units competing for product, customers, and internal support resources, may not support the creation of an effective organizational culture. These units are unlikely to align to support the overall success of the business.
- **Create value and belief statements**: Use employee focus groups, by department, to put the mission, vision, and values into words that state their impact on each employee's job.
- **Practice effective communication**: Keeping all employees informed about the organizational cultural change process ensures commitment and success. Telling employees what is expected of them is critical for effective organizational cultural change.
- **Redesign your approach to rewards and recognition**: Management will likely need to change the reward system to encourage the behaviours vital to the desired organizational culture.
- **Review all work systems**: Such as employee promotions, pay practices, performance management, and employee selection to make sure they are aligned with the desired culture. As an example, you cannot just reward individual performance if the requirements of your organizational culture specify team work. An executive's total bonus cannot reward the accomplishment of his department's goals without recognizing the importance of him playing well with others on the executive team to accomplish your organizational goals.

8.6 Matching People with Organizational Culture[7]

Being aware of an organization's culture at all levels is important because the culture defines acceptable and unacceptable behaviour. In some cultures, for example, creativity is stressed. In others, the status quo is valued. Some cultures are more socially oriented, while others are task-oriented, "business only" environments. In some company's teamwork is key. In other's, individual achievement is encouraged and valued. An organization's culture also determines the way in which employees are rewarded. Management tends to focus on a dominant source of motivation, such as pay, status, or opportunity for personal growth and achievement. The accessibility of management and the ways in which decisions are made are reflections of an organization's culture as well.

It is important for individual values to match organizational culture because it helps the organization for achieving the common or collective goal. An organization will operate more productively as a whole when key values are shared among the majority of its members. To that end, employees need to be feeling ease with the desired behaviours encouraged by the organization so that individual motivated and group productivity remain high.

All of this is of key importance to managers. Supervisor usually set the tone by exerting core values that form the overall dominant culture shared by the majority of an organization's members. So, if management does not take the time to understand the culture that motivates an organization, problems are to be expected. New procedures and activities will be very hard to implement if they do not interconnect with the organization's culture.

For making congenial environment for workers' or workers' will accept the new changes, management starts an effort at the process of hiring. Management can foster the development of a positive culture by employing people who share the same values and vision that the organization have. To do this, employers can spend time with prospects before they enter the organization as new employees. Once new hires are indoctrinated with the organization's values, they will form an objective perception of the environment that will solidify the organization's personality or culture.

In addition to hiring people who fit the organization, managers need to have a solid understanding of the dynamics of culture and how to transform it so that they can direct activities in a manner that gets results. Some ways to continually transmit the culture of an organization in a productive way include telling stories, having corporate "rituals," and using symbolic language when referring to the organization's mission. Firm-sponsored social events and mentorship programs may be effective as well.

Having a positive and aligned culture benefits the organization in many ways. One important benefit is a high level of productivity. The destructive influence of hiring someone who does not share the same set of values, goals and commitment espoused by the organization will weaken a strong chain of links and bonds. An employee's performance depends on what is and what is not proper among his or her peers, which in turn affects that individual's behaviour and motivation to participate and contribute within the organizational framework.

An effective means of keeping employees aligned with the values and goals of an organization is by developing a culture that encourages employees to focus on a higher purpose for their work. Values that support this kind of cohesive operation include the idea that people are basically, good, rational and interested in achievement. Leaders that unify an organization believe that everyone has something to contribute to the organization and decision-making should involve people at all levels within the organization.

Creating an environment where people enjoy and value their work is key. To do this effectively, leaders must be sure to communicate clear expectations for every member of the organization. These expectations should be supported by the words and actions of managers who regularly let people know how their work is important to the organization. Individuals should be given assignments that are consistent with their strengths and interests, and opportunities for continued learning and growth should be provided as well.

The importance of understanding organizational culture cannot be overlooked. The bottom line for managers who want to create a culture of success is to start with creating a positive environment. Bring in people whose values are in line with the organization's culture, and continue to acknowledge success and involve the whole organization in maintaining an environment that allows people to enjoy working hard to meet the company's goals.

REFERENCES

1. Joanne Martin, *Cultures in Organizations*, Oxford University Press, New York, 1992, p.3.
2. W.B. Turnstall, *Cultural Transition at AT & T*, Sloan Management Review, 25, 1983, pp. 1-12.
3. Charles W.L. Hill, and Gareth R. Jones, *Strategic Management*. Houghton Mifflin, 2001.
4. Gareth Morgan, *Images of Organization. Thousand Oaks*, CA: Sage Publications, 1997.
5. Cameron, K., & Quinn, R., *Diagnosing and Changing Organization Culture*, Addison- Wesley, New York, 1999.
6. humanresources.about.com/.../**organizationalculture**/.../**culture**_change_2.htm.
7. Asim Khan, "*Matching People with Organizational Culture*" Business Management Group, Inc.,CA.

❍❍❍

CHAPTER 9

LEADERSHIP

9.1 INTRODUCTION

For running successfully the companies need an efficient and impressive leader, who facilitate workers to do work. Leadership is a process of influencing the behaviour of other workers' to work willingly and enthusiastically for achieving preplanned goals. Leaders are not compared with manager because the visions of both are different. Leaders' source of power is their personal abilities and manager is authority delegated. Leaders inspire workers' to work hard but manager control the activity of workers'. Good leaders are made not born. If you have the desire and willpower, you can become an effective leader. In this chapter we define leadership. Then take a look of principle and process of leadership. Discuss importance and quality of good leader. And lastly, discuss the theories of leadership.

9.2 CONCEPT AND MEANING

Leadership is a process by which a person influences others to accomplish an objective and directs the organization in a way that makes it more cohesive and coherent. Leaders carry out this process by applying their leadership attributes, such as beliefs, values, ethics, character, knowledge, and skills.

Leadership is the ability to influence a group towards the achievement of a vision or set of goals.[1]

Leadership is interpersonal influence exercised in a situation and directed through communication process, towards the attainment of a specified goal or goals.[2]

It is the quality of the behaviour of the individuals whereby they guide people or their activities in an organized effort.[3]

It is the ability to shape the attitude and beahviour of others, whether in formal or informal situations.[4]

A simple definition of leadership is that leadership is the art of motivating a group of people to act towards achieving a common goal. Put even more simply, the leader is the inspiration and director of the action. He or she is the person in the group that possesses the combination of personality and skills that makes others want to follow his or her direction.[5]

9.3 Importance of Leadership

According to Peter Drucker, "an effective leader is one who can make ordinary men do extraordinary things, make common people do uncommon things. Leadership is a lifting of a man's sights to a higher vision, the raising of man's standard to a higher performance, the building of a man's personality beyond its normal limitations.[6]

There are few common importances are:

- **Motivating workers**—A good leader always motivate their followers for doing work hard and with perfection.
- **Overcome the barriers**—They make the path of their workers' easy. If any problem faced by workers' it should be overcome with providing necessary resources to perform their task.
- **Maintains integrity**—Leader should maintain institutional integrity and his organization's distinctive identity. They integrate the needs of the individual with those of the group so that the goals are easily reached.
- **Act as arbitrator**—When group experiences internal difference, whether based on emotional or intellectual clashes, a leader can often resolve the difference. He acts as an arbitrator to prevent serious group splintering.[7]
- **Parental approach**—Leaders show personal concern for the workers'. Providing an adequate reward structure to encourage performance of their followers. They delegate the authority where needed and inviting participation from the side of workers' when possible.

9.4 Qualities of Good Leader

The leader is expected to play many roles and, therefore, must be qualified to guide others to organizational achievement and must also be capable handler of interpersonal relations.[8]

Some other qualities that good leader has:

- Flexibility
- Technical mastery
- Enthusiasm
- Fairness
- Paternalism

- Decisiveness
- Friendliness
- Tolerance and patience
- Persuasiveness
- Intellectual
- Stability in behaviour
- Communication skill
- Knowledge of human relation
- Initiative

9.5 Principles of Leadership

To help you *be*, *know*, and *do*; (U.S. Army, 1973)[9] follow these eleven principles of leadership:

1. Know yourself and seek self-improvement—In order to know yourself, you have to understand your *be*, *know*, and *do*, attributes. Seeking self-improvement means continually strengthening your attributes. This can be accomplished through self-study, formal classes, reflection, and interacting with others.
2. Be technically proficient—As a leader, you must know your job and have a solid familiarity with your employees' tasks.
3. Seek responsibility and take responsibility for your actions—Search for ways to guide your organization to new heights. And when things go wrong, they always do sooner or later—do not blame others. Analyze the situation, take corrective action, and move on to the next challenge.
4. Make sound and timely decisions—Use good problem solving, decision making, and planning tools.
5. Set the example—Be a good role model for your employees. They must not only hear what they are expected to do, but also see. *We must become the change we want to see*—Mahatma Gandhi.
6. Know your people and look out for their well-being—Know human nature and the importance of sincerely caring for your workers.
7. Keep your workers informed—Know how to communicate with not only them, but also seniors and other key people.
8. Develop a sense of responsibility in your workers—Help to develop good character traits that will help them carry out their professional responsibilities.
9. Ensure that tasks are understood, supervised, and accomplished—Communication is the key to this responsibility.
10. Train as a team—Although many so called leaders call their organization, department, section, etc. a team; they are not really teams...they are just a group of people doing their jobs.

11. Use the full capabilities of your organization—By developing a team spirit, you will be able to employ your organization, department, section, etc. to its fullest capabilities.

9.6 The Process of Great Leadership

The road to great leadership (Kouzes & Posner, 1987)[10] that is common to successful leaders:

- **Challenge the process**—First, find a process that you believe needs to be improved the most.
- **Inspire a shared vision**—Next, share your vision in words that can be understood by your followers.
- **Enable others to act**—Give them the tools and methods to solve the problem.
- **Model the way**—When the process gets tough, get your hands dirty. A boss tells others what to do, a leader shows that it can be done.
- **Encourage the hearts**—Share the glory with your followers' hearts, while keeping the pains within your own.

9.7 Leadership Theories

(A) Great Man Theory

This theory is based on the assumptions that leaders are born and not made and the great leaders will arise when there is a great need.

Early research on leadership was based on the study of people who were already great leaders. These people were often from the aristocracy, as few from lower classes had the opportunity to lead. This contributed to the notion that leadership had something to do with breeding. This was easy to verify, by pointing to people such as Eisenhower and Churchill, let alone those further back along the timeline, even to Jesus, Moses, Mohammed and the Buddha.

(B) Trait Theory

This theory is based on the assumptions that people are born with inherited traits. There are some traits particularly suited to leadership and people who make good leaders have the right (or sufficient) combination of traits.

Early research on leadership was based on the psychological focus of the day, which was of people having inherited characteristics or traits. Attention was thus put on discovering these traits, often by studying successful leaders, but with the underlying assumption that if other people could also be found with these traits, then they, too, could also become great leaders.

Stogdill (1974) identified the following traits and skills as critical to leaders.

Traits	Skills
• Adaptable to situations	• Clever (intelligent)
• Alert to social environment	• Conceptually skilled
• Ambitious and achievement-orientated	• Creative
• Assertive	• Diplomatic and tactful
• Cooperative	• Fluent in speaking
• Decisive	• Knowledgeable about group task
• Dependable	• Organized (administrative ability)
• Dominant (desire to influence others)	• Persuasive
• Energetic (high activity level)	• Socially skilled
• Persistent	
• Self-confident	
• Tolerant of stress	
• Willing to assume responsibility	

Exhibit 1: Traits and Skills

McCall and Lombardo (1983) researched both success and failure identified four primary traits by which leaders could succeed or 'derail':

- Emotional stability and composure: Calm, confident and predictable, particularly when under stress.
- Admitting error: Owning up to mistakes, rather than putting energy into covering up.
- Good interpersonal skills: Able to communicate and persuade others without resort to negative or coercive tactics.
- Intellectual breadth: Able to understand a wide range of areas, rather than having a narrow (and narrow-minded) area of expertise.

(C) Behavioural Theory

Leaders can be made, rather than are born and successful leadership is based in definable, learnable behaviour. These are the assumptions of behavioural theory. Behavioural theories of leadership do not seek inborn traits or capabilities. Rather, they look at what leaders actually do. If success can be defined in terms of describable actions, then it should be relatively easy for other people to act in the same way. This is easier to teach and learn then to adopt the more ephemeral 'traits' or 'capabilities'.

(i) Role Theory

The assumptions of role theory are people define roles for themselves and others based on social learning and reading. People form expectations about the roles that they and others will play. People delicately encourage others to act within the role expectations they have for them and they will act within the roles they adopt.

We all have internal schemas about the role of leaders, based on what we read, discuss and so on. We subtly send these expectations to our leaders, acting as *role senders*, for example through the balance of decisions we take upon ourselves and the decisions we leave to the leader.

Leaders are influenced by management expectation, particularly if they are sensitive to the people around them, and will generally conform to these, playing the leadership role that is put upon them by others. Within organizations, there is much formal and informal information about what the leader's role should be, including 'leadership values', culture, training sessions, modeling by senior managers, and so on. These and more (including contextual factors) act to shape expectations and behaviours around leadership.

Role conflict can also occur when people have differing expectations of their leaders. It also happens when leaders have different ideas about what they should be doing *vs.* the expectations that are put upon them.

(ii) The Managerial Grid

Leaders may be concerned for their people and they also must have some concern or the work to be done. The question is, how much attention to they pay to one or the other? This is a model defined by **Blake and Mouton** in the early 1960s.

Concern for People				
	High	Country Club management		Team management
	Medium		Middle of the road management	
	Low	Impoverished management		Authority-compliance
		Low	Medium	High
		Concern for Production (Task)		

Exhibit 2: The Managerial Grid

Impoverished management

Leader put minimum effort to get the work done and basically lazy approach that avoids as much work as possible.

Authority-compliance

Strong focus on task, but with little concern for people. Focus on efficiency, including the elimination of people wherever possible.

Country club management

Care and concern for the people, with a comfortable and friendly environment and collegial style. But a low focus on task may give questionable results.

Middle of the road management

A weak balance of focus on both people and the work. Doing enough to get things done, but not pushing the boundaries of what may be possible.

Team management

People are committed to task and leader is committed to people. The concern for production and people both are high.

(D) Participative Leadership

People are more committed to actions where they have involved in the relevant decision-making. People are less competitive and more collaborative when they are working on joint goals. When people make decisions together, the social commitment to one another is greater and thus increases their commitment to the decision.

A Participative Leader, rather than taking autocratic decisions, seeks to involve other people in the process, possibly including subordinates, peers, superiors and other stakeholders. Often, however, as it is within the managers' whim to give or deny control to his or her subordinates, most participative activity is within the immediate team. The question of how much influence others are given thus may vary on the manager's preferences and beliefs, and a whole spectrum of participation is possible, as in the table below:

< Not participative				Highly participative >
Autocratic decision by leader	Leader proposes decision, listens to feedback, then decides	Team proposes decision, leader has final decision	Joint decision with team as equals	Full delegation of decision to team

Exhibit 3: Spectrum of Participation

There are many varieties on this spectrum, including stages where the leader sells the idea to the team. Another variant is for the leader to describe the 'what' of objectives or goals and let the team or individuals decide the 'how' of the process by which the 'how' will be achieved (this is often called 'Management by Objectives').

The level of participation may also depend on the type of decision being made. Decisions on how to implement goals may be highly participative, whilst decisions during subordinate performance evaluations are more likely to be taken by the manager.

(i) Lewin's Leadership Styles

Kurt Lewin and colleagues did leadership decision experiments in 1939 and identified three different styles of leadership, in particular around decision-making.

Autocratic—In the autocratic style, the leader takes decisions without consulting with others. The decision is made without any form of consultation. In Lewin's experiments, he found that this caused the most level of discontent. An autocratic style works when there is no need for input on the decision, where the decision would not change as a result of input, and where the motivation of people to carry out subsequent actions would not be affected whether they were or were not involved in the decision-making.

Democratic—In the democratic style, the leader involves the people in the decision-making, although the process for the final decision may vary from the leader having the final say to them facilitating consensus in the group.

Laissez-Faire—This style is to minimize the leader's involvement in decision-making, and hence allowing people to make their own decisions, although they may still be responsible for the outcome. Laissez-faire works best when people are capable and motivated in making their own decisions, and where there is no requirement for a central coordination, for example in sharing resources across a range of different people and groups.

(ii) Likert's Leadership Styles

Rensis Likert identified four main styles of leadership, in particular around decision-making and the degree to which people are involved in the decision.

Exploitive authoritative—In this style, the leader has a low concern for people and uses such methods as threats and other fear-based methods to achieve conformance. Communication is almost entirely downwards and the psychologically distant concerns of people are ignored.

Benevolent authoritative—When the leader adds concern for people to an authoritative position, a 'benevolent dictatorship' is formed. The leader now uses rewards to encourage appropriate performance and listens more to concerns lower down the organization, although what they hear is often rose-tinted, being limited to what their subordinates think that the boss wants to hear. Although there may be some delegation of decisions, almost all major decisions are still made centrally.

Consultative—The upward flow of information here is still cautious and rose-tinted to some degree, although the leader is making genuine efforts to listen carefully to ideas. Nevertheless, major decisions are still largely centrally made.

Participative—At this level, the leader makes maximum use of participative methods, engaging people lower down the organization in decision-making. People across the organization are psychologically closer together and work well together at all levels.

(E) Situational Leadership

This theory is based on assumption that the best action of the leader depends on a range of situational factors.

When a decision is needed, an effective leader does not just fall into a single preferred style, such as using transactional or transformational methods. In practice, as they say, things are not that simple. Factors that affect situational decisions include motivation and capability of followers. This, in turn, is affected by factors within the particular situation. The relationship between followers and the leader may be another factor that affects leader behaviour as much as it does follower behaviour.

The leaders' perception of the follower and the situation will affect what they do rather than the truth of the situation. The leader's perception of themselves and other factors such as stress and mood will also modify the leaders' behaviour.

(i) Hersey and Blanchard's Situational Leadership

Leaders should adapt their style to follower development style (or 'maturity'), based on how ready and willing the follower is to perform required tasks (that is, their competence and motivation). There are four leadership styles (S1 to S4) that match the development levels (D1 to D4) of the followers. The four styles suggest that leaders should put greater or less focus on the task in question and/or the relationship between the leader and the follower, depending on the development level of the follower.

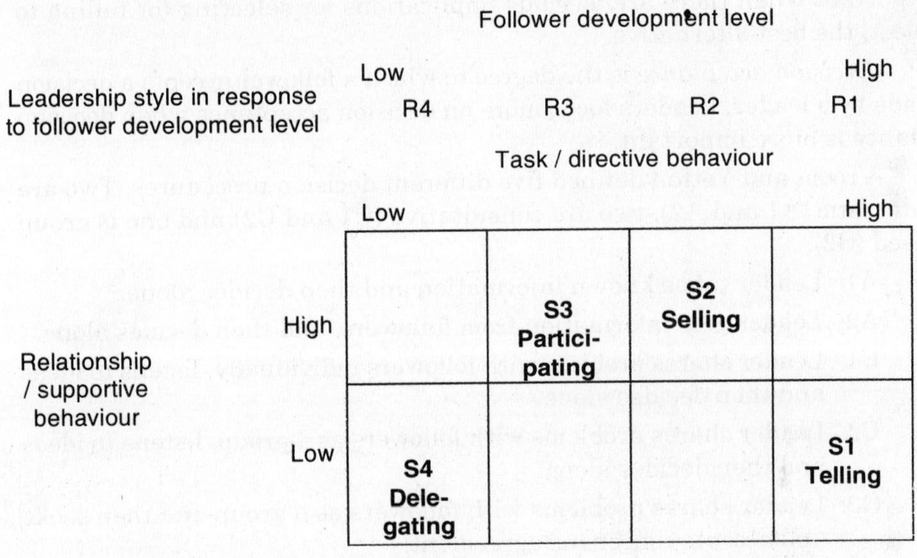

Exhibit 4: Hersey and Blanchard's Situational Leadership

S1: Telling/Directing

Follower: R1: Low competence, low commitment/Unable and unwilling or insecure

Leader: High task focus, low relationship focus

S2: Selling/Coaching

Follower: R2: Some competence, variable commitment / Unable but willing or motivated

Leader: High task focus, high relationship focus

Note: S1 and S2 are leader-driven.

S3: Participating/Supporting

Follower: R3: High competence, variable commitment/able but unwilling or insecure

Leader: Low task focus, high relationship focus

S4: Delegating/Observing

Follower: R4: High competence, high commitment/able and willing or motivated

Leader: Low task focus, low relationship focus

Note: S3 and S4 are follower-led.

(ii) Vroom and Yetton's Normative Model

The basic assumption of this theory is decision acceptance increases commitment and effectiveness of action. Participation increases decision acceptance.

Decision quality is the selection of the best alternative, and is particularly important when there are many alternatives. It is also important when there are serious implications for selecting (or failing to select) the best alternative.

Decision acceptance is the degree to which a follower accepts a decision made by a leader. Leaders focus more on decision acceptance when decision quality is more important.

Vroom and Yetton defined five different decision procedures. Two are autocratic (A1 and A2), two are consultative (C1 and C2) and one is group based (G2).

A1: Leader takes known information and then decides alone.

A2: Leader gets information from followers, and then decides alone.

C1: Leader shares problem with followers individually, listens to ideas and then decides alone.

C2: Leader shares problems with followers as a group, listens to ideas and then decides alone.

G2: Leader shares problems with followers as a group and then seeks and accepts consensus agreement.

Situational factors that influence the method are relatively logical:

- When decision quality is important and followers possess useful information, then A1 and A2 are not the best method.
- When the leader sees decision quality as important but followers do not, then G2 is inappropriate.
- When decision quality is important, when the problem is unstructured and the leader lacks information/skill to make the decision alone, then G2 is best.
- When decision acceptance is important and followers are unlikely to accept an autocratic decision, then A1 and A2 are inappropriate.
- When decision acceptance is important but followers are likely to disagree with one another, then A1, A2 and C1 are not appropriate, because they do not give opportunity for differences to be resolved.

- When decision quality is not important but decision acceptance is critical, then G2 is the best method.
- When decision quality is important, all agree with this, and the decision is not likely to result from an autocratic decision then G2 is best.

(iii) Path-Goal Theory of Leadership

The Path-Goal Theory of Leadership was developed to describe the way that leaders encourage and support their followers in achieving the goals they have been set by making the path that they should take clear and easy.

In particular, leaders:

- Clarify the path so subordinates know which way to go.
- Remove roadblocks that are stopping them going there.
- Increasing the rewards along the route.

Leaders can take a strong or limited approach in these. In clarifying the path, they may be directive or give vague hints. In removing roadblocks, they may scour the path or help the follower move the bigger blocks. In increasing rewards, they may give occasional encouragement or pave the way with gold.

This variation in approach will depend on the situation, including the follower's capability and motivation, as well as the difficulty of the job and other contextual factors.

House and Mitchell (1974) describe four styles of leadership:

SUPPORTIVE LEADERSHIP

Considering the needs of the follower, showing concern for their welfare and creating a friendly working environment. This includes increasing the follower's self-esteem and making the job more interesting. This approach is best when the work is stressful, boring or hazardous.

DIRECTIVE LEADERSHIP

Telling followers what needs to be done and giving appropriate guidance along the way. This includes giving them schedules of specific work to be done at specific times. Rewards may also be increased as needed and role ambiguity decreased (by telling them what they should be doing).

This may be used when the task is unstructured and complex and the follower is inexperienced. This increases the follower's sense of security and control and hence is appropriate to the situation.

PARTICIPATIVE LEADERSHIP

Consulting with followers and taking their ideas into account when making decisions and taking particular actions. This approach is best when the followers are expert and their advice is both needed and they expect to be able to give it.

ACHIEVEMENT-ORIENTED LEADERSHIP

Setting challenging goals, both in work and in self-improvement (and often together). High standards are demonstrated and expected. The leader shows faith in the capabilities of the follower to succeed. This approach is best when the task is complex.

(F) Contingency Theory

The leader's ability to lead is contingent upon various situational factors, including the leader's preferred style, the capabilities and behaviours of followers and also various other situational factors are the assumption of this theory.

Contingency theories are a class of behavioural theory that contends that there is no one best way of leading and that a leadership style that is effective in some situations may not be successful in others.

An effect of this is that leaders who are very effective at one place and time may become unsuccessful either when transplanted to another situation or when the factors around them change.

This helps to explain how some leaders who seem for a while to have the 'Midas touch' suddenly appear to go off the boil and make very unsuccessful decisions.

(i) Fiedler's Least Preferred Co-worker (LPC) Theory

The basic assumption is leaders prioritize between task-focus and people-focus. Relationships, power and task structure are the three key factors that drive effective styles.

Fiedler identified that a Least Preferred Co-worker scoring for leaders by asking them first to think of a person with which they worked that they would like least to work with again, and then to score the person on a range of scales between positive factors (friendly, helpful, cheerful, etc.) and negative factors (unfriendly, unhelpful, gloomy, etc.). A high LPC leader generally scores the other person as positive and a low LPC leader scores them as negative.

High LPC leaders tend to have close and positive relationships and act in a supportive way, even prioritizing the relationship before the task. Low LPC leaders put the task first and will turn to relationships only when they are satisfied with how the work is going.

Three factors are then identified about the leader, member and the task, as follows:

- *Leader-member Relations*: The extent to which the leader has the support and loyalties of followers and relations with them are friendly and cooperative.
- *Task Structure*: The extent to which tasks are standardized documented and controlled.
- *Leader's Position-power*: The extent to which the leader has authority to assess follower performance and give reward or punishment.

The best LPC approach depends on a combination of three. Generally, a high LPC approach is best when leader-member relations are poor, except when the task is unstructured and the leader is weak, in which a low LPC style is better.

#	Leader-Member Relations	Task Structure	Leader's Position- Power	Most Effective Leader
1	Good	Structured	Strong	Low LPC
2	Good	Structured	Weak	Low LPC
3	Good	Unstructured	Strong	Low LPC
4	Good	Unstructured	Weak	High LPC
5	Poor	Structured	Strong	High LPC
6	Poor	Structured	Weak	High LPC
7	Poor	Unstructured	Strong	High LPC
8	Poor	Unstructured	Weak	Low LPC

Exhibit 5: LPC Approaches

(ii) Cognitive Resource Theory

Intelligence and experience and other cognitive resources are factors in leadership success. Cognitive capabilities, although significant are not enough to predict leadership success. Stress impacts the ability to make decisions. These are the assumptions for cognitive resource theory.

Cognitive Resource Theory predicts that:

1. *A leader's cognitive ability contributes to the performance of the team only when the leader's approach is directive.*
2. *Stress affects the relationship between intelligence and decision quality.*

   When there is low stress, then intelligence is fully functional and makes an optimal contribution. However, during high stress, a natural intelligence not only makes no difference, but it may also have a negative effect.
3. *Experience is positively related to decision quality under high stress.*

   When there is a high stress situation and intelligence is impaired, experience of the same or similar situations enables the leader to react in appropriate ways without having to think carefully about the situation. Experience of decision-making under stress also will contribute to a better decision than trying to muddle through with brain-power alone.
4. *For simple tasks, leader intelligence and experience is irrelevant.*

When subordinates are given tasks which do not need direction or support, then it does not matter how good the leader is at making decisions, because they are easy to make, even for subordinates, and hence do not need any further support.

(iii) Strategic Contingencies Theory

Intra-organizational power depends on three factors: problem skills, actor centrality and uniqueness of skill. If you have the skills and expertise to resolve important problems, then you are going to be in demand. And by the law of supply and demand, that gives you're the upper hand in negotiations. It also gives you power from the reciprocity created.

(G) Transactional Leadership

The basic assumption behind this theory is people are motivated by reward and punishment; Social systems work best with a clear chain of command. When people have agreed to do a job, a part of the deal is that they cede all authority to their manager. The prime purpose of a subordinate is to do what their manager tells them to do.

The transactional leader works through creating clear structures whereby it is clear what is required of their subordinates, and the rewards that they get for following orders. Punishments are not always mentioned, but they are also well-understood and formal systems of discipline are usually in place.

The early stage of Transactional Leadership is in negotiating the contract whereby the subordinate is given a salary and other benefits, and the company (and by implication the subordinate's manager) gets authority over the subordinate.

When the Transactional Leader allocates work to a subordinate, they are considered to be fully responsible for it, whether or not they have the resources or capability to carry it out. When things go wrong, then the subordinate is considered to be personally at fault, and is punished for their failure (just as they are rewarded for succeeding).

The transactional leader often uses *management by exception*, working on the principle that if something is operating to defined (and hence expected) performance then it does not need attention. Exceptions to expectation require praise and reward for exceeding expectation, whilst some kind of corrective action is applied for performance below expectation.

Whereas Transformational Leadership has more of a 'selling' style, Transactional Leadership, once the contract is in place, takes a 'telling' style.

LEADER-MEMBER EXCHANGE (LMX) THEORY

Leader-Member Exchange Theory, also called *LMX* or *Vertical Dyad Linkage Theory*, describes how leaders in groups maintain their position through a series of tacit exchange agreements with their members.

In-group and Out-group

In particular, leaders often have a special relationship with an inner circle of trusted lieutenants, assistants and advisors, to whom they give high levels of responsibility, decision influence, and access to resources. This in-group pays for their position. They work harder, are more committed to task objectives, and share more administrative duties. They are also expected to be fully committed and loyal to their leader. The out-group, on the other hand, are given low levels of choice or influence.

This also puts constraints upon the leader. They have to nurture the relationship with their inner circle whilst balancing giving them power with ensuring they do not have enough to strike out on their own.

The LMX Process

These relationships, if they are going to happen, start very soon after a person joins the group and follow three stages:

1. ***Role taking***: The member joins the team and the leader assesses their abilities and talents. Based on this, the leader may offer them opportunities to demonstrate their capabilities.
2. ***Role making***: In the second phase, the leader and member take part in an unstructured and informal negotiation whereby a role is created for the member and the often-tacit promise of benefit and power in return for dedication and loyalty takes place.

   Trust-building is very important in this stage, and any felt betrayal, especially by the leader, can result in the member being relegated to the out-group.
3. ***Routinization***: In this phase, a pattern of ongoing social exchange between the leader and the member becomes established.

Success Factors

Successful members are thus similar in many ways to the leader (which perhaps explains why many senior teams are all white, male, middle-class and middle-aged). They work hard at building and sustaining trust and respect.

To help this, they are empathetic, patient, reasonable, sensitive, and are good at seeing the viewpoint of other people (especially the leader). Aggression, sarcasm and an egocentric view are keys to the out-group washroom.

The overall quality of the LMX relationship varies with several factors. Curiously, it is better when the challenge of the job is extremely high or extremely low. The size of the group, financial resource availability and the overall workload are also important.

(H) Transformational Leadership

The basic assumptions are people will follow a person who inspires them. A person with vision and passion can achieve great things. The way to get things done is by injecting enthusiasm and energy.

Working for a Transformational Leader can be a wonderful and uplifting experience. They put passion and energy into everything. They care about you and want you to succeed.

Developing the vision: Transformational Leadership starts with the development of a vision, a view of the future that will excite and convert potential followers. This vision may be developed by the leader, by the senior team or may emerge from a broad series of discussions. The important factor is the leader buys into it, hook, line and sinker.

Selling the vision: The next step, which in fact never stops, is to constantly sell the vision. This takes energy and commitment, as few people will immediately buy into a radical vision, and some will join the show much more slowly than others. The Transformational Leader thus takes every opportunity and will use whatever works to convince others to climb on board the bandwagon.

In order to create followers, the Transformational Leader has to be very careful in creating trust, and their personal integrity is a critical part of the package that they are selling. In effect, they are selling themselves as well as the vision.

Finding the way forwards: In parallel with the selling activity is seeking the way forward. Some Transformational Leaders know the way, and simply want others to follow them. Others do not have a ready strategy, but will happily lead the exploration of possible routes to the promised land.

The route forwards may not be obvious and may not be plotted in details, but with a clear vision, the *direction* will always be known. Thus finding the way forward can be an ongoing process of course correction and the Transformational Leader will accept that there will be failures and blind canyons along the way. As long as they feel progress is being made, they will be happy.

Leading the charge: The final stage is to remain up-front and central during the action. Transformational Leaders are always visible and will stand up to be counted rather than hide behind their troops. They show by their attitudes and actions how everyone else should behave. They also make continued efforts to motivate and rally their followers, constantly doing the rounds, listening, soothing and enthusing.

It is their unswerving commitment as much as anything else that keeps people going, particularly through the darker times when some may question whether the vision can ever be achieved. If the people do not believe that they can succeed, then their efforts will flag. The Transformational Leader seeks to infect and re-infect their followers with a high level of commitment to the vision.

One of the methods the Transformational Leader uses to sustain motivation is in the use of ceremonies, rituals and other cultural symbolism. Small changes get big hurrahs, pumping up their significance as indicators of real progress.

Overall, they balance their attention between action that creates progress and the mental state of their followers. Perhaps more than other approaches, they are people-oriented and believe that success comes first and last through deep and sustained commitment.

(i) Bass' Transformational Leadership Theory

Awareness of task importance motivates people and focus on the team or organization produces better work are the assumption of this theory.

Bass defined transformational leadership in terms of how the leader affects followers, who are intended to trust, admire and respect the transformational leader.

(ii) Burns' Transformational Leadership Theory

Association with a higher moral position is motivating and will result in people following a leader who promotes this. Working collaboratively is better than working individually.

Burns defined transformational leadership as a process where leaders and followers engage in a mutual process of 'raising one another to higher levels of morality and motivation.' Transformational leaders raise the bar by appealing to higher ideals and values of followers. In doing so, they may model the values themselves and use charismatic methods to attract people to the values and to the leader.

Burns' view is that transformational leadership is more effective than transactional leadership, where the appeal is to more selfish concerns. An appeal to social values thus encourages people to collaborate, rather than working as individuals (and potentially competitively with one another). He also views transformational leadership as an ongoing process rather than the discrete exchanges of the transactional approach.

REFERENCES

1. Robbins, *Organizational Behaviour*, Pearson Education, 2008, p. 440.
2. Robert Tannenbaum et al., *Leadership and Organization: A Behavioural Science Approach*, McGraw-Hill, New York, 1961.
3. Bernard, Chester I., *The Nature of Leadership in Organization and Management.*
4. Hodge, B.J., and Johnson, H.G., *Management and Organizational Behaviour*, John Wiley & Sons, New York, 1970, p. 250.
5. http://www.skagitwatershed.org/~donclark/leader/leadcon.html
6. Drucker, Peter, F., *Management: Task, Responsibility, Practices*, Harper & Row, 1973.
7. Applewhite, *Organizational Behaviour*, p. 388.
8. Dubing, Robert, *The World of Work: Industrial Society and Human Relations*, Prentice-Hall, Englewood Cliffs, 1958, p. 393.
9. Lamb, L.F., McKee, K. B. (2004). Applied Public Relations: Cases in Stakeholder Management. Mahwah, New Jersey: Lawrence Erlbaum Associates. Routledge U.S. Army Handbook (1973).
10. Kouzes, James M. & Posner, Barry Z. (1987). *The Leadership Challenge.* Jossey-Bass, San Francisco.

CHAPTER 10

GROUP DYNAMICS

10.1 INTRODUCTION

Human beings exhibit some characteristic behaviour patterns in groups. People involved in managing groups and group members themselves can benefit from studying theories and doing practical exercises which help them to better understand people's behaviour in groups and group dynamics.

People may underestimate the importance of society and group memberships on their lives. Whilst people sometimes undertake solo journeys but by and large much of our experiences of life involves being engaged with others and groups. The nature of these groups can be quite varied, from a family going for a walk, to the crowd at a football game, to an internet discussion group, to a group of fellow workers.

Given the diverse, yet common occurrence of groups, what is the nature and pattern of such *group experiences*? The social dynamics which occur within groups over time vary from group to group, but also illustrate some commonalities. In this particular chapter we discuss the concept and feature of group dynamics. After that group formation and development are taking into consideration. In next section, put some types of group and give the reasons why individual want to join particular group. And lastly discuss structure and degree of cohesiveness of group.

10.2 CONCEPT AND MEANING

Group exists in every organization and they affect the behaviour of their members. They not only affect the behaviour of individuals but also influence the work performed by them which ultimately affect the organization. Such groups are created by the organization as well as by organization members for their own satisfaction.

A group is defined as 'two or more individuals, interacting and mutually dependent on each other, who have come together to achieve particular objectives' or 'group are consisting two or more person who are interacting with one another in such a way that each person influence and influenced by each others.' In simple words, group means two or more individual who share common values, norms and interest.

Dynamics comes from the Greek word meaning 'force'. Hence group dynamics refers to the study of force operating within groups. Group dynamics is concerned with the interaction and forces between group members in social situations.

A group is "two or more people who share a common definition and evaluation of themselves and behave in accordance with such a definition" (Vaughan and Hogg, 2002, p. 200).

Group dynamics is the branch of social psychology that studies the psychodynamics of interaction in social groups.

According to Robert, group is 'a collection of two or more interacting individuals with a stable pattern of relationships between them, who share common goals and who perceive themselves as being a group'. A group is thus, an aggregation of people who interact with other, are known of each another and have a common objective and perceive them to be a part of a group. Because they interact and influence each other, groups develop a number of dynamic processes that separate them from a random collection of individuals.

Group dynamics refers to the interactive nature of individuals within the contexts of a group. These interactions between individuals within the group are distinctly different than in one-on-one interactions. Group dynamics also refers to the study of the nature of groups.

Kurt Lewin (1943, 1948, and 1951) is commonly identified as the founder of the movement to study groups scientifically. He coined the term *group dynamics* to describe the way groups and individuals act and react to changing circumstances.

The psychological aspect or conduct of an interpersonal relationship. This is the study of the interaction between people with a common objective in a closed environment.

According to business directory group is a interaction of complex intra- and inter-personal forces operating in a group which determine its character, development, and long-term survival.

10.3 Features of Group

(i) To form a group there should be at least ***two or more individuals*** involved. There is no maximum limit of the group but if group are being so large than communication becomes little bit difficult. Some time rules and regulations of the organization play an important role in formal group formation and meaningful interaction among the members in the case of informal group.

(ii) ***Interaction*** is one of the main features of group. All the group members must be interact either by face to face communication or by using some mechanical devices like writing, telephone, internet, etc. It is not compulsion that all the members of the group to interact each other simultaneously, but each member must interact at least occasionally with one or more members of the group.

(iii) ***Developing Leadership***. The purpose of any group is all the members of the group must be know each other and to complete some objective. For this reason they collectively choose a leader among themselves and granted authority by members to make decisions, take action and other activity which will be related to group. The criteria of selection of leader based upon their performance and some time particular situation also help in to designate leader.

(iv) All the members of the group have some ***collective identity*** and they all are aware about their membership. They must have the feeling that he or she is the part of the group.

(v) ***Group Norms*** are rules or guidelines of accepted behaviour which are established by a group and used to monitor the behaviour of its members. Informal group establish their own group norm with taking consideration of each members concern. In very structured formalized group these norms become law or operation laws. And each member should behave according to those particular laws.

(vi) ***Group Cohesiveness*** is a degree to which group members are attached to each others and are motivated to reside in the group. It shows the extent of liking of each member towards others.

(vii) The ultimate result of group membership is ***satisfaction*** of members. If members were satisfied they are more productive, reduce conflicts, coordinated, motivated, participative and many more.

10.4 Group Formation and Development

The most basic theory explaining affiliation is ***'propinquity'***. This interesting word means simply that person affiliated with one another because of geographical proximity. For example, the theory would predict those workers who work nearer in workplace are more likely to form group then the other workers. Or workers who work in the same area of the plant/office close to one another would more probably form into groups than would those who are not physically located together.

Homan's interaction theory is a more comprehensive theory of group formation. The theory is based on activities, interactions and sentiments. They are directly related to one another. The more activity person shares, the more numerous will their interaction and the stronger will be their sentiments. This theory had a great deal to the understanding of group formation and process. The major element is 'interaction'. Individual in a group interact with one another not just in a physical propinquity sense, but also to achieve many group goals, such as cooperation and problem solving.

Balance theory of group formation states that persons are attracted to one another on the basis of similar attitudes toward commodity, relevant object and goals. Individual X will interact and form a group with individual Y because of common attitude and values (Z), both propinquity and interaction plays a role in balance theory.

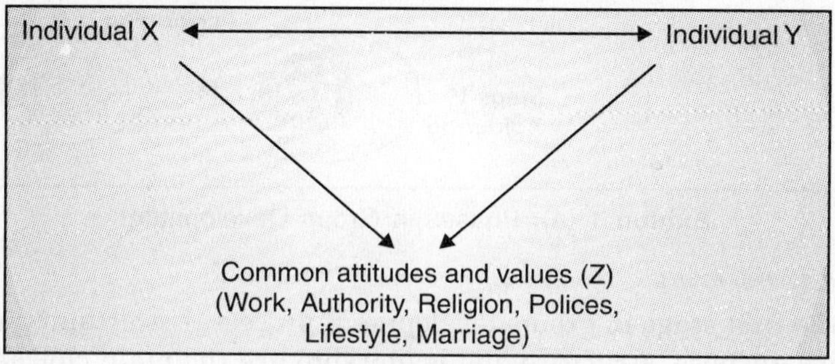

Exhibit 1: Balance Theory

Exchange theory is based upon reward and cost outcomes of interaction. These two are common outcomes for making an interaction with other or simply helpful in affiliation or group formation. Rewards from interaction gratify needs, while costs incur anxiety, fatigue, frustration etc.

Four Stage Model of Group Development

Hare has given four stages for group development. These are:

1. *Latent*—This stage stands for latent pattern, maintenance and tension reduction. It is marked by the group's natural need to reach agreement as to its purposes, work methods and expectation and participation obligation. This agreement reduces the tension surroundings the group's direction, priorities and maintenance in the problem solving process.
2. *Adaptation*—At this stage, the group generate critical information necessary to solve the problem at hand. It lays out fact and identifies the necessary skills and resources required for solution and also participants identify and essential role that are key to the problem solving efforts.
3. *Integration*—It requires flexibility, reassessment and innovation on the part of their members and leaders. Find out the alternatives which are necessary to move the group in the final stage.
4. *Goal Attainment*—This is the last stage, in which the solution has been finally found out.

Phase in Group Development

Bruce Tuckman (1965) proposed the four-stage model called Tuckman's Stages for a group. Tuckman's model states that the ideal group decision-making process should occur in four stages:

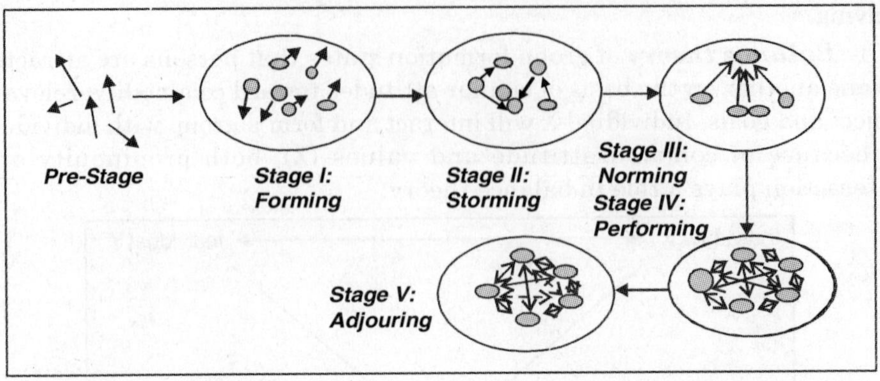

Exhibit 1 (a): Phases in Group Development

Stage I: Forming

It is the first stage in group development process. Uncertainty about the group's purpose, structure and leadership are the main characteristics of this stage. Members are pretending to get on or get along with others. This stage is complete when members have begun to think of themselves as a part of a group.

Stage II: Storming

Intra group conflicts are the essential part of this stage. Members accept the existence of the group, but there is resistance to the constraints that the group imposes on individuality. There is also conflict over who will control the group. When this stage is complete, there will be a relatively clear hierarchy of leadership within the group.

Stage III: Norming

At this stage close relationship, cohesiveness, and trust developed among the group members. This stage is complete when the group structure solidifies and the group has assimilated a common set of expectations of what defines correct member behaviour.

Stage IV: Performing

The group structure at this stage is fully functional and accepted to all members of the group. Group energy has moved from getting to know and understands each other to performing the task.

Tuckman added a 5th stage 10 years later:

Stage V: Adjourning

Actually the group development process is completed on performing stage, when the particular groups are stat doing performing than automatically their development process completed. This stage is for temporary groups, having characterized by concern with wrapping up activities rather than task performance.

10.5 Types of Groups

1. ***Formal and Informal Groups***—*Formal groups* are governed by prescribed rules and regulations of concern organization. They are created and maintained to fulfill specific needs or task of the organization. These groups are permanent like top management team, work units in different departments of the organization or temporary like they made for some specific task to perform and when such task are completed they disappear. Five members making up a counseling team are the example of formal group.

   Informal groups created on the basis of voluntary and spontaneous requirements. They give their member a sense of social satisfaction. These groups are generally small in size, having indefinite structure, communications flow in all direction especially horizontal, authority is given by the group members, group member's behaviour are regulated by their own norms, values and beliefs. Three members of different department having lunch with each other are the example of informal group.

2. ***Task and Command Group***—Task group consist of those members who are from either same or different department come and contact with each other for completing a particular task or job. They are basically temporary in nature when that task is accomplished they get back to their departments and position. A task group is usually formed to solve the problem or perform an activity that involves a number of organizational units. Like problem of absenteeism is increases day by day and for solving that problem management create a task group consisting of members (supervisor, manager, counsellor) who are going to check the problem and give suggestion also about how this problem will be overcome.

   Command group consist of those individuals who report directly to their superior or manager. It is determined by the organization chart.

3. ***Primary and Secondary Group—Primary Groups*** consist of those members who have intimate face-to-face association and co-operations. They are usually small in size and it is based on intimate relationship. Like family, friendship groups (those brought together because they share one/more common characteristics) or neighbourhood groups.

   The members of the *secondary groups* have not interest in the problem and pleasure of others. It is more formal, general and isolated. There is no continues interaction, intimacy, co-operation and association as primary group have.

10.6 Why Individual Join the Group?

Most of the individual join the informal groups because some of their needs will be satisfied. They work in vocational groups because they must make a living, they join social groups because they need the companionship of others and they join clubs for reason of prestige. E.V. Schneider holds that informal groups are meant to afford the workers:

(*i*) Relief from monotony, boredom and fatigue.

(*ii*) Opportunity to acquire status.

(*iii*) An increased flow of emotional responses.

(*iv*) Opportunity for independence.

(*v*) Increased security.

Beach lists five reasons which he claims, are responsible for the formation of groups:

(*i*) *Companionship & Friendship*—A group gives to a person a feeling of belonging and makes it possible for him to socialize with his/her friends.

(*ii*) *Security & Protection*—A group can be a source of security and protection against management, especially if a member of the group has made mistake and need to keep the foreman from discovering them.

(*iii*) *Advance their own Interest*—They may try to secure benefits such as better and higher piece rate or in the case of office workers, large desks, longer lunch hours or other symbols of status including favourable working conditions.

(*iv*) *Need for Assistance/Advice on one's job*—Some times individual wants or need some short of advice or assistance for their betterment.

(*v*) *Communicating Information*—Group serves as a means of communicating information about the company or organization which does not come through official channels or comes faster on the grapevine/informal communication.

Stephen P. Robbins gives six reasons of why the people join the groups:

(i) *Security*—By joining a group, individuals can reduce the insecurity of "standing alone". People feel stronger, have fewer self doubts and are more resistant to threats when they are part of a group.

(ii) *Status*—Inclusion in a group that is viewed as important by others provides recognition and status for its members.

(iii) *Self Esteem*—Groups can provide people with feeling of self worth. That is, in addition to conveying status to those outside the group, membership can also give increased feelings of worth to the group members themselves.

(iv) *Affiliation*—Groups can fulfill social needs. People enjoy the regular interaction that comes with group membership. For many people, these on-the-job interactions are their primary source for fulfilling their needs for affiliation.

(v) *Power*—What cannot be achieved individually often becomes possible through group action. There is power in numbers.

(vi) *Goal Attainment*—There are times when it takes more than one person to accomplish a particular task—there is a need to pool talents, knowledge or power in order to complete a job. In such instances, management will rely on the use of a formal group.

10.7 Group Structure

Work group are not simply an aggregation of workers. They have some specific structure for group performance that develops over a period of time. The structure gives a prescribe behaviour which will be expected from the group members. The structure variables that influence the behaviour of the group are:

- ***Group Status***—Status is defined as a social ranking within a group and is assigned to individuals on the basis of position in the group or individual characteristics. Status can be check by the salary or wage level, seniority, interaction or popularity, responsibility, nature of work, work schedule of individual. Individuals can find themselves in a conflict situation when they move between group whose status criteria is different or when they join the group whose members have different background.
- ***Group Roles***—*Shakespeare said*, "The entire world is a stage, and all the men and women merely players". Every individual are required to play there role. *Luthans* says, "A role consists of a pattern of norms and is directly related to the theoretical use of the term. It is a position that can be acted out by an individual". According to *Alan Bater*, "As a pattern of prescribe behaviour a role is a bundle of norms, and as a pattern of actual behaviour a role is a one side of set of social relationship". Therefore, a role is a pattern of behaviour of individual that is expected when he/she interact with others. There are certain attitudes and actual behaviour consistent with a role, and they create the *role identity*. An individuals views of how he/she is supposed to act in a given circumstances is a *role perception*. Role expectation are defines as how other individuals believe a person should be act in a given circumstances.
- ***Group Norms***—Every group have some acceptable standards behaviour that is shared by the group members. Group norms tell members what they ought and ought not to under certain situations. According to *Argyle*, "group norms are rules or guidelines of accepted behaviour which are established by a group and used to monitor the behaviour of its members. *Performance norms* set the standards for their member how to do particular job effectively and how increase level of output. *Social arrangement* norms include interaction with others, with whom they go for lunch, friendship inside and outside the job etc. *Appearance norms* consist of appropriate dress, how to express loyalty to work or organization and many more. *Allocation of resource norms* can originate in the group or in the organization and cover things like pay, assignments of difficult tasks and allocation of new tools and equipments. These are the common classes of norms.

- ***Group Size***—Group size also influence the behaviour of their members. If group consist of few members or simply say that *smaller group* are frequently communicate with other members of the group with face to face interaction. So on that kinds of group behaviour are little bit goes informal they set their standard concerning all the member background, liking, customs and tradition. But this will not happened to the *large size group* because members are in large numbers and they communicate with each others with the help of some mechanical devices. And the prescribed behaviour is made by some committee with or without participation of all the members of the large group.
- ***Group Cohesiveness***—Explain in next section.
- ***Group Leadership***—Leader also influence the members behaviour in making group structure. If leader are autocratic they set the standard behaviour for group according to their own interest without having concern of members. If they are participative than he/she discussed with members before imposing prescribe behaviour.

10.8 Group Cohesiveness

Cohesiveness in a group is achieved when the group appears to be very attractive to its group members. In such type of cohesiveness, individuals value their group membership and have a very strong enthusiasm and motivation to remain members of the group.

Cohesiveness is defined as a degree to which group members are attracted to each other and are motivated to stay in the group.

According to Business Diectonary.com group cohesiveness is the extent to which the members of the group find staying together to be in mutual interest.

It is the extent to which group members are loyal and committed to the group and to group members also. In a highly cohesive group the members effectively achieve their goal with the support and trust of the other member. A group that lack cohesiveness will not support to one another and also find difficulties in the attainment of objectives.

There are many factors which influencing the group cohesiveness like,

- When ***group size*** is large than interaction become difficult among members which lower the degree of cohesiveness.
- The greater the ***dependencies*** on each other will resultant into higher degree of cohesiveness.
- ***Intra-group competition***. Group cohesiveness is low if members are competing amongst themselves.
- ***Inter-group competition***. When two groups compete, members of each group get united and the group gets solidified.

- ***Member turnover***. If member frequently leave the group and new member join the group. Because new member are not aware so much as older member about the group hence, the group become less cohesive.
- The more ***homogeneous the group***, i.e. the more members share similar characteristics and backgrounds, the greater the cohesiveness or vice-versa.
- If group members experience the ***group or collective success*** it get strengthened the cohesiveness.
- If members share same ***tradition and custom*** this will definitely make the strong interaction and cohesiveness among the members.

The ultimate of any organization is achieving the high production level. Most of the time, organization trying to find out the way by which they can achieve their target without any interruption. They now felt that apart from physical facilities there are some psychological satisfaction if given to worker than it will definitely increase the production level. For that reason the importance of group cohesiveness are taken into consideration. The relationship of cohesiveness and productivity depends on the group performance. As the performance and degree of cohesiveness is high than it resultant into high productivity. Other dimensions are shown in the exhibit 3.

		Group Cohesiveness	
		High	*Low*
Group Performance	*High*	High productivity	Moderate productivity
	Low	Decrease in productivity	No significant effect on productivity

Exhibit 2: Cohesiveness—Productivity Relationship

Advantage of Group Cohesiveness

- Group members are regular at their work.
- Members of cohesive group have no anxiety at the workplace.
- They have high moral and satisfaction level also high.
- Cohesiveness increase productivity.
- It reduces intra group conflicts.
- Quick transmission of messages.
- Members become participative.
- Problem of absenteeism reduces.
- Members become more loyal and committed to group norms.

❍❍❍

CHAPTER 11

WORK ENVIRONMENT

11.1 INTRODUCTION

Most of human relation experiments indicated that there are social factors which affect the production. Somehow, this phenomenon is incomplete because a production is done by worker or a group of workers' with their bond or combined efforts but environment where they work is also affect their efficiency. Image the situation where employees worked under the low intensity of light or proper ventilation is not there, is that possible to give 100 per cent effort in that particular environment? The answer is no and the particular company also suffer the losses as well as facing health related and personal problem of workers. In this chapter we discuss the concept of work environment and also the major factors which affect the work environment like noise, music, light and others.

11.2 CONCEPT AND MEANING

Work environment is designed to establish and maintain physical conditions that allow workers' to concentrate on their work without any disturbance. These disturbances may be arising from the noise of the machines, improper ventilation, humidity and temperature of workplace, inadequate facility of drinking water and other amenities. Unfavourable working conditions slowdown the workers' activities and production process also. They increase the problem of absenteeism, turnover, and grievance and generally contribute to inefficiency. There is no doubt that people generally prefer delightful to distasteful environment and that when attention is paid to creating a favourable working environment, as well as to actual job performance methods, overall niceness prevails.

Working conditions has to ensure that it complies with all applicable laws and regulations. In India, the **Factories Act 1948** is enacted primarily with the object to regulate the conditions of work in manufacturing establishments coming within the definition of term 'Factory' as used in the

Act. According to Factories Act 1948[1], Chapter 3 deals with the 'health of the workers' with reference to such matters as cleanliness, disposal of wastes and effluents, ventilations, dust and fume, artificial humidification, overcrowding, lighting, drinking water, latrines and urinals and spittoons (section 11 to 20)

11.3 Requirement of Suitable Working Environment

Are the factories requiring suitable working condition for their workers'? Production is increased with adequate working conditions? Workers' efficiency increased if working environment is pleasant? All such questions to be answered by the quotation: *'The quality of employees will be directly proportional to the quality of life you maintain for them'* —**Charles E. Bryan.**

In the factories like low illuminations which resultant into eye strain, headache, fatigue, increased number of accident, low quality of work, low output which also create low morale and satisfaction among the workers. These changes also affect the social climate of the factory. With better working conditions workers' feel that something is being done for them. This provides psychological satisfaction which helps in to maintain congenial environment with increased efficiency. Therefore, suitable working condition is required for high production.

In short,

- For higher production.
- For higher efficiency of workers'.
- Increased morale and satisfaction.
- Reduce boredom and monotony.
- Reduce fatigue.
- Better communication between the workers' itself and with the management.
- Encourage innovations.
- Reduce absenteeism and turnover.
- Reduce accident proneness.
- Provide healthy environment and many more.

Noise

Noise is undesirable and unwanted sound. Not all sound is noise. What may be considered as music to one person may be noise to another? Noise means any type of disturbance or any loud, meaningless, unpleasant and discontent sound is referred to noise. Noises are sound, which are harmful, disruptive, distracting and irritating. When noise becomes too intense it not only affect the work of individual but also causes both psychological and physical problems. It may also reduce the efficiency of workers which resultant into low productivity, cause fatigue and various health disorders. Sometime noise in factory temporary or permanently damage the heavily capacity of workers' and it also create barriers to communication.

Noise not only affects the morale of the workers' by creating unpleasant conditions but also creates unfavourable attitude towards the management. Therefore, noise as a disturbing factor of working environment should be carefully attended to by the management.

Experimental Studies

Pollock and Bartlett (1932) conducted a study on students who were asked to do all kinds of tasks from, physical to mental work under noisy and calm situations. The results indicated that to begin with, noise produced slight deficiency in the beginning of test. But there was quick habituation and adjustment after sometime and hence their efficiency did not decrease. Especially with regard to mental work, it was noted that speed decreased due to noise.[2]

Culbert and Posner (1960) examined the degree to which individuals can successfully adapt to noise. They found that after several weeks individual even adapted to a noise as intense as jet aircraft.[3]

Park and Payne (1963) found that average performance was not affected by intense noise. What they did find was that variability of performance become much greater. Also important in their study was the fat that they only found this effect for a boring, easy task. With a task of high difficulty they observe no noise effect at all.[4]

Tobias (1972) stated that flight inspectors showed a moderate average hearing loss, flight instructors and commercial pilots showed mild to moderate average loss and agriculture pilots' uniform hearing losses.[5]

From the studies it was not cleared that whether noise actually affect the working of employees'. But it was clear that in some cases noisy situation is favourable while in other not. The effect of noise depends upon the nature of task performed by the employees. If task require high mental or psychological thinking that noise affect that particular task.

Control of Noise

According to Oakley (1945), there are two general approaches to noise abatement[6].

1. Find out the source of noise and try to stop them.
2. Noise may be prevented from reaching the people.

Other ways

- Locating noisy air-compressors and other equipment away from the site boundary, along with creating temporary barriers to physically block the noise.
- Proper construction planning and scheduling techniques.
- Regular and thorough maintenance of operating machinery.

- Machines should be designed and manufactured which cause less noise or soundless machines.
- Barriers should be installed at places to safeguard the human ears from damage.

Illumination

The illuminance (lighting level) requirement depends upon such things as the visual performance necessary for the task involved and general comfort and amenity requirement. To be able to carry out any work effectively and accurately proper and appropriate lighting is essential. The quality of lighting in a workplace can have a considerable effect on productivity. A proper lighting system for a work station takes into account the visual demands of the task(s) and balances general or ambient lighting with task specific lighting to achieve comfort, efficiency and accuracy. With adequate lighting workers can produce more products with fewer mistakes, which can lead to a 10-50 % increase in productivity. Good lighting can decrease errors by 30-60 % as well as decrease eye-strain and the headaches, neck pain and nausea, and other disorders.

Adequate lighting allows workers to concentrate better on their work which increases their productivity. The level of lighting that workers need varies depending on the nature of the task, the sharpness of the workers' eyesight, and the environment in which the work is done. For example, detailed work, such as inspection, assembling of small parts or technical drawing, needs a great deal of light. Common work, on the other hand, such as loading or unloading materials, handling of materials or packaging, requires less light.

Difficulties of Illumination

- **Shadow** will affect the amount of illumination, and its impact on people in working areas will depend on the task being performed and on the disposition of desks, work benches etc. the remedy is to use physical large luminaries or to increase their numbers.
- **Glare** occurs when there is too much direct or reflected light within the field of view. The most common cause of glare results from looking directly at unscreened lamps from normal viewing angles. Glare causes a decrease in contrast which results in decreased visibility and physical discomfort. Glare from sunlight coming through windows can be reduced by using exterior or interior blinds but this reduces the amount of natural lighting. It may be more effective to rearrange the workplace so that the windows are not in the normal direct field of view.
- **Luminance** is the amount of light reflected or coming from a light source or surface. It is important that there is not a great difference between the luminance levels for the task and that of the surrounding area. Luminance levels for the immediate area surrounding the tasks should

be one third that of the task. The further from the task the less light is needed.

- **Reflectance** is the percentage of light falling on a surface that is reflected. In an office the most reflective surface should be the ceiling; the least reflective should be the floor and in between are the reflectance of walls and furniture. In general, reflections from surfaces within the field of view should be minimized. Colour and finish are used to control the reflectance of a surface. A totally black surface reflects no light. For a white surface the reverse is true. Also a matte finish reflects less light than a shiny one of the same colour.
- **Contrast** is the relationship between the light coming from an object and the immediate background, such as words on paper. High contrast is important for fine detail work. Using a black pen in place of a pencil for handwritten copy will increase the contrast and improve the readability.
- The reflection of light falling on a coloured surface produces a **Coloured effect** in which the amount of colour reflected depends upon the light source and the colour of the surface. The choice of lamp is important if colour effect is required and can be as important a consideration as the illuminance itself. It can affect both the mood and the perception of size in a workplace. Some of the colour effects are as :
    - Blues and greens are considered relaxing or soothing.
    - Pastel colours reduce the impact of colour.
    - Cool colours such as blues and greens can make a space seem larger.
    - Orange, yellow and brown colours are thought to be stimulating.
    - Red and violet are considered alarming or aggressive.
    - Reds and oranges can make a space seem smaller. Different types of lights will influence how colours are perceived. If the light source is not coordinated with the colour of a work area colours may be perceived as off or strange. Visibility may be more different.

Experimental Studies

Ferree and Rand conducted tests on 550 people; 100 were in each 10-year age range from 10 to 60 years, 50 subjects were over 60 years of age. Approximately 70% of these people preferred less than 15 foot-candles for reading 10-point type (average book text type); 50% preferred less than 11.3 foot-candles. Individual differences are evident in this type of experiment, as in every other in psychology. These authors found a wide variation in the preference expressed in each age group. The people above 35 years of age tend generally to prefer more light for reading than those below 35.[7]

The Electric Lamp Manufacture's Association in 1943 gave sufficient evidence to support that quality of output can be increased in factories. A study conducted by the National Industrial Fatigue Research Board (1929) indicated that there is decrement in efficiency due to inadequate illumination. Optimum illumination is, therefore, required for better efficiency and comfort.

In a tile-pressing factory, Admas found that when illumination was increased from 1.7-4.7 foot candles output increased by 6%. Admas thus view that this improvement in production is largely due to the tonic effect of increased illumination.[8]

Tips for reducing adverse effect of illumination

- Fit the lighting to the visual demands of the task when designing or changing any work station or area.
- Clean all the essential elements in workplace at regular interval.
- Use indirect multiple light sources for both task and ambient lighting whenever possible.
- Replace light bulbs and tubes which have blown or are reduced in brightness.
- Design or adjust lighting so that direct and reflected glare is not in the field of view.
- Position light sources so that the light comes from the side.
- Use adjustable shades on windows to account for the changes in daylight.

Atmospheric Conditions

Humidity

The degree of moisture in the air needs to be controlled within certain limits. Excessive levels of moisture (high humidity) can seriously interface with the body's ability to sweat and can cause considerable discomfort. Where the production process requires high humidity, such as in paper-making, exposure time should be kept to a minimum. A dry atmosphere can cause dryness of throat and dehydration. Normal comfort levels of humidity lie between 40% to 50% relative humidity but may vary slightly between different types of work. Extended exposure to a relative humidity below 30% can give rise to adverse pulmonary health effects.

Experimental Studies

Vernon, Bedford and others did a study on coal miners under varying conditions of temperature and humidity. The results suggest that workers took 7 minutes rest per hour under the most favourable conditions. But when the conditions were the most unfavourable they took 22-40 minutes rest every hour. Moreover, when conditions were more unfavourable, they took more time to feel the cold, were involved in accidents very frequently and lost more time due to sickness.[9]

The findings of the study by the New York Ventilation Commission showed that fall in output were 9% when air was stagnant. But it was 24% when a temperature was high and air was stagnant. It is, however, important to note that natural ventilation is always preferable to artificial devices. Moreover the ventilating system should be of such nature that it can filter the air also. It should remove dust, etc. from the air. This controls the temperature and humidity.[10]

Ventilation

For survival proper air required to every individual and become more important who work in a factory. When individual work together they exhale poisonous gas and the air become little bit polluted and unhealthy for the workers. It also increases the humidity and the temperature of the work place. During that physiological and psychological changes were noticed such as rapid increase in pulse rate, heart beat, loss of weight and physical weakness etc. improper ventilation create an environment uneasy for worker to perform their task. So, it is important that proper ventilation in workplace required. Under the **Factories Act 1948 (section 13)** there is a provision regarding health that effective and suitable ventilation shall be made in every workroom for securing and maintaining efficiency of workers' and also give them ease and work satisfaction.

Experimental Studies

The New York Ventilation Commission conducted some experimental studies, the results of which showed that mental work can be performed as effectively under humid, hot and stagnant air conditions as under optimal conditions. Though frequent rest pause may be necessary under adverse atmospheric conditions, it was really strange to note that even under the most unfavourable conditions mental work was very little affected.[11]

Long Working Hour

Earlier employers pretend that with increase in working hour the productivity also increases. Therefore, the more emphasis on to increase the length of the working hour. When doing this activity the number of accidents in workplace and the problem of absenteeism also increase which resultant into low production. The working hours of contract workers are regulated through the provisions of the Factories Act, 1948, Plantation Labour Act, 1951 and Mines Act, 1952, as the case may be. The Factories Act, 1948 provides that normally an adult worker shall not be allowed to work for more than 9 hours in a day and 48 hours in a week. As regards rest interval, the Act stipulates that no worker shall work for more than 5 hours before he has rest interval of at least half an hour. Long working hour not only affects the production but also leads to fatigue which become the main cause of dissatisfaction among the workmen in their workplace. Co-relation between the long working hour and others are as follows:

- **Physical health**—The physical health of the workers' deteriorate day by day when they work for a long time. There is also link between long hours and maladaptive health behaviours such as smoking, which can in turn increase the risk of some health problems. However, there are so many other factors that can affect health that long working hours is likely to be just one of many.

- **Long hours and fatigue**—There is an association between working long hours and fatigue.
- **Long hours and stress and psychological health**—Long working hours can lead to stress or mental ill health, although this is somewhat equivocal. Working long hours is probably associated with stress, but so are many other work and non-work factors. The key is perhaps to ascertain why an individual is working long hours in the first place as the way an individual thinks about their job and the amount of control they have over their job will mediate the long hours stress/psychological health relationship.
- **Safety and accidents**—It is likely that fatigue associated with working long hours will have a strong impact on safety and accidents.
- **Performance**—The evidence is far from conclusive with regard to the performance effects of working long hours. The studies are relatively robust in that performance is often measured both subjectively and objectively. What could perhaps be said about the literature is that it supports the evidence for a link between working long hours and fatigue, in that performance is often used as an indirect measure of fatigue.
- **Work-life balance**—Workers' perceive that working long hours leads to poor work-life balance. However, this was based on self-report measures. Control over when an individual works is very important to the extent to which working long hours will impact on home and family life, with those people who can control how long they work perceiving less of a negative impact on work-life balance.

Experimental Studies

Cross-sectional survey of male day-shift workers in a chemical factory using the Self-Rating Depression Scale (SDS) and the Cumulative Fatigue Symptoms Index (CFSI) done by Shouji Nagashima and others. Working hours were subdivided into six groups and odds ratios were calculated for positive outcomes on the SDS and CFSI using logistic regression analysis. The result was a total of 715 workers participated. In the group working 260-279 h/month, the odds ratios for SDS and 'irritability', 'anxiety' and 'chronic tiredness' of the CFSI were significantly increased. In the group working 280 h/month, the odds ratios on CFSI for 'general fatigue', 'physical disorders', 'anxiety' and 'chronic tiredness' were likewise significantly increased. The present results clarified that working hours should be <260 h/month in order to minimize fatigue symptoms in male day workers.

Many researchers believe the link is stress, certainly with regard to the ill health outcomes associated with working long hours. Park, Kim,

Chung and Hisanaga (2001) and Spurgeon et al. (1997) argue that long hours act as a direct stressor and also an indirect stressor on employees. The indirect stressor mechanism means that working longer hours leads to employees being exposed to other workplace stressors for longer.

Tips for reducing adverse effect of Atmospheric Conditions

- Maier (1970) has suggested that supplying the workers with salt tablets would relieve some of the weakness and time losses caused by excessive perspiration in the summer.
- Workers' are advised to wear apparel according to the condition of ventilation so that they can get maximum comfort and ease.
- Provide adequate break between the works but make sure they should be adequate otherwise it leads work breakdown.
- Proper ventilation should be in the factory, natural as well as artificial.
- The need and comfort of the manual workers as compared to mental workers should be looked into first, because the adverse effects of humidity and temperature on manual workers are high.

Music

For making work environment more peaceful and effective introduce music during working hour. It was great practice for making employees more relaxed and energies for doing their work. Music gives strength to the employee's satisfaction and also liking of music also impact on their work. Some of the employers have introduced music in an even more informal way by encouraging their employees to sing. But some time it creates stagnancy in work like women workers' will stop work and listen with attention when some star is broadcasting and the star is on the air more often than the boss would like. When music introduced to a work it may increases production to some extent, but there is also the possibility of wastage when music diverts attention and disturbs concentration.

Experimental Studies

Blum and Naylor (1968) expressed the views that "possibly music influence production to the maximum extent when its rhythm is compatible with the employees' rhythm of work, or when it tends to pace him.'[12]

Music has an extremely favourable effect upon production, especially in repetitive work. He stated that music probably produces its major direct effect when the individual's capacity for attention is not absorbed by this work, in this circumstance, music appears to direct unused attention from brooding, talking or off the job activities.[13]

REFERENCES

1. Mamoria, Gankar, *Dynamics of Industrial Relations*, Himalaya Publications, p. 698.
2. Pollock, K.G. and Bartlett, F.C. *Two Studies in the Psychological Effects of Noise*, Industrial Health Res. Board, Rep. No. 65, London, 1932.
3. Culbert, S.S., and M.I.Posner, Human Habituation to an Acoustical Energy Distribution Spectrum. *Journal of Applied Psychology*, 1960, 44, 263–266.
4. Park, J.F.,Jr., and M.C.Payne, Jr., Effect of Noise Level and Difficulty of Task in Performing Division. *Journal of Applied Psychology*, 1963, 47, 367–368.
5. Tobias, J.V. *Auditory Effects of Noise on Aircraft Personnel*, F.A.A. Office of Aviation Medicine Report, 1972, November, No. 72, p.7.
6. Oakley, C.A., *Men at Work*, Hodder and Stoughton Ltd., University of London Press Limited, 1945.
7. Ferree, C.E., and G. Rand. Work and its Illumination. *Personnel Journal*, 1940(a), 19, 55–64.
8. Mohanty, G., *Industrial Psychology and Organizational Behaviour*, Kalyani Publication, p. 364.
9. Vernon, H.M. and Warner, C.G. Objective and Subjective Test for Noise, Personnel Journal, 1932, 11, pp. 141–149.
10. Mohanty, G., *Industrial Psychology and Organizational Behaviour*, Kalyani Publication, p. 384.
11. Mohanty, G., *Industrial Psychology and Organizational Behaviour*, Kalyani Publication, p. 385.
12. Blum, M.L. and Naylor, J.C. *Industrial Psychology: Its Theoretical and Social Foundations*, Harper and Row, Publishers, New York, 1968.
13. Smith, H.C. Music in Relation to Employee Attitudes, Piece Work Production and Industrial Accidents, *Applied Psychology Monograph*, No. 14, 1947.

CHAPTER 12

ENGINEERING PSYCHOLOGY

12.1 INTRODUCTION

A machine, no matter how automatic, requires a man to handle it. For the perfect operation of machine, a capable and competent operator is required. The system of human engineering developed as a solution to such problems. When engineers realized that man unlike the machine cannot be redesigned, they started with man and designed the machine around the man to suit his abilities and capabilities keeping in view the various limitations of the human operators.

It was further recognized that as long as men operate machines must be designed according to their skills and capabilities. For this purpose the knowledge and skills of psychologist are utilized by the engineers. A human engineering psychologist is mostly interested in knowing and studying the characteristics of machine and it is his job to determine how well a person can work with the machines, what are the difficulties he might face etc. In this chapter we explore the engineering psychology concepts with their importance and problems or limitations. Development of engineering psychology is also discussed under this chapter.

12.2 CONCEPT AND MEANING

During the Second World War a rapid expansion has taken place in the area of human engineering, popularly known as engineering psychology. It is also called applied psychophysics, system research and the man-machine system.

Engineering psychology owes its existence to a type of cooperative research where experts from different fields like engineers, statisticians, medical men, physicists and psychologists have made their significant contributions. Engineering psychology deals with human interaction to systems and equipment. According to Oxford English Dictionary, "engineering psychology is the management of industrial labour, especially, regarding the relationships between people and machines".

Engineering psychology is the science of human behaviour and capability, applied to the design and operation of systems and technology (Stanton, N. 1996).

The Blum (1956) remarks, "Human engineering is that endeavour which seeks to match human beings with modern machines so that their combined output will be comfortable, safe and more efficient".

The area of knowledge dealing with the capabilities and limitations of human performance in relation to design of machines, jobs, and other modifications of the human's physical environment also known as human engineering.

12.3 Importance / Need of Human Engineering

- Engineering psychology emphasizes that all machinery and tools or equipment in workplace should be designed accordingly human operator.
- For convenience or increasing effectiveness of operator all the tools or machinery are so arranged that it can be easily approached.
- It provides ease to operators which definitely helps to maintain the physical or mental health of operator.
- It seeks to ensure that human capabilities, limitations and tendencies are considered in the design of the machines and it must be designed in such a way that individual of average capacity of skill can handle it without difficulties.
- It reduces the motion or movement of the operator which results in less fatigue from the concerned job.
- It gives the feeling of safe and comfortable to the operator and he can perform efficiently and finish the work in less time.

12.4 Development of Human Engineering

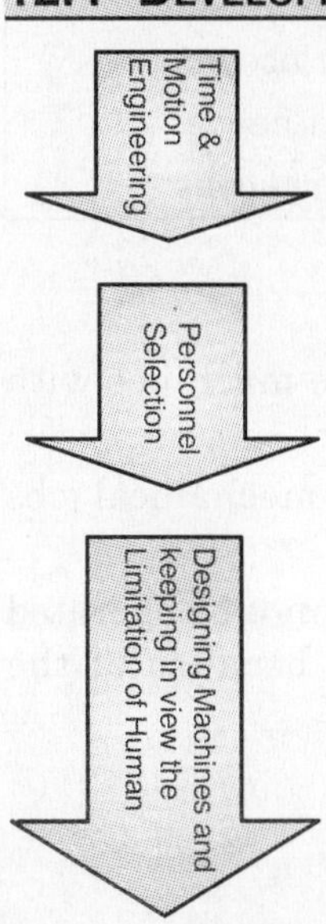

1. *Time and Motion Engineering*: Engineering psychology is just an extension of the time and motion study. The famous Taylor (Father of Scientific Management) states that the time relation and sequence of motion are utilized to find out the one best way of doing work. Mrs. and Mr. Gilbreth showed how a man can operate a machine in the best possible way by using maximum motion in minimum time. In this way, a lot of time was saved, workers were also less fatigued and worked comfortably. Thus, the time and motion study contributed to the first phase of engineering psychology.

2. *Personnel Selection*: This concept is based on realization of human variability and recognition *i.e.*, individual difference; all human being does not have the same kind of skill or capability. Thus, only the best fitted person for a job is selected. Problems are more crucial where complex machines are to be handled with superior abilities are required. In such case, personnel selection on the basis of skill, knowledge, ability, expertise is absolutely required.
3. *Designing Machines, keeping in view, limitation of Human Abilities*: With the development of engineering psychology, there was the realization occurred that the design of machines is not as important as the fact how such machines can be operated efficiently and of course handled easily by the workers without any difficulties. This becomes the most significant task of engineering psychologists. Hence task required to operate the machine should not be beyond the capacity of the individual.

A brief analysis of the three stages of development of engineering psychology indicates that the primary object of the engineering psychology is to develop a science to deal adequately with the design of machines for human use. The aim of the engineering psychologist is, therefore, to see how efficiently and economically a person can deal with the machines.

Differentiate between Engineering and Engineering Psychology	
Engineering	**Engineering Psychology**
An engineer is concerned with the physical aspects of the machine	An engineering psychologist is mostly interested in the psychological aspects of the man-machine system
In engineering, the machine is designed first and there is no consideration whatsoever, for the human being who usually operates the machine	It has a purpose to design the machine in accordance with the human needs, abilities and limitations

12.5 Problems of Human Engineering

- Machines run much faster, but man cannot operate the machines with the same speed.
- Untrained people employed in certain complicated and mechanical jobs take a long period to reach the standards.
- Various electronic and radio communication devices cannot be operated by the human beings most efficiently and speedily because of the physiological and psychological limitations.

- Machines or equipments should be designed accordingly, operator has also become one of the problems because of individual differences *i.e.*, ability, skill, knowledge, experience etc.

REFERENCES

1. Stanton, N. (1996). "Engineering Psychology: Another Science of Common Sense?". *The Psychologist* **9** (7): 300–303. Retrieved 2 July 2011.
2. http://www.answers.com/topic/human-factors-engineering-1#ixzz3BtkYEcIQ.
3. http://www.oxforddictionaries.com/definition/english/human-engineering.

❍❍❍

CHAPTER 13

INDUSTRIAL FATIGUE

13.1 INTRODUCTION

Fatigue is an important phenomenon in industrial psychology because it creates many problems including stress, weakness, tiredness, exhaustion and of course decrease in productivity. Employee recognize fatigue as a feeling of tiredness or pain, he regards it as intrinsically unpleasant which reduce their efficiency. For this and many more other reasons of industrial fatigue need investigation, both physiological and psychological point of view. It was clear from the many studies that proper training result in correct work methods which can do much to prevent the onset of fatigue or at least in reducing fatigue adverse effects. Any type of muscular work will result in fatigue because doing muscular work the expenditure of energy is at a faster rate than its recovery. Depending on the strength, stamina and preparation of individual fatigue is manifested at different rates in different individual. By the use of effective motivational practices fatigue can be successfully eliminated or at least reduce its effects in this chapter.

13.2 CONCEPT AND MEANING

Fatigue of workers is a complex phenomenon resulting from various factors in technically innovated modern industries, and it appears as a feeling of exhaustion, lowering of physiological functions, breakdown of autonomic nervous balance, and decrease in work efficiency. On the other hand industrial fatigue is caused by excessive workload, remarkable alteration in working posture and diurnal and nocturnal rhythms in daily life.

Fatigue can be a symptom of a medical problem, but more commonly it is a normal physiological reaction to exertion, lack of sleep, boredom, changes to sleep-wake schedules, or stress. Fatigue, also known as weariness, tiredness, exhaustion, or lethargy, is generally defined as a feeling of lack of energy. Fatigue is not the same as drowsiness, but the desire to sleep may accompany fatigue. Apathy is a feeling of indifference that may accompany fatigue or exist independently.

Gilbreth (1911) holds the view that due to unsatisfactory and unsuitable working conditions, fatigue is caused and hence there is a daily loss of 20% workers due to decrease in production. Adverse effect is also found in the individuals and on the welfare of the society.

Health of Munitions Workers Committee defined fatigue as "the sum of the results of activity which show themselves in a diminished capacity for doing work".

Muscio (1921)[1] defines fatigue as "a condition caused by activity in which output produced by that activity tends to be relatively poor and the degree of fatigue tends to vary directly with the poorness of output". Muscio, however, is not satisfied with this definition because fatigue cannot be directly measured and because diminished output may also be cause of distraction. The most accepted definition of fatigue is "reduction in the ability to do work caused by changing in the chemical and psychological level".

According to British Association Committee fatigue is "diminution of the capacity for work which follows excess of work or lack of rest and which is recognized on the subjective side by a characteristic malaise".

According to Viteles[2], "tension, speed, subjection to specification of work and a decrease in the enjoyment of work leads to fatigue".

According to business directory, "employee burnout characterized by physical or emotional exhaustion, resulting in lowered job productivity and performance. The employee becomes tired of doing the job, which results in poor motivation. The fatigue may be caused by such factors as understaffing, unpleasant surroundings, and high pressure".

In an intensive study called "Fatigue and hours of service of interstate truck drivers" (1941) the term fatigue is defined as an altered psychological and physiological state in relation to the states of recovery or normal capacity.

'Fatigue is caused by length or intensity of some activity in a gainful occupation', defined by Maier (1970)[3].

Fatigue is a widely used term related to a physiological and psychological state. Although it is given as a synonym for drowsiness and tiredness it is often mistakenly associated with sleepiness. Both, fatigue and sleepiness are characterized by a decrease in memory, reaction time, information processing, decision-making and vigilance, but one can be fatigued without being sleepy.[4]

Fatigue is considered an internal precondition for unsafe acts because it negatively affects the human operator's internal state. Research has generally focused on pilots, truck drivers, and shift workers.

13.3 Types of Industrial Fatigue

Fatigue can be both physiological and psychological.

- Physiological fatigue is the inability to continue functioning at the level of one's normal abilities. A person with physiological fatigue cannot lift as heavy a box or walk as far as he could if not fatigued. Muscular fatigue resulting from prolonged physical work, are the example.

- Psychological, on the other hand, rather manifests in sleepiness or slowness. A person with psychological fatigue may fall asleep, may react very slowly, or may be inattentive. With micro sleeps, the person may be unaware that he was asleep. Sensory (degradation of sensory perception) and cognitive fatigue, or alertness, intellectual fatigue are the examples of psychological fatigue.

Fatigue also differentiated by acute and cumulative fatigue

- Acute fatigue is experienced perhaps at the end of a long day, and
- Fatigue where you may still feel tired even after a night's sleep this comes under cumulative fatigue.

'Acute fatigue' has been recently explored by Jansen, Kant and van den Brandt (2002). They looked at the relationship between the need for recovery from work, prolonged fatigue and psychological distress in a large sample (N = 12,095) from the Netherlands. They conceptualized need for recovery as the "*need to recuperate from work-induced fatigue, primarily experienced after a day of work.*" They found that the need for recovery was a separate concept from prolonged fatigue.

Konz (1998a) recognizes that fatigue is likely to be related to long daily work hours especially if there is a lack of sleep; whereas occasionally, it will be due to long weekly work hours (cumulative fatigue). Many of the studies that we consider in this review use weekly working hours as their measure of 'long hours' and not daily hours. This means that cumulative fatigue may well be being measured as opposed to acute fatigue.

13.4 Why Do We Get Fatigued?

Despite the absence of an agreed scientific definition, there has still been research on fatigue. Rogers et al. (1999) note that several different mechanisms can contribute to how fatigued an individual is, for example, loss of sleep, length of working hours, age, health status, general sleep quality, experience at work and motivation and home/family life and responsibilities and commuting times.

For example, a recent article (DeFrank, Konopaske and Ivancevich, 2000) discusses 'travel stress' and notes the many ways that "executives" may be fatigued through business travel. These include missing out on good quality sleep because of unfamiliar or noisy hotels, or working late to complete jobs before departing on a business trip.

For Konz (1998), one of the main reasons that people become fatigued is insufficient rest. This can result from working at the wrong time (shift work) or working too many hours. He suggests that prolonged overtime of over 12 hours a day and 55 hours a week should be avoided. He also alerts us to the fact that an individual will have less of a chance of getting sufficient sleep if a long working day is extended by a long commute or moonlighting (working a second job). In addition, he notes that fatigue can occur for other reasons, for example:

- Too much, or too little stimulation at work.
- A large fatigue dose i.e., through too intensive work and not enough chance to rest.
- Lack of opportunity for different work tasks.
- Not taking sufficient short breaks while at work (fatigue increases exponentially with time).
- Having insufficient time to recover from fatigue. For Konz, long-term fatigue occurs when fatigue is carried over into the next day.

In conclusion, there are many different factors that may affect how fatigued an individual may become. Factors that are directly related to long hours include spending too much time doing work tasks and being exposed to 'stressors' in the work environment, and missing out on sufficient sleep due to long work hours.

13.5 Fatigue Symptoms

Some of the common fatigue symptoms are following:

- Weakness, lack of energy, tiredness, exhaustion
- Passing out or feeling as if you are going to pass out
- Palpitations (feeling your heart beating)
- Dizziness
- Vertigo is the feeling that you or your environment is moving or spinning. It differs from dizziness in that vertigo describes an illusion of movement. When you feel as if you yourself are moving, it's called subjective vertigo, and the perception that your surroundings are moving is called objective vertigo.
- Shortness of breath

13.6 Industrial Studies on Fatigue

United States Public Health Service conducted a study on 889 interstate truck drivers in three cities—Baltimore, Nashville and Chicago to find out the relationship between working hour and fatigue. This is one of the most valuable studies in the field of industrial psychology. The objectives of this study were:

- To determine if various period of truck driving would produce demonstrable and significant psycho physiological changes;
- To investigate the nature of these changes; and
- To discover whether a characteristic pattern of psycho physiological response occurs after long hours of driving.

The sixteen factors which were considered as contributing to fatigue in truck drivers were:

1. Performance of a skilled operation requiring a high degree of alertness and attention.
2. Nervous strain due to driving under adverse conditions.
3. Muscular exertion in loading and unloading and in the repair and maintenance of vehicles.
4. General irregularity of habit as a result of long distance hauls.
5. Failure to obtain satisfactory rest or sleep during rest periods or when off duty.
6. Physical condition.
7. Constant use of the eyes, frequently under unfavourable conditions such as glare, etc.
8. Social factors in the environment or occupational tradition possibly promoted by enforced absence from home.
9. Monotony inducing sleepiness.
10. The consumption of coffee and alcohol.
11. Exposure to all types of weather conditions.
12. Exposure to toxic fumes and gases.
13. Economic insecurity, that is, fear of losing one's job especially in the case of older men.
14. Noises
15. Vibration
16. Sedentary occupation—the effect of posture.

Crowden (1932)[5] classify muscular work in industry into three general types:

(i) Heavy muscular work that is too strenuous for a steady, continues rate of work to be maintained. Examples of this type of work are loading trucks, building roads and possibly mining coal.

(ii) Moderate heavy work that is continuous and which the rate of expenditure of effort is much lower than in the first type and is somewhat balanced by the rate of recovery. Examples of this type of work include machines tending and many other kinds of factory work.

(iii) In this type muscular work in the industry is light, speed work which involves a relatively small expenditure of energy but which often require a postural stain that cause unnecessary fatigue. Example is office work.

Crowden found that in a 50 yard borrow run the worker expends approximately 8% of his energy in raising and lowering the handles, 22% in attaining a wheeling speed and in stopping, and the remaining 70% in the run itself. This study shows the tremendous inefficiencies that would result from interfering with the run once it is stared. While studying the energy cost of moderately heavy work, Bedale (1924) found that carrying a load with a yoke as a milk-maid does is the most economical method from the point of view of expenditure of bodily energy. Any method of carrying weights which requires postural strain and displacement of the body when walking is more costly.

Crowden holds the view that light speed work involves little expenditure of energy, but that there may be considerable fatigue because of the cramped or uncomfortable position maintained by the worker.

According to Blum & Naylor, the men who had been driving prior to being tested performed less efficiently on the average than those who had not driven on tests of the functions like (i) aiming, (ii) resistance to glare and (iii) speed of eye movement.

The data on these tests, however, do not differentiate consistently between drivers who worked from 1 to 10 hours and those who worked over 10 hours. In items 1–7 this difference does occur. The heart rate decreased slightly with hours of driving. The average white cell count was higher in men who had driven since sleeping than in men who had not drivers since sleeping. No relationship was found between hours of driving and ability to estimate the size of known objects, differentiate white cell counts, hemoglobin content of the blood, acidity of the urine, specific gravity of urine, visual acuity and the total base and potassium concentration of blood serum.

13.7 Causes and Remedies of Industrial Fatigue

- Industrial fatigue may be occurring by **unfavourable or unsatisfactory work environment**. Unsatisfactory or unfavourable work environment include improper facility of illumination, ventilation, humidity, tempera- ture and problem of noise. All these factors lead to headache, eye strain and some time irritation and weakness. For minimizing these influences on the work, employers must take care of the factory layout.
- **Long working hour** also gives support to industrial fatigue. Long working hours can lead to stress or mental ill health, decreased production, rate of accident also increases. The remedy for avoiding fatigue is simple to regulate the laws regarding working hour.
- When machine are designed only taking consideration of work not worker who perform the task on that machine. Not stress on the comfort and ease to perform the task then it leads to a problem like workers' do unnecessary work and also it leads to extra expenditure of energy or effort. This comes out in the form of fatigue. To remove unnecessary fatigue, machines should be constructed (improving the design of machine) in such a way that workers would feel comfortable while doing work. One of the best method to minimize fatigue from **bad design of machine**

by practicing time and motion study where wrong, unnecessary and useless movements should be avoided and productivity automatically increases.

- **Inadequate rest periods** also cause of industrial fatigue. Most of the studies suggest that frequent short rest intervals look like to be more effective than a few longer ones. Too long rest intervals may create disturbance and also workers loses the continuity of the work or gets out of the mood for it. The solution for this problem is to introduce rest periods in between working hours should be depending upon the nature of the work.
- Physical and mental health also causes the fatigue in workplace. In the case of a physically weak worker there is quick onset of fatigue compared to healthy worker. Emotional disturbance in work place as well as outside the work place, lack of adjustment with surrounding, domestic problem and many more may consume a lot of energy which cause fatigue as a result of mental illness. Therefore, employer provides free medical facilities and also ensures that their workers are aware about the health problems and remedy for the same. For overcome the mental illness workers should be given proper counseling and guidance for a healthy and tension free mental life.

13.8 Effects of Industrial Fatigue

- Reduced performance and productivity in the workplace.
- Increase the possibility of absenteeism and turnover.
- Increase the risk of accidents and injuries occurring.
- Ability to think clearly.
- Headache, eye strain, muscular pain etc.
- Lack of concentration.
- Irritability, anxiety etc.
- Poor judgements.
- Reduced capacity for effective interpersonal communication.
- Fatigue and irregular sleeping habit disrupt circulation rhythms.
- Lack of sleep cause heart disease, high blood pressure, stomach infection, diabetes, depression, asthma and many more.
- Women's reproductive health can also be affected by fatigue like increased risk of miscarriage, low birth weigh, higher occurrence of premature birth.

REFERENCES

1. Muscio, B., Is a Fatigue Test Possible, *British Journal of Psychology*, 1921, 12: pp.31-46.
2. Viteles, M.S., *Industrial Psychology*, Norton, 1932.
3. Maier, N.R.F. *Psychology in Industry*, Oxford and IBH Publishing Co., New Delhi, 1970.
4. http://www.hse.gov.uk/research/hsl_pdf/2003/hsl03-02.pdf
5. Crowden, G.P., *Muscular Work, Fatigue and Recovery*, Pitman, London, 1932.
6. J.C. Stutts, J.W. Wilkins, and B.V. Vaughn. *Why do People have Drowsy Crashes: Input from Drivers Who Just Did*? Technical report, AAA Donation for Trac Safety, University of North Carolina Highway Research Center - School of Medicine, 1999.

❍❍❍

CHAPTER 14

INDUSTRIAL BOREDOM

14.1 Introduction

A worker is an important asset of the company. Without their effort or contribution employers may not achieve the high production target. An employer motivates their workers' for doing well by different means like monetary benefits and non-monetary facilities. They tried to give good and well arranged working environment to their workers. Apart from that some time workers not fully give their effort to concern task. There are many factors but here we take consideration on a specific factor that is boredom. Boredom is considered as one of the most important psychological factor which adversely influence on workplace and also productivity. It is the common belief that boredom and dissatisfaction are very common in our present method of production. But to what extent a state of boredom really affects production needs careful consideration. In this chapter define the concept of boredom, what are their causes and remedies taken by employers discussed. And lastly we talk about the effect and steps for minimizing boredom.

14.2 Concept and Meaning

Boredom is commonly referred to as mental fatigue or psychological fatigue which leads to work decrement. Boredom is often associated with jobs that are repetitive. It is usually associated with work that is basically uninteresting to the workers who perform that particular task.

According to Maier (1970), "It is claimed that repetitive work makes robots of men and that it destroys such human values as pride in workmanship and individuality".[1]

Boredom is an emotional state experienced during periods lacking activity or when individuals are uninterested in the activities presented to them. The first record of the word boredom is in the novel Bleak by Charles Dickens, written in 1852, in which it appears six times, although the expression *to be a bore* had been used in the sense of "to be tiresome or dull" since 1768.

Boredom is a condition characterized by perception of one's environment as dull, tedious, and lacking in stimulation. This can result from leisure and a lack of aesthetic interests.

Boredom has been defined by C.D. Fisher in terms of its central psychological processes: "an unpleasant, transient affective state in which the individual feels a pervasive lack of interest in and difficulty concentrating on the current activity."[2]

M. R. Leary and others describe boredom as "an affective experience associated with cognitive attention processes."[3]

These definitions make it clear that boredom arises not from a lack of things to do but from the inability to latch onto any specific activity.

There are three types of boredom, all of which involve problems of engagement of attention. These include times when we are prevented from engaging in something, when we are forced to engage in some unwanted activity, or when we are simply unable, for no apparent reason, to maintain engagement in any activity or spectacle.[4]

14.3 Causes and Remedies of Boredom

- **Repetitive Nature of Work**

  Boredom caused by repetitive work. When workers do the same job over prolonged period of time, then the chance of being bored from that particular work is on high. It is true fact that, when the work repeated it becomes machine like and require no logical work, attention, concentration on the part of the worker which resultant into boredom. The best method to overcome the boredom at this stage is 'job rotation' or exchange of jobs. By this worker become more attentive, they concentrate of new task which automatically encourage them to do work.

  In a study by Wyatt (1929)[5] some people were engaged in cutting cigarette papers and making cigarette alternatively, at an interval of 1 ½ hours. Their performance was better than those who were engaged in either of the tasks for the tasks for the whole day. Maier (1970) found that because of exchange of the jobs improvement in work was noticed.

  Similarly, in a laboratory study of assembling bicycle chains, Wyatt (1929) observed that output increased from 2.4 to 5 due to change in work. Wyatt and Frasner concluded that reduction in output is constantly noted, especially where there is constant complaint of boredom. Thus, variability in the same job should be permitted as far as possible.

- **Rest Pause**

  Rest pauses if lengthy lead to boredom. A long rest pause usually creates disturbance in different types of mental work because the worker loses the continuity and interest of work.

  The remedy is to introduce frequent and short rest pauses seem to be more effective. The amount of rest pause varies with the nature of work because manual work require more frequent rest pause as against mental work.

- **Ambience**

  Unfavourable ambience also creates boredom. When an employee dislikes their workplace automatically after some time they get bored.

  One of the remedy to overcome this problem is introduction of music. Music at workplace helps in reducing boredom, improving the mental state of workers and raising the level of production and efficiency. A study by Kerr (1945)[6] suggested that music not only improved production, it also improved the attitude of the workers and had a favourable effect on their mental state.

  Smith (1947)[7] reported a finding which revealed that there was an average increase of 7% in the day shift and 17% in the night shift with the introduction of music. However, McGehee and Gardner (1949)[8] did not find any improvement in production due to the introduction of music.

- **Intelligence**

  One of the causes of boredom is intelligence. It is quite seemed unusual that the most important asset of the workers' leads boredom. The reason behind that worker with low intelligence may be satisfied with the job like floor cleaning but under such situations an intelligent worker will not find any interest and job satisfaction.

  How to overcome this problem is one of the major concerns for employer. Here, employers try to designate the work based on employee's capability and interest and of course their personal profile will definitely minimize the chance of being bored.

- **Incomplete Task**

  If work not completed at time worker develop a sense of dissatisfaction which create sometime boredom. If management divides the task into different subparts and when a part is completed the employee experiences a feeling of completion. Maier (1970), "Task completion represents a form of motivation inherent in the nature of job and therefore is one of the most practical ways for creating interest".

14.4 Effects of Boredom

- Reduction in the efficiency of the worker.
- Losing interest on particular task.
- Boredom lacks feeling of satisfaction.
- Downfall in production.
- Various health problems like, sleepiness, nervousness, anxiety, laziness etc.
- Workers become sarcastic.
- Lack of concentration and many more.

14.5 How to Reduce Boredom?

- Psychological *guidance* and counseling should be given to neurotic workers. Because neurotic workers lose interest in the job and get bored very quickly.
- If repetitive work is made entirely automatic or semi-automatic, the feeling of boredom can be reduced to a considerable extant.
- Group discussion can be used to reduce boredom.
- Feeling of progress in their experience when introduced amongst the workers in workplace it will avoid boredom.
- Introduction of social events also reduce the work boredom like picnic, formal get-*to-gather* etc.
- Encourage informal group in workplace this will differently reduce the boredom.
- Boredom reduces by giving employees responsibility and opportunities of judgements.

REFERENCES

1. Maier, N.R.F. *Psychology in Industry*, Oxford and IBH Publishing Co., New Delhi, 1970.
2. Fisher, C.D. (1993). Boredom at work: A neglected concept. *Human Relations*, 46, 395–417, p. 396.
3. Leary, M.R., Rogers, P.A., Canfield, R.W., & Coe, C. (1986). Boredom in Interpersonal Encounters: Antecedents and Social Implications. *Journal of Personality and Social Psychology*, 51, 968–975, p. 968.
4. Cheyne, J.A., Carriere, J.S.A., & Smilek, D. (2006). Absent-mindedness: Lapses in conscious awareness and everyday cognitive failures. *Consciousness and Cognition*, 15, 578–592.
5. Wyatt, S., Langdon, J.N. and Stock, F.G.L. Fatigue and Boredom in Repetitive Work, *Industrial Health Res. Bd.*, 1937, Rep. No. 77.
6. Kerr, W.A. Effects of music on factory production, *Applied Psychology*, Monogr, 1945.
7. Smith, H.C. Music in relation to employee attitude piecework production and industrial accident, *Applied Psychology*, Monogr, 1947, pp.14.
8. McGehee, W. and Gardner, J.E. Music in a complex industrial job, *Personnel Psychology*, 1949, 2, pp. 405–417.

❍❍❍

CHAPTER 15

INDUSTRIAL ACCIDENT AND SAFETY

15.1 INTRODUCTION

With the introduction of machines in the workplace the tasks become easy for the workers' to perform. But one of the dark sides of the mechanization is occurrence of injuries. Some time it will be resultant from the number of factors related to workers and some time the cause of injuries occurred by working condition. Employers have a responsibility to provide safe working condition and to preserve their workers. Industrial safety has direct influence the production process. If employers accurately and fairly check the safety measures it will be definitely prevent accidents and ensure regular flow of work. Because if they should pay adequate attention to industrial safety it will be not only benefited to the workers' but also fulfill the interest of the employers also. In this chapter first we discuss the meaning and concept of accident and safety, accident cause, accident proneness their cost and measurement. After that we elaborate the industrial safety and method for reducing accident or safety measures.

15.2 CONCEPT AND MEANING

The word accident is derived from the Latin verb ***accidere***, signifying "fall upon, befall, happen, chance." An accident, often causing serious injury that is job-related in that it usually happens on a work site such as a factory floor or a construction site. Or an unexpected and undesirable event, especially one resulting in damage or harm.

According to the Factories Act, 1948, it is "an occurrence in an industrial establishment causing bodily injury to a person who makes him unfit to resume his duties in the next 48 hours".

An industrial accident may be defined as "an occurrence which interferes with the orderly progress of work in an industrial establishment".[1]

According to T.W. Harrell, "Accidents are not only expensive, but they also lower the morale of the workers and in addition result in lower production".[2]

Heinrich (1959) defines an accident as an unplanned and uncontrolled event in which the action or reaction of an object, substance, and person results in personal injury or the productivity thereof.

Accident not only costly to industrial economy but they also results in injuries, pain or even death of the worker involved. It will also lower the morale and satisfaction of the worker and decrease the rate of production. Therefore, industries work hard to find out the causes of accident and also provide safety measures to reduce the accidents.

In common accident may be defined as, some sudden and unexpected event taking place without expectation, upon the instant, rather than something that continues, progresses or develops; something happening by chance; something unforeseen, unexpected, unusual, extraordinary, or phenomenal, taking place not according to the usual course of things or events, out of the range of ordinary calculations; that which exists or occurs abnormally, or an uncommon occurrence.

15.3 Causes of Industrial Accidents

Accidents are usually the result of a combination of factors, each one of which may vary from situation to situation.[3] According to Glimer (1971), unsafe acts and unsafe conditions may interact in such a way that an accident may be caused by both. Also these two factors may be separately responsible for accidents.[4]

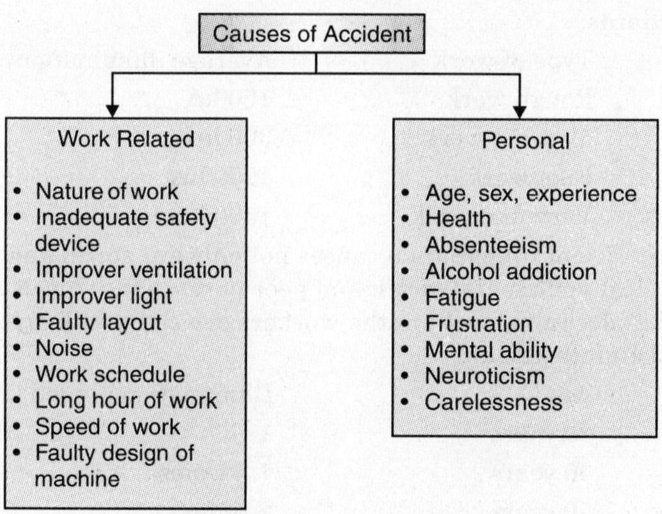

Exhibit 1: Causes of Accidents

Work Related

- ***Nature of work***—Plenty of accident in the workplace are by the nature of work. Slippery and greasy floors, locations of machines also lead to accidents.

- ***Inadequate safety device***—Safety devices are the part of work and need utilization when required such as gloves, rubber sole, ear blocker, goggles, glasses, particular clothes. But all safety devices if not properly working than it will lead to accidents. While making a survey of accidents, Stephenson (1927) came to the conclusion that many of the safety devices to be wear by the workers are actually not used by them, perhaps because of resistance or because they consider this to be an insult to their intelligence and efficiency.
- ***Improver ventilation***—This is also cause accident because by the moisture workers feel uncomfortable to perform the task and it will be resultant into minor or some time major accidents. Extremes of heat and cold are harmful to the human body. This is experienced as follows:
  - Below 12 deg C–Uncomfortably cold
  - Below 20 deg C–Cold
  - 24–30 deg C–Comfortable
  - Above 38 deg C–Uncomfortably hot
  - Above 42 deg C–Intolerably hot
- ***Improver light***—To control industrial accidents illumination should be proper and optimum. Stanley's (1966) study indicates that 25% of the accidents are due to artificial lighting. Excessive glare causes eye strain and it becomes one of the frequent causes of accident as viewed by DeSilva (1942). Comfortable work environment should have the following lighting standards:

Type of work	Average illumination
Rough work	150 lux
Medium work	300 lux
Fine work	1000 lux
Very fine work	1500 lux

Insufficient illumination causes not only eye strain and vision defects, but physical and mental strain and poor performance levels. A factor often ignored in declining trend in the workers eye sight with age. This has also to be taken into account

Age	Illumination needed
30 years	1
40 years	1.5 times
50 years	2 times
60 years	3 times

- ***Faulty layout***—Optimum arrangement of physical resource within the prescribed area called layout. Like sequential location of machines i.e. machine should be placed according to task which was performed first than second than third and so on. If they are not properly done definitely it will lead to accidents.

- ***Noise***—If induced hearing loss or occupational deafness is caused by prolonged exposure. Continuous prolonged exposure to higher than permissible levels of noise causes vision changes, heart and circulatory disturbances and behaviour changes.

  Permissible levels of noise in the work environment are as follows:

Hours of exposure	Noise level, Decibels
8	90
6	92
4	95
3	97
2	100
1	105
1/2	110
1/4	115

- ***Work schedule***—One of the most important causes of industrial accident is work schedule. Many of studies shown that workers who work in night shift are more inclined to accident as compared to day shift.
- ***Long hour of work***—If worker work across their allotted time (prescribed time for doing particular task) usually eight hours a day, they get tired easily and with resultant into fatigue, muscular pain, stress etc. which lead accident.
- ***Speed of work***—When speed of work rises and definitely frequency of accidents also rises. And it will more on night shift as compared to day shift. Excessive speed also introduces fatigue which may lead to accident.
- ***Faulty design of machine/ equipment***—Some time worker not understand the process of operating machinery because of their faulty design. They not properly control the equipments. It will increase the chance of accident and create an unsafe working environment.

PERSONAL

- ***Age, sex, experience***—Younger workers are more prone to accident as compared to older ones. As workers gain experience the possibility of accident reduced. Sex also influence the rate of accident, female workers are more inclined to accident as male. Vernon (1945) has found that there is a significant relationship between young age and less experience and the accident rate. Approximately 50% of the employees had accidents in their first 6 months, and only 5% had accidents after they had two and a half years of experience.
- The Metropolitan Insurance Company suggests, on the basis of age, that the younger people are the greatest sufferers. In a textile mill it was found that among the younger group, for every 100 workers 80 were involved in accidents, whereas the number of accidents was 12 in the 30–35 years age group.

- ***Health***—Poor health and low energy lead to accident. Health not only includes physical but also mental health. If worker's physical or mental health deteriorates it increases the chance of accident.
- ***Absenteeism***—Workers who are regular in their work are less prone to accident as compared to absentee. From the attendance record of a company from last few years showed a direct relationship between accidents and absenteeism. In a sample of 289 employees, 200 employees who had no accidents averaged 15 absences, while the remaining 89 who had accidents, averaged 24 absences.(Hill, 1955).
- ***Alcohol addiction***—At the state of drunkenness individuals' does not control over their action. They did not understand the clearly picture of work which may lead accidents. It not only influences the work of individual but also affect the family, friends and co-workers relationship with the particular individual.
- **Fatigue**—Fatigue caused by many reasons like long working hour, unfavourable working condition, inappropriate rest periods, faulty machine, physical and mental health and many more. From all these reasons workers loses attention and concentration on work resultant into accidents. Musico (1922) found that there is a constant increase in accidents as hours pass, both in the morning and evening spells, but they are higher in the morning than in the end hours. He further found that the maximum number of accidents occurred at 11 a.m. and again between 5 and 6 p.m.
- ***Frustration***—Doob (1961) clearly indicates that frustration causes a person to be accident-prone, especially when he shows aggressive, regressive or fixative actions as a reaction to frustration.
- ***Mental ability***—Some studies found that worker with low mental ability are more prone to accident as compared to others but some studies shown that there is no correlation among intelligence and mental ability. Chamber (1939) found that very few accident prone individuals were above average in intelligence and learning ability, dependability and industry. But it was recommended to management that before assigning the task or job to worker makes sure that particular task is compatible to their mental ability.
- ***Neuroticism***—A worker who is neurotic are more inclined to accident. Many of psychologists said that there is positive relation between neuroticism and accident. Neurotic worker get fatigue easily, lose their confidence, feeling unsatisfied and many more and obviously they all the cause accident. Management should be more emphasis on the problem and remedies of neuroticism.
- ***Carelessness***—Carelessness is the prime cause of accident. A little bit carelessness some time introduces huge accident. Carelessness can be removed by regular reminders to be careful.

15.4 Accident Proneness

Whatever the cause of accident some worker is more prone to another. A worker who is accident-prone in one specific situation may not be so in other. If two workers are operated on similar machine under identical situation, one may commit more accidents than the other. The first worker will be called an 'accident-prone operator'.

Harrell (1964), "Accident-proneness is the continuing tendency of a person to have accidents as a result of his stable and persisting characteristics". Accident proneness is a condition in which a "human being is mentally inclined, strongly disposed, attitudinally addicted or personally destined to become continually involved in an on-going and never-ending series of accidents or injuries".[5]

In the opinion of Blum and Naylor (1968), "accidents do not distribute themselves by chance, but happen frequently to some men and infrequently to others as a logical result of combination of circumstances". The reoccurrence of accident may be came by difference in mental ability and experience, muscular weakness, visual disability, hearing capacity, emotional instability and many more.

15.5 Accident Cost

There are some direct and indirect costs incurred in accident. Which not only affect the victim family as well as worker itself but also affect the production as well as employers.

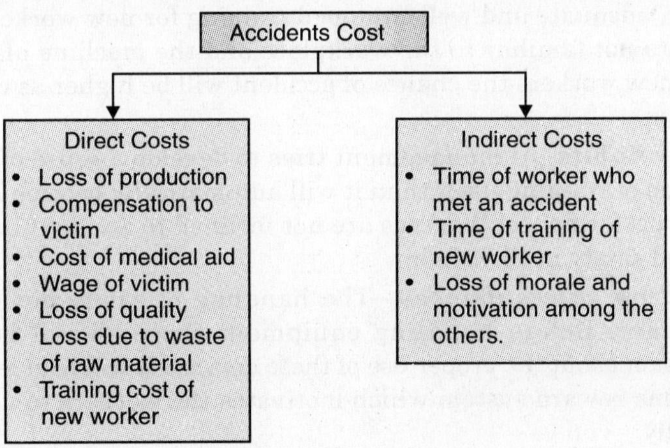

Exhibit 2: Accident Cost

15.6 Accident Measurement

Accident frequency rate and severity rate are the two main statistical ratios which have been used to gather accident information.

The National Security Council of the United States has given the following formulae for the computation of frequency rate and severity rate. The frequency rate is the number of time cost accidents (or injuries which have disabled an employee) per 1, 000, 000 man-hours worked. The severity rate, on the other side, is the total number of days charged or lost because of accidents per 1, 000, 000 man-hours worked.[6]

$$\text{Accident frequency rate} = \frac{\text{Number of disabling work injuries} \times 1{,}00{,}000}{\text{Total number of man-hour worked}}$$

$$\text{Severity rate} = \frac{\text{Number of man day lost} \times 1{,}000{,}000}{\text{Total number of man-hour worked}}$$

15.7 Industrial Safety

Accidents have many causes and it will happen at any time. If employer provide safe work environment to workers than automatically it minimizes the occurrence of accident. Industrial safety contributes to team work, high satisfaction and morale and but obvious high productivity.

15.8 Safety Measures

There is some safety measure which if seriously considered than it will be helpful to not only workers but also employer of the particular concern:

- ***Appropriate training programmes***—For minimizing the impact of accident in workplace employers must ensure that there should be a proper, adequate and well equipped training for new workers. Because they are not familiar to the workplace and the machine also and with these new workers the chance of accident will be higher as compared to another.
- ***Safety habits***—If management tries to develop a sense of security at the time of training itself than it will automatically become habit at the actual performance. Workers are not inclined to accident because they adopted safety in their habit.
- ***Handling safety devices***—The handling of safety devices is very important. Before handling equipment there should be a proper discussion about the proper use of these devices. It will lead less accident. Put some reward system which motivates the workers to use machine carefully.
- ***Safety campaigns***—Promote awareness about safety among the workers. It can be done by posters, slogans etc. or organize an effective accident prevention week which create awareness about how to minimize accident in workplace, what safety measures should be if taken for doing flawless work.

- ***Housekeeping***—Poor housekeeping like wet or dry, slippery and greasy floors, bad arrangement of machines, material leads accident. For maintaining a safe work place housekeeping details must be attended to.
- ***Adequate selection***—Selection of workers at workplace should be done by proper tests. Assign task to individual according to their compatibility. If work or task is compatible to worker than chance of accident should be minimized and of course workers will be satisfied and feel less fatigue.
- ***Actuarial methods***—The actuarial method emphasis finding the cause of accidents based on actual data and developing reduction of conducted accident programmes from that angle. Mcfarland and Moseley's (1954)[7] clearly indicate that accident repeaters committed many more violations than did accident-free-drivers. The number of vibrations of accident repeaters is much greater than proportional expectations. They liable to believe that a man drives as he lives. Speed in private driving and violations which reflect attitude towards authority seem to be characteristic of repeaters. In brief the actuarial method involves studying accidents statistics to determine based upon statistical data those things which seem to be related to accident frequency. (Blum & Naylor)[8].
- ***Regular inspection***—For the conduction of sound working it was recommended that regular inspection should be done on workplace. The inspector checks all the availability of proper working environment for workers and if any dissimilarity exists they counsel the worker and also inform the management.
- ***Safety education programmes***—Accidents can be reduced by safety education programmes which was conducted by management and workers groups. Regular foremen's meetings can be effective in reducing accidents. The United States Department of Labour (1947) has issued a "Guide to Industrial Accident Prevention Through a Joint Labour-Management Safety Committee"[9] which suggests some points for a safety committee:
  - (*i*) Make immediate and detailed investigation of accident reports.
  - (*ii*) Develop accident data to indicate accident sources and injury rates.
  - (*iii*) Develop or revise safe practice and rules to comply with plant needs.
  - (*iv*) Inspect the plant to detect hazardous physical conditions or unsafe work methods.
  - (*v*) Recommended changes or additions to protective equipment and device to eliminate hazards.
  - (*vi*) Promote safety and first aid training for committee members and workers.
  - (*vii*) Participate in advertising safety and in selling the safety progamme to workers.
  - (*viii*) Conduct regular scheduled meetings.

Considerable work is being performed by the Committee of Highway Safety Research of the National Academy of Sciences in 1952[10]. This committee serves as a center for the collection of information related to accidents and is also engaged in outlining desirable research programmes. The following summary statements may be made from the committee's data:

(*i*) 70% to 90% of automobile accidents are due wholly or in part of human errors or lapses.

(*ii*) The accidents records kept have value as a general index but are of questionable value as a criterion for research on accident causes.

(*iii*) Many drivers having multiple accidents in one period are accident free in a later period.

(*iv*) Factors leading to accidents are largely correctable or may be compensated for by greater caution.

(*v*) Drivers between 18 and 25 years of age have far more than their proportionate share of accidents.

(*vi*) The effect of intensive safety education and enforcement campaigns has been shown to be immediate but temporary.

(*vii*) Psychological driver tests are probably of more values as educational as selection devices.

(*viii*) Clinics for accidents repeaters have been shown to have values. Whether this is due to increased knowledge, attitude change or motivation is not known.

United Nations Economic Commission for Europe has concentrated its efforts on preventing industrial accidents and especially their transboundary effects in its region, which stretches from Canada and the United States in the west to the Russian Federation in the east. Its work led to the adoption of the *Convention on the Transboundary Effects of Industrial Accidents*. It was signed by 26 UN/ECE member countries and the European Community and entered into force on 19 April 2000.[11]

The following measures may be carried out for safety, depending on national laws and practices, by Parties, competent authorities, operators, or by joint efforts:

1. The setting of general or specific safety objectives;
2. The adoption of legislative provisions or guidelines concerning safety measures and safety standards;
3. The identification of those hazardous activities which require special preventive measures, which may include a licensing or authorization system;
4. The evaluation of risk analyses or of safety studies for hazardous activities and an action plan for the implementation of necessary measures;
5. The provision to the competent authorities of the information needed to assess risks;

6. The application of the most appropriate technology in order to prevent industrial accidents and protect human beings and the environment;
7. The undertaking, in order to prevent industrial accidents, of the appropriate education and training of all persons engaged in hazardous activities on-site under both normal and abnormal conditions;
8. The establishment of internal managerial structures and practices designed to implement and maintain safety regulations effectively;
9. The monitoring and auditing of hazardous activities and the carrying out of inspections.

There are some ways by which the **ILO** is to control of the causes of major industrial accidents and also recommend safe operation of major hazard installations.[12]

1. Works management should control major hazard installations by sound engineering and management practices, for example by:
   (*a*) Good plant design, fabrication and installation, including the use of high-standard components;
   (*b*) Regular plant maintenance;
   (*c*) Good plant operation;
   (*d*) Good management of safety on site;
   (*e*) Regular inspection of the installation, with repair and replacement of components where necessary.
2. Works management should consider the possible causes of major accidents, including:
   (*a*) Component failure;
   (*b*) Deviations from normal operation;

Safe Operation of Major Hazard Installations

- The primary responsibility for operating and maintaining the installation safely should lie with works management.
- Good operational instructions and sound procedures should be provided and enforced by works management.
- Works management should ensure that workers operating the installation have been adequately trained in their duties.
- Accidents and near misses should be investigated by works management.

Office of Labour Commissioner, Govt. of NCT of Delhi, the Delhi Factories Rules, 1960 mentioned duties of inspector—

The inspector shall—

(*a*) inspect the industrial activity or isolated storage at least once in a calendar year,

(b) send annually status report on the compliance with the Rules by occupiers to the Ministry of Environment and Forests through the Directorate General Factory Advice Service and Labour Institutes and Ministry of Labour, Government of India,

(c) enforce direction and procedure in respect of industrial activities or isolated storage covered under the Factories Act, 1948 and in respect of pipelines up to a distance of five hundred meters from the outside of the perimeter of the factory, regarding—

(i) Notification of the major accidents as per rules 61-UC (1) and 61-UC(2);

(ii) Notification of sites as per rules 61-UE and 61-UF;

(iii) Safety Reports and Safety Audits as per rules 61-UH to 61-UJ;

(iv) Notification of sites as per rules 61-UE and 61-UF;

(v) Notification of sites as per rules 61-UE and 61-UF;

(vi) Safety Reports and Safety Audits as per rules 61-UH to 61-UJ;

(vii) Preparation of "on-site Emergency Plans" as per rule 61-UK and involvement in the preparation of "Off-site Emergency Plans" in consultation with District Collector or District Emergency Authority.

61-UC. Notification of Major Accidents

(1) Where a major accident occurs on a site or in a pipeline, the occupier, shall, within 48 hours, notify the Inspector and Chief Inspector of that accident, and furnish thereafter to the Inspector and Chief Inspector a report relating to the accident in installments, if necessary, in Schedule[5].

(2) The Inspector and Chief Inspector shall, on receipt of the report in accordance with sub-rule (1) of this rule, undertake a full analysis of the major accident and send the requisite information to the Ministry of Environment and Forests through the Directorate General Factory Advice Service and Labour Institutes and Ministry of Labour, Government of India.

61-UE. Notification of Site

(1) An occupier shall not undertake any industrial activity or isolated storage unless he has submitted a written report to the Chief Inspector containing the particulars specified in Schedule 6 at least 90 days before commencing that activity or before such shorter time as the Chief Inspector may agree and for the purposes of this sub-rule, an activity in which subsequently there is or is liable to be a threshold quantity given in Column 3 of Schedules 2 and 3 or more of and additional hazardous chemical shall be deemed to be a different activity and shall be notified accordingly.

(2) The Chief Inspector within 60 days from the date of receipt of the report in accordance with sub-rule (1) of this Rule shall examine and

on examination of the report if he is of the opinion that contravention of the provisions of the Act or the rules made there under has taken place, he may issue notice for obtaining compliance.

61-UF. Updating of the Site Notification

Where an activity has been reported in accordance with rule 61UE (1) and the occupier makes a change in it (including an increase or decrease in the maximum quantity of a hazardous chemical to which this rule applies which is or is liable to be at the site or in the pipeline or at the cessation of the activity) which affects the particulars specified in that report or any subsequent report made under this rule, the occupier shall forthwith furnish a further report to the Inspector and the Chief Inspector.

61-UH. Safety Reports and Safety Audit Reports

(1) Subject to the following sub-rules of this rule an occupier shall not undertake any industrial activity or isolated storage to which this rule applies, unless he has prepared a Safety Report on that industrial activity containing the information specified in Schedule 7 and has sent a copy of that report to the Chief Inspector at least ninety days before commencing that activity.

(2) After the commencement of these rules, the occupiers of both the news and the existing industrial activities or isolated storages shall arrange to carry out safety audit by a competent agency to be accredited by an Accreditation Board to be constituted by the Ministry of Labour, Government of India in this behalf. Further, such auditing shall be carried out as under:

(*a*) Internally once in a year by a team of suitable plant personnel.

(*b*) Externally once in two years by a competent agency accredited in this behalf.

(*c*) In the year when an external audit is carried out internal audit need not be carried out.

(3) The occupier within 30 days of the completion of the audit shall send a report to the Chief Inspector with respect to the implementation of the audit recommendation.

61-UJ. Requirement for Further Information to be sent to the Inspector and the Chief Inspector

Where in accordance with rules 61-UH and 61-UI, and occupier has sent safety report and safety audit report relating to an industrial activity of isolated storage to the Inspector and the Chief Inspector may, by a notice served on the occupier require him to provide such additional information as may be specified in the notice and the occupier shall send that information to the Inspector and the Chief Inspector within ninety days.

REFERENCES

1. Mamoria, C.B., Gankar, *Personnel Management*, Himalaya Publication, p. 789.
2. Harrell. T.W. *Industrial Psychology*, Oxford & IBH, New Delhi, 1964, p. 196.
3. Kirpatrick, Donald J., "Supervisory Inventory on Safety", Personnel Administration, Vol. 8, No.4, 1964, pp. 32–34.
4. Glimer, V.B.H., *Industrial and Organizational Psychology*, McGraw-Hill, Kausaka Publications, 1971.
5. Sikula A.F., *Personnel Administration and Human Resource Management*, John Wiley & Sons, New York, 1997, p. 335.
6. Mamoria, C.B., Gankar, *Personnel Management*, Himalaya Publication, p. 794.
7. Mcfarland, R.A., and A.L. Moseley, *Human Factors in Highway Transport Safety*, Harvard School of Public Health, Boston, 1954.
8. Blum, M.L. & Naylor, J.C., Industrial Psychology: Its Theoretical and Social Foundations, New Delhi, 2002.
9. U.S.Department of Labour, *Guide to Industrial Accident Prevention through a Joint Labour-Management Safety Committee*, Labour Information Bulletin, February 1947.
10. National Academy of Sciences, National Research Council, *The Field of Highway Safety Research*, National Research Council, Washington, D.C., 1952.
11. United Nations Economic Commission for Europe, Preventive measures for industrial safety, *Convention on the Transboundary Effects of Industrial Accidents*, 2000.
12. *Prevention of Major Industrial Accident*, Code of Practice, Geneva, International Labour Office, 1991 pp. 8-9
13. Government of NCT of Delhi, Office of Labour Commissioner, The Delhi Factories Rules, 1960.

❍❍❍

CHAPTER 16

JOB ANALYSIS

16.1 INTRODUCTION

A job is a bundle of tasks that performed by workers' in organization. Job analysis is often described as the cornerstone of successful employee selection efforts and performance management initiatives. A job analysis involves the systematic collection of information about a job. It is an accurate study of the various components of a job. It is not only concerned with analysis of the duties and conditions of work but also with the individual qualification and experience of the workers'. If organization carefully done job analysis than they get maximum production with increased efficiency of workers'. This chapter describes the job analysis, their importance in industrial psychology and different methods of job analysis.

16.2 CONCEPT AND MEANING

Job analysis is a formal and detailed examination of job. Job analysis is the process of gathering and organizing detailed information about various jobs within the organization so that managers can better understand the process through which they are performed most effectively.[1] Job is synonyms of work. Work is understood as physical and mental activity that is carried out at a particular place and time, according to instruction, in return for money.[2]

Job analysis includes job description and job specification. Job description includes tasks and responsibilities of a job. Job title, duties, machines, tools and equipment, working conditions and hazards comes under job description.

The capabilities that the job holder should possess for doing a particular job from part of job specification. Education, experience, training, skills, communication are a part of job specification. Whatever the particular job demanded there are certain abilities required to discharge the task. Job analysis is important if an organization is to fully understand the skills and competencies required to perform a particular job.

Job Analysis

Job Description

A statement containing items such as:

- Job title
- Location
- Job summary
- Duties
- Machines, tools and equipment
- Materials
  Supervision given or received
- Working condition
- Hazards

Job Specification

A statement of human qualification necessary to do the job. Usually contains such items as:

- Education
- Experience
- Training
- Judgement
- Initiative
- Physical effort
- Physical skills
- Responsibilities
- Communication skills
- Emotional characteristics
- Unusual sensory demands such as sight, smell, hearing.

Exhibit 1: Job Analysis Contents

There is a list of eleven items of job analysis suggested by Viteles' (1932) known as Guide of Job Analysis:

1. Identification of the job
2. Number employed
3. Statement of duties
4. Machines used
5. Analysis of operations
6. Conditions of work
7. Pay and non-financial incentives
8. Relation to other allied jobs (place in the organization)
9. Opportunities for transfer and promotion
10. Time and nature of training
11. Personal requirements:
    (*a*) General (e.g., age, marital status)
    (*b*) Physical
    (*c*) Educational
    (*d*) Previous experience
    (*e*) General and special abilities
    (*f*) Temperamental and character requirements

Job analysis is a important part of working efficiency, besides promoting smooth working relationships among the employees. Effective training programmes, efforts to reduce fatigue, fair personnel police and many other measures leading to efficiency cannot be introduced effectively unless the basic and preliminary step of job analysis has been taken carefully.

16.3 Importance of Job Analysis

Lawshe and Satter (1944) have pointed out four primary importance of job analysis:

- To find out the derivation of training content.
- For setting up of personnel specifications.
- For the improvement of job efficiency.
- For establishment of wage structure.

16.4 Job Analysis Methods

There are many different methods which may be used to obtain data for a job analysis. Some are the listed below:

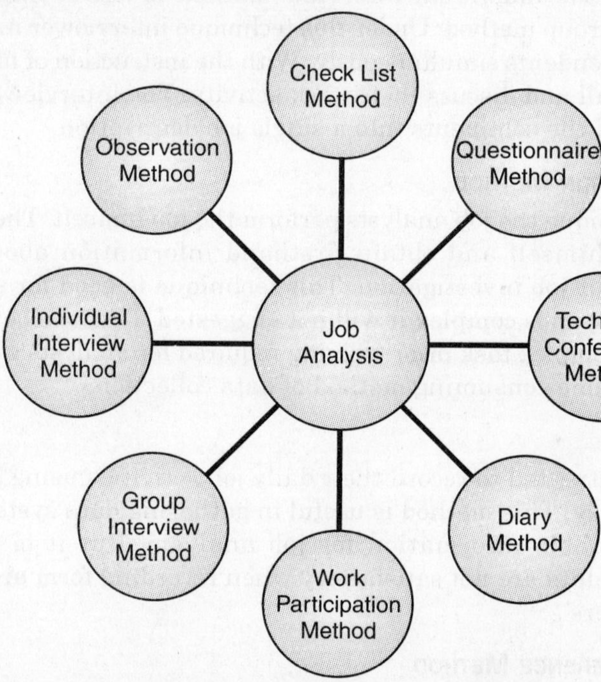

Exhibit 2: Methods of Job Analysis

Checklist Method

Under this technique of collecting data for job analysis, workers' check the task that he performs from a long list of possible task statements. It requires lots of preliminary work to prepare the check list for collecting appropriate task statements. Check list method are easily administered to large group and easy to tabulate.

Observation Method

Observation method actually conducted at the place of job or work. The observers examine the task which was performed by worker through simple observation without interrupting work, and made their conclusion. The advantage of this method is the production process never stopped.

Individual Interview Method

In this method representatives are selected and interviewing usually outside or the actual job situation. The interview is structured and should be done with the help of experienced and qualified interviewers. It has not been done by the single interview, but a series of individual interview provide accurate data for job analysis. This technique is costly and time consuming but if done with care it provides complete picture of the job.

Group Interview Method

Group interview method is an extension of individual interview method. The advantage over the individual interview method is the savings in time obtained by the group method. Under this technique interviewer interviewed the group of respondents simultaneously. With the instruction of interviewer respondents recall and discuss their work activity. The interviewer collects and combines all the comments into a single job description.

Work Participation Method

Under this technique the job analysts perform the job himself. They learned by doing work himself and obtain firsthand information about all the characteristics for job investigation. This technique is good for simple job but as the job becomes complex it will not suggested. Because before doing that particular complex task prior training required for analysts which leads into costly and time consuming method of data collection.

Diary Method

Workers' are instructed to record their daily job activities using some type of logbook or diary. This method is useful in gathering data systematically which give valuable information for job analysis. But it is also time consuming, and data are not satisfactory when recording form are not kept simple for workers'.

Technical Conference Method

Under this method job analyst get information from expert rather than actual job performer. These experts are basically the supervisors who have extensive knowledge of job. The analyst discusses all the characteristics of job with experts. The main drawback of this method is the expert are not actually perform the task themselves. They give information to analyst on the basis of their own previous experience.

Questionnaire Method

Here, job performer gives the detailed information about the job via survey method. Under this technique a well prepared questionnaire related to job activity imposed to workers' and job analyst examine the responses. The method is useful for people who write easily but not so good for collecting data from low-level workers' who have little facility for self-expression. It is also time consuming and lengthy process to analyze the data obtained.

REFERENCES

1. Denisi, Griffin, *Human Resource Management*; Biztantra, New Delhi, p. 155.
2. John Bratton and Jeffrey Gold, *Human Resource Management*; Palgrave, MacMillan, 2008, p. 116.
3. Dale S. Beach, Personnel–*The Management of People at Work*, p. 166.
4. Mohanty, G., *Industrial Psychology and Organizational Behaviour*, Kalyani Publisher, 1999, p. 100.
5. Blum, Naylor, *Industrial Psychology*, CBS Publication, pp. 94–95.

❍❍❍

CHAPTER 17

RECRUITMENT AND SELECTION

17.1 INTRODUCTION

The manpower is the most important asset of the organization. Without their contribution or effort an organization can never achieve their goals. From the process of goal setting to the implementation, manpower contributes much more or we can say that without manpower any organization does not survive. For effective use of manpower proper planning should be considerable. Planning for placing right person, at right place for doing right work, at a right time. For this reason it is quite more important to recruit and select those people who are right. In this chapter, we examine the methods, source, detailed process of recruitment and selection. We start by aims and objective of recruitment. Then we look at process of recruitment, factor affecting recruitment and source of recruitment. And finally discuss the process of selection.

17.2 CONCEPT AND MEANING

Recruitment is the process of attracting potential candidates for a particular job vacancy. Recruitment forms the first stage in the process which continues with selection and ceases with placement of the candidates.[1] According to Edwin B. Flippo, "Recruitment is the process of searching the candidates for employment and stimulating them to apply for jobs in the organization". Recruitment is the activity that links the employers and the job seekers.

Recruitment is the process of locating and encouraging potential applicants to apply for existing or anticipated job opening.[2] Recruitment is the process of developing a pool of qualified applicants who are interested in working for the organization might reasonably select the best individual or individuals to hire for employment.[3] In simple words, recruitment is the process of attracting qualified applicants for a specific job. The process begins when application are brought in and ends when the same is finished. The result is a pool of applicants, from where the appropriate candidate can be selected.

According to businessdictionary.com, "Process of identifying and hiring best-qualified candidate (from within or outside of an organization) for a job vacancy, in a most timely and cost effective manner".

According to Yoder and others, "Recruitment is a process to discover the source of manpower to meet the requirement of the staffing schedule and to employ effective measures for attracting that manpower in adequate number to facilitate effective selection of an efficient working force."[4]

In simple words, recruitment refers to the process of screening and selecting qualified people for a job at an organization or firm. Or recruitment is the process of attracting prospective employees and stimulating them for applying job in a organization.

Recruitment is a continuous process whereby the firm attempts to develop a pool of qualified applicants for the future human resources needs even though specific vacancies do not exist. Usually, the recruitment process starts when a manger initiates an employee requisition for a specific vacancy or an anticipated vacancy.

Thus, recruitment enables the organization to select suitable employees for different jobs. It is the most important function of the personnel department. It is concerned with the discovery of the source of manpower and tapping of the sources so that the potential employees are properly evaluated and the new employees are placed and inducted to fill up the vacant position in the organization.

Recruitment is a two-way street: it takes a recruiter and recruitee. Just as the recruiter has a choice whom to recruit or whom not, so also the prospective employee has to make the decision if he should apply for that organizations' job. The individual makes this decision usually on three different bases (*i*) the objective factor (pay, benefits, location, opportunity etc.) (*ii*) critical contact (behaviour of the recruiter, the nature of physical faculties etc.) (*iii*) subjective factor (personality patterns, the image of organization i.e. choices are made on a highly personal and emotional basis.)[5]

17.3 Need of Recruitment

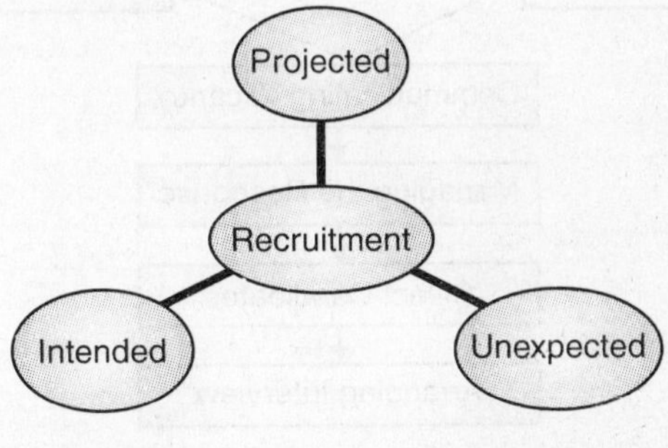

Exhibit 1: Need of Recruitment

1. **Projected:** Projected needs are those movements in personnel, which an organization can predict by studying trends in internal and external environment.
2. **Intended:** That needs arising from changes in organization and retirement policy.
3. **Unexpected:** Resignation, deaths, accidents, illness give rise to unexpected needs.

17.4 Objectives of Recruitment

- Recruitment aims at developing and marinating adequate supply of labour force according to the need of the organization.
- To provide sufficiently large group of qualified candidates, so that suitable candidates can be selected out of them.
- Hiring the right kind of candidate on the right job.
- It facilitates the maximum pool of candidate with minimum cost.
- Meet the organization's legal and social obligation regarding the composition of its workforce.
- Recruitment is the process which associates the employers with the employees.
- Help to reduce the probability that job applicants once recruited and selected will leave the organization only after a short period of time.
- Attract and encourage more and more candidates to apply in the organization.

17.5 Process of Recruitment

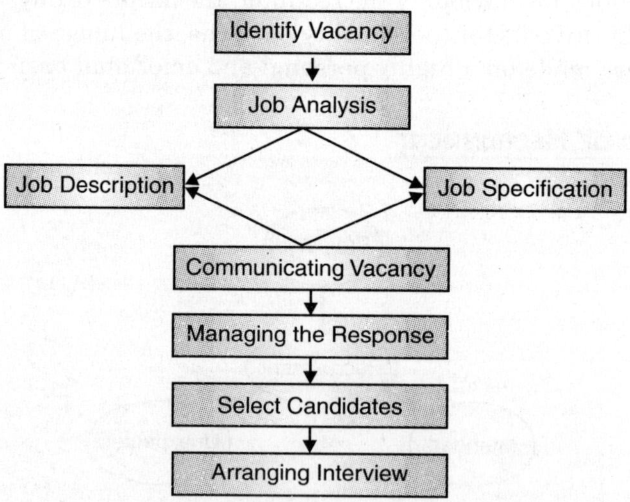

Exhibit 2: Process of Recruitment

1. **Identify Vacancy:** The recruitment process begins when human resource department get a requisition from other department. How many personnel are required in a particular department? What are their qualifications? This type of question is analyzed at this stage.
2. **Job Analysis:** It is a procedure by which pertinent information is obtained about a job, i.e., it is detailed and systematic study of information relating to the operations and responsibilities of a specific job.[6] At this stage of recruitment detailed analysis should be considered or prepare complete job analysis which include both job description (which includes title, location, duties, working condition, hazards etc.) and job specification (which includes qualification, experience, age limit required etc.)
3. **Communicating Vacancy:** The next step in the process of recruitment is communicating vacancy to desired applicant which can be done by advertisement in newspapers, radio, television, on internet etc.
4. **Managing the Response:** It is crucial task and should be done by well-qualified staff because if any flaws exist in this stage it may leads to call for interview an undesirable candidate or organization miss an opportunity to recruit desirable candidate.
5. **Select Candidates:** It is as more important as previous stage which should be done with sincerity. Here the HR department selects the candidates who are suitable for the particular job or profile.
6. **Arranging Interview:** This is the last stage in the recruitment process which leads to the initiation of selection process. The suitable candidates which are selected in previous stage should call for interview and arrange interview for those candidates.

17.6 Factor Affecting Recruitment

Recruitment not done in isolated environment there are some factor which influence or affect recruitment policy of any organization. Mainly there are two types of factor which affect the recruitment. One is internal which comes under with in the organization and another one is external factor which is outside of the organization.

Internal Factors

1. **Organizational Strategy**

   The recruitment should be affected by organizational strategy. Growth and expansion plan of organization may affect the recruitment process. What are the business plan of organization and how their plan could be implemented? The entire questions affect the recruitment process in the organization.

2. **Organizational Size**

   It is but obvious, the size of the organization affect the recruitment process. Organization are of two types one is small where number of employees are not very huge, need of manpower is limited and may be recruitment process will be easy. On the other hand, big or large organization needs more manpower and for this reason their recruitment process are frequent.

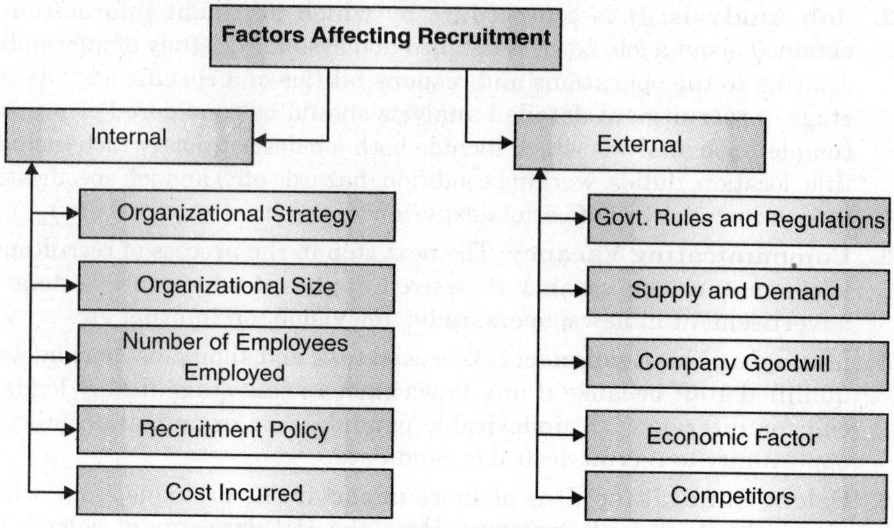

Exhibit 3: Factors Affecting Recruitment

3. **Number of Employees Employed**

   If organization had sufficient manpower and for any task new employees required it may be fulfilled by the exiting employees themselves otherwise, they recruit new applicants.

4. **Recruitment Policy**

   If recruitment policy is simple, easy to approachable, less time taken, at adequate time and other related factor influence not only candidates who wish to join organization but also for organization personnel who planned recruitment policy and other related staff.

5. **Cost Incurred**

   Cost incurred in recruitment also affects the process. Because recruitment cost not only include the organization money but also time and efforts of their personnel which is more costly than money.

EXTERNAL FACTORS

1. **Government Rules and Regulations**

   Various government rules and regulations prohibiting discrimination in hiring and employment have direct impact on recruitment practices. For example, Government of India has introduced legislation for reservation in employment for scheduled castes, scheduled tribes, physically handicapped etc.

2. **Supply and Demand**

   Supply and demand of the specific skill in the market place also affect the recruitment process of the organization. If the organization has a demand for more professionals and there is limited supply in the market for the professionals demanded by the company, then the company will have to depend upon internal sources by providing them special training and development programs.

3. **Company Goodwill**

   Image of the employer can work as a potential constraint for recruitment. An organization with positive image and goodwill as an employer finds it easier to attract and retain employees than an organization with negative image. Goodwill of a company is based on what organization does and affected by industry.

4. **Economic Factor**

   Economic factor of country or even world also affect the recruitment process. Like what is going on the present scenario when the recession is faced by the whole world the possibilities of recruitment in different organizations is minimal and most of the organization retrenched their employees.

5. **Competitors**

   The recruitment policies of competitors also affect recruitment of other organizations. To face the competition in the market, many a times the organizations have to change their recruitment policies according to the policies being followed by the competitors.

17.7 Source of Recruitment

Every organization has the opportunity of choosing the candidates for its recruitment processes from two types of sources one is internal and other is external. The sources within the organization itself (like transfer of employees from one department to other department, promotions) to fill a position are known as the internal sources of recruitment. Or candidates who are already working in an organization come under internal source.

Recruitment candidates from all the other sources who are outside the organization are known as the external sources of recruitment.

Internal Sources

1. **Promotions**

   The employees are promoted from one department to another in same organization with more benefits and greater responsibility based on efficiency and experience of a particular employee.

2. **Upgrading and Demotion**

   Employees are upgraded or even demoted according to their performance which was assigned to him/her.

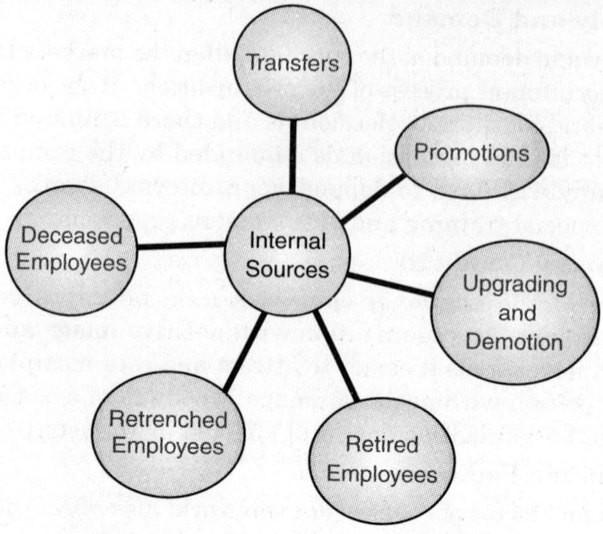

Exhibit 4: Internal Source of Recruitment

3. **Transfers**

   The employees are transferred from one department to another according to their performance and experience. With little benefits or no benefits.

4. **Retired Employees**

   It may also be recruited once again in case of shortage of qualified human resources or increase in load of work. Recruitment of such people save time and costs of the organizations as the people are already aware of the organizational culture and the policies and procedures.

5. **Retrenched Employees**

   Retrenched employees are also source of useful recruitment for the organization. They better know the organization policy and practices and when they again recruited most of the cost reduced.

6. **Deceased Employees**

   The dependents and relatives of deceased employees and disabled employees are also source of internal recruitment.

External Sources

1. **College Students**

   Various management institutes, engineering colleges, medical colleges etc. are a good source of recruitment. Where well qualified executives, engineers, medical staff etc. are recruited by the companies. They provide facilities for interviews and placements in their campus. This source is known as Campus Recruitment.

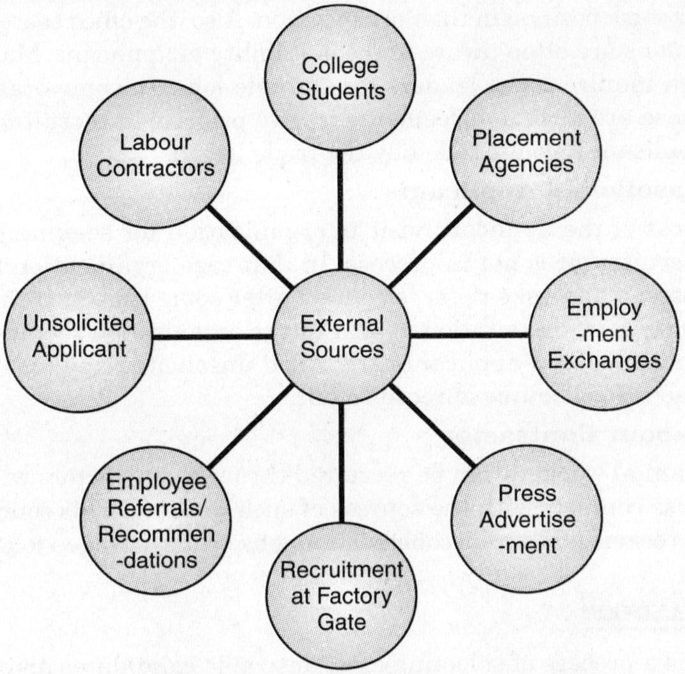

Exhibit 5: External Source of Recruitment

2. **Placement Agencies/Consultancy**

   They charge a small fee from a candidate. They play a role of third party where they provide required number of candidates to the organization with significant qualification. And they also charge some little amount as a fee from the respective candidate.

3. **Employment Exchange**

   Government establishes public employment exchanges throughout the country. They provide clearing house for jobs and job information. These exchanges provide job information to job seekers and help employers in identifying suitable applicants.

4. **Press Advertisement**

   Advertisement of the vacancy in the newspaper and other related magazine or journal is also a good source of recruitment. Where candidate response on job vacancy according to their matched profile.

5. **Recruitment at Factory Gate**

   If a permanent worker is not present than unskilled workers may be recruited at the factory gate. More competent among these may be recruited to fill permanent vacancies in the organization.

6. **Employees Referrals and Recommendation**

   Many organizations have prepared system where the existing employees of the organization can refer their friends and relatives for some position in their organization. Also, the office bearers of trade unions are often aware of the suitability of applicant. Management can inquire these leaders for suitable jobs. In some organizations these are formal agreements to give priority in recruitment to the applicant recommended by the trade union.

7. **Unsolicited Applicants**

   Most of the applicant visit to organization for seeking jobs when recruitment is not in process. In that case organization kept their resume and asks them to contact after some time or if there is any vacancy in organization in near future organization should call them. These types of applicants are called unsolicited applicants. This is also a good source of recruitment.

8. **Labour Contractor**

   Manual workers can be recruited through contractors who sustain close contacts with the sources of such workers. This source is used to recruit labour for construction jobs or daily wages jobs.

17.8 Selection

Selection is a process of selecting most desirable candidates among others for a particular job. Picking candidate who have relevant qualification to fill jobs in an organization.

17.9 Objective of Selection

Selection process is to determine whether an applicant meets the qualification for a specific job and to choose the applicant who is most likely to perform well in that job. In other words, to find out which job applicant will be successful, if hired.

17.10 Process of Selection

Selection is generally a series of hurdles or steps. Each one must be successfully cleared before the applicant proceeds to the next. There is no hard and fast rule that every organization have same pattern or process of selection. Organization have there own policy of selection even for different job profile may be have different selection process.

1. **Invite Application:** It is first step of selection process. For successfully complete the process of selection it is required that number of applicants should be in large. At the time of receiving application office manager or even receptionist entertain the candidate thus it makes good image of organization in the mind of applicants. They meet tactfully with applicant's i.e. friendly and courteous. If jobs are not available at that time the applicant may be asked to contact the HR department after a suitable period of time.

2. **Screening of Application:** Whatever the application received by organization is now screened with certain criteria like education, experience, age and other related information for a particular job. This helps in to remove undesirable application. From here the rejection will started, applicant who desirable comes to next stage and who are not will be rejected at this initial stage.
3. **Preliminary Interview:** When the large numbers of applicants are available, the preliminary interview is desirable both of the applicant seeking employment and of the company also. In preliminary interview perspective are given the necessary information about the nature of the job and information taken by applicants like their education, skills, salary demanded, reason for leaving previous jobs etc.
4. **Application Blank:** Application blank is one of the easiest and common method by which company gets the maximum information on various aspects of the candidate's academic, social, demographic, working experience and references. It is widely acceptable device for getting information from a prospective applicant which will enable a management to make a proper selection and the particular information should be in their own hand-writing.

Application blank may be very long or comprehensive and sometime brief are used. It includes:

- *Personal data*—Address, contact number, email ID, sex, and identification marks etc.
- *Physical data*—Height, weight, and health condition.
- *Educational data*—Levels of formal education like class X, XII, graduation, PG etc., marks obtained any other professional education acquired.
- *Employment data*—Past experience, job profile, promotions, reason for leaving previous job, last salary drawn and expected etc.
- *Extra curricular activities*—NSS, NCC, sports, games, debate, quiz etc. at school, college, university, state or national level and of course prize won on these events.
- *Reference*—Name of two or more individual who certify the suitability of an applicant to a particular job.

5. **Psychological Test:** The next step in the process of selection is very important because from here the main and critical test of candidature begins. What kind of psychological test is used for judging the candidate is another important decision. A test is standardized, having objective to measure of a candidates' behaviour, performance or attitude. Some of the commonly used test are as follows:
   - Attitude test (measure an candidates' potential to learn certain skills like clerical, mechanical, mathematical, etc.)
   - Intelligence test (mental ability, ability to understand instruction, take decisions etc.)

- Personality test (the way he/she present themselves, co-operative, calm, relaxed, good communicator etc.)
- Achievement test (typing test, shorthand test, tally, knowing latest technology)
- Simulation test

6. **Interview:** When the candidate passed their psychological test then the next step is to face interview. Interview is a face to face interaction between interviewer and interviewee. The interviewer check that the particular candidature is suitable for specified job or not and interviewee gets maximum information about their job profile, salary, etc. There are many types of interview like structured and unstructured interview, selection interview, panel interview, stress interview etc.
7. **Reference Checking:** The use of references is common in most selection procedure. It helps in checking out the candidate character, their qualification what they have, their experience is appropriate or not other related data should be authenticated or not. These references may be from candidate's who are familiar with the candidate's information. The personnel department checks reference carefully.

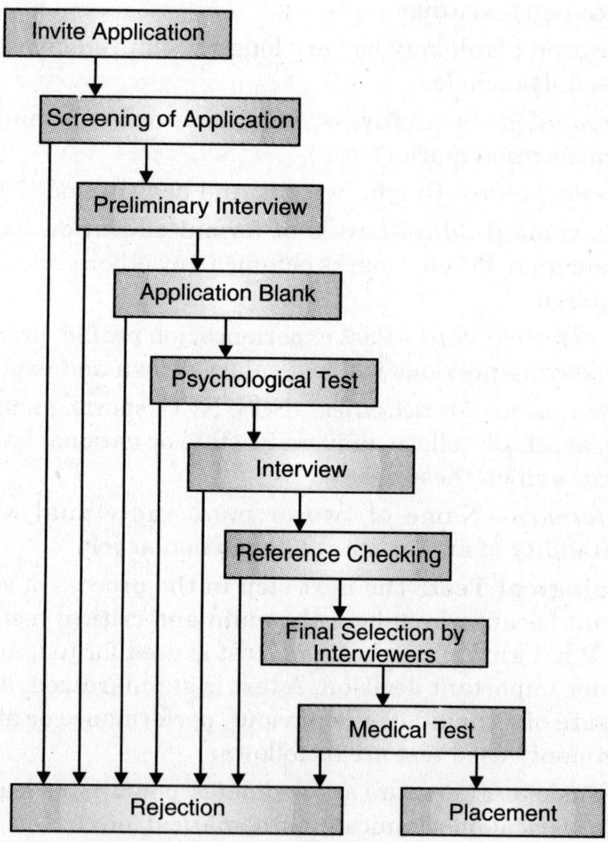

Exhibit 6: Selection Process

8. **Final Selection by Interviewers:** After completing the entire above step now final selection should be done by the interviewers.
9. **Medical Test/Physical Examination:** Physical or medical examination reveals whether or not a candidate possess physical qualities like acute hearing, clear vision, high stamina, clear tone of voice. 'Physical examination should disclose the physical characteristics of the individual that are significant from the standpoint of his efficient performance of the job he may enter or of those jobs to which he may reasonably expect to be transferred or promoted', says Dale Yoder.
10. **Placement:** The final step in selection process is placement of candidate to their job and work place.

REFERENCES

1. Kempner, T. (Ed.), *Handbook of Management*, Weidenfield and Nicolson, Landon, 1971, p. 310.
2. A. Barver, "*Recruiting Employees*", Thousand Oaks, CA: Sage, 1998.
3. James A. Breaugh, *Recruitment: Science and Practice* (Boston, Mass.:PWS-Kent, 1992).
4. Robbins, Stephen P., Personnel: *The Management of Human Resource*, Prentice Hall Inc, Englewood Cliffs, New Jersey, 1978, p.75.
5. Behling, O.Labovitz, G. and M. Gainer, "*College Recruiting; A Theoretical Base*", Personal Journal, No.47, 1968, pp. 13–19.
6. Flippo, E.B., *Personnel Management*, 1980, Fifth edition, p. 110

❍❍❍

CHAPTER 18

INTERVIEW

18.1 INTRODUCTION

An interview is typically used to evaluate or select candidates for specific job or we can simply say it leads hiring decision. Interviews are a widely used tools to access people's experiences, attitudes, and feelings of reality. The interview is usually followed by the evaluation of submitted résumés from interested candidates, then selecting a small number of candidates for interviews. The job interview is considered one of the most useful tools for evaluating the potential or the prospect of employees. An interview also allows the candidate to evaluate the respective organization's culture and what they expect from their candidates. If there are many interested candidates who have applied for one position than multiple rounds of interview may be used and this requires major participation of personnel department. Once the candidate has been interviewed, the organization typically selects most desirable and appropriate candidate for the job. In this chapter we discuss the meaning, importance and types of interview.

18.2 CONCEPT AND MEANING

The word 'interview' means 'view between' or 'sight between'. It suggests a meeting between two persons for the purpose of getting a view of each other, or for knowing each other. An interview is a means of two-way communication where both the parties either interviewee or interviewer can exchange their thoughts and ideas for respective job.

Interview is a conversation in which one person (the *interviewer*) extracts some information from another person (the *subject* or *interviewee*).

Interview is the face-to-face interaction between interviewer and interviewee. Interviewer is a person or group of persons from employer' side or employer who himself conducts or take an interview. Interviewee is the person or candidate who had been judged or evaluated by interviewer for specific job position.

According to Millar, an interview is 'A face-to-face dyadic interaction in which one individual plays the role of interviewer and the other takes on the role of interviewee, and both of these roles carry clear expectation concerning behavioural and attitudinal approach. The interview is requested by one of the participants for a specific purpose and both participants are willing contributors.'

Interviews are one of the most popularly used devices for employee selection. Interviews vary in the extent to which the questions are structured, from totally unstructured and free-wheeling conversation to a set list of questions each applicant is asked (Dipboye et.al.). Many studies have shown that structured interviews are more valid than unstructured, that is, they are more accurate in predicting which applicants will make good employees (Wiesner et.al.).

18.3 TYPES OF INTERVIEW

Basically interview can be broadly divided into two parts–structured and unstructured interviews.

STRUCTURED INTERVIEW

When the interviews are conducted in a proper, organized and in a predetermined way it is called structured interview. Under this type of interview, all the questions which will be asked during the interview are decided previously by the experts. The time duration is also fixed for each candidate. It is also called directive interview.

The basic purpose of this interview is to ensure that each interview is conducted with exactly the same questions in the same order. This ensures that answers can be reliably aggregated and that comparisons can be made between candidates with confidence. Although this type of interview lacks the free flow exchange of information and some time it becomes its disadvantage. Structured interview is widely used for the research purposes and it has been advocated for use in the recruitment process as well, though the practice has not been so popular.

UNSTRUCTURED INTERVIEW

When the interview does not follow the set procedure or any set format but in which the interviewer may have to consider some key points or questions before going to interview table. Under unstructured interview, interviewers take an opportunity to proceed on the responses of candidate in friendly and non-threating conversation. An unstructured interview allows the interviewer to build better rapport with the interviewee along with a normal conversation. It is also called non-directive interview.This type of interview is much more casual and unrehearsed. It depends on free flowing conversation which tends to focus on candidates' personal qualities as they relate to the work but questions about skills and strengths can also be asked and should be answered as formally as in a structured interview. In an unstructured interview, interviewer is able to discover important information about the candidate which may not seem relevant before the interview. Although it is time consuming but if properly conducted then it leads better results.

Apart from these two types of interview, following are the other types of interview have been popular in corporate world:

1. **Promotion Interview:-** Persons due for promotion are interviewed even if there is no competition. The interview is likely to be informal and serves as induction into a new team, with new responsibilities and clarifications about nature of duties, responsibilities and expectations are made during a promotion interview. If there is competition for promotion, the interview helps in the selection process and may also serve as an opportunity for a discussion of career opportunities for candidate.
2. **Appraisal or Assessment Interview:-** An appraisal interview is one of the methods of periodical assessment of employees. Annual appraisal interview is the best method for judging employee's attitudes. A face-to-face confidential talk is an opportunity for both, they discuss on several issues.

   This interview is more a discussion than question-answer. The focus is on the career development, shortcomings, areas which need improvement, training need, opportunities for promotion etc.
3. **Exit Interview:-** An exit interview is given to an employee who has resigned. The organization can –
   - Find out the precise reason for the employee's decision to leave.
   - Get feedback on employee's attitudes of the organizations policies.
   - Give the final pay cheque or information about when it will be ready and how it will be handed over.
   - Give information about PF, group insurance and how and when the dues will be paid.
   - Check that all books, manuals, tools, equipments which were issued to the employee have been returned.
4. **Problem Interview:-** A problem interview is a meeting with a problematic employee. An employee whose performance or behaviour is unsatisfactory in spite of warning represents a problem. An interview is more likely to suggest a solution than warnings and notices.

   The reason for the employee's poor performance can be found out in a face-to-face talk; it may be domestic problems, health, lack of training or dissatisfaction with job, environment etc. Many organizations have facilities for counseling staff: the employee may be offered a session with the counselor.

5. **Stress Interview:-** As the name suggests, a stress interview puts the candidate into difficult situations in order to test her/his reaction in stress. This method is used for selection for the positions in which the person must be able to face difficult situations without getting upset. A stress interview tests such qualities as courage, tact, cool temper, and self-command, which is needed when, confronted with groups.
6. **Selection Interview:-** The most important objective of the selection interviews is to assess the suitability of the candidates for specific jobs.

   Employment interviews are usually taken by a panel of interviewers. An interview may take anything from 10 minutes to 45 minutes or even longer. Interviewers spend more time on good candidates. They have to gather enough information about the candidates to be able to assess their suitability to join the organization.

The candidates too must find out about the organization, its employee policies and culture, what it expects the recruits to do and what opportunities it offers for career development.

18.4 Importance of Interview

- It is an important part of manpower planning (manpower planning is the function of HR department where organization can assess the requirement of staff in organization and also suggests the way how to fulfill that positions).
- Without interview, selection or hiring process could not be completed.
- By the interview, organization can analyze the capabilities, skills and knowledge of the candidate.
- A candidate also gets benefited by interview because at the time of interview he/she can also have an opportunity to know about the organization in a better way.
- The interview serves as a two-way process for the exchange of information. The interviewer has the opportunity to learn more about the candidate's background. The candidate also has the chance to ask questions to gain additional insight regarding the expectations of the job and to get a better feel for the organization's culture.
- Interview not only helps in the selection process, but through this process organizations get an opportunity to diagnose their employees' routine or specific problems like the cause of dissatisfaction towards their work, peer group or organization and solve them.

18.5 Interview Preparation

- The candidate is expected to be properly groomed and formally dressed. Clean and well-cut nails, properly combed hair and general personal hygiene are very important. Well-fitting clothes, neat footwear and a suitable handbag or briefcase are the normal requirements of formal appearance.

- For freshers, it is necessary to revise and have up-to date knowledge of their subject or specialization.
- It is beneficial to go with Information about the interviewing company in advance like its owners/directors, its product, its turnover, share capitals etc.
- Honesty in answering questions is the best policy. Dishonesty generally makes a bad impression.
- Self-assessment takes time and should be done carefully and patiently before going for interview.
- Important current issues in the country and in the world will be asked at the time of interview. So it will suggest to candidates that they should regularly read newspapers, watch TV news and discussion on current issues for current affairs.

REFERENCES

1. Owen Hergie (1997), The Handbook of Communication Skills, Psychology Press, New York, p. 385.
2. Dipboye, R.L., Macan,T., & Shahani-Denning, C. (2012). The selection interview from the interviewer and applicant perspectives: Can't have one without the other. In N. Schmitt (Ed.), The Oxford handbook of personnel assessment and selection (pp. 323–352). New York City: Oxford University.
3. Wiesner, W.H., & Cronshaw, S.F. (1988). A meta-analytic investigation of the impact of interview format and degree of structure on the validity of the employment interview. Journal of Occupational Psychology, 61(4), 275–290.
4. Minichiello, V., Aroni, R., Timewell, E., & Alexander, L. (1990). *In-depth Interviewing: Researching people.* Hong Kong: Longman Cheshire Pty Limited.

❍❍❍

CHAPTER 19

RELIABILITY AND VALIDITY OF RECRUITMENT TEST

19.1 INTRODUCTION

Reliability and validity are two technical properties of a test that indicate the quality and usefulness of the test. These are the two most important features of a test. Management should examine these features when evaluating the suitability of the test for organization use. Reliability estimates the consistency of test measurement, or more simply the degree to which an instrument measures the same way each time it is used in under the same conditions with the same subjects. Validity, on the other hand, involves the accuracy of measurement and what management supposed to measure. Validity is more important than reliability because if an instrument does not accurately measure what it is supposed to, there is no reason to use it even if it measures consistently.

19.2 IMPORTANCE OF RELIABILITY AND VALIDITY TEST ON RECRUITMENT

An employment test is considered "good" if the following can be said about it:

- The test measures what it claims to measure consistently or reliably. This means that if a person were to take the test again, the person would get a similar test score.
- The test measures what it claims to measure. For example, a test of mental ability does in fact measure mental ability, and not some other characteristic.
- The test is job-relevant. In other words, the test measures one or more characteristics that are important to the job.
- By using the test, more effective employment decisions can be made about individuals. For example, an arithmetic test may help you to select qualified workers for a job that requires knowledge of arithmetic operations.

The degree to which a test has these qualities is indicated by two technical properties: reliability and validity.

19.3 Reliability Test

Reliability is the extent to which a test is repeatable and gives up consistent scores. Test reliability refers to the degree to which a test is consistent and stable in measuring what it is intended to measure. Most simply put, a test is reliable if it is consistent within itself and across time. A measure is considered reliable if a person's score on the same test given twice is similar. It is important to remember that reliability is not measured, it is estimated.

The goal of estimating reliability (consistency) is to determine how much of the variability in test scores is due to measurement error and how much is due to variability in true scores. Measurement errors are essentially random a person's test score might not reflect the true score because of the following reasons:

- *Test taker's temporary psychological or physical state*: Test performance can be influenced by a person's psychological or physical state at the time of testing. For example, differing levels of anxiety, fatigue, or motivation may affect the applicant's test results.
- *Environmental factors*: Differences in the testing environment, such as room temperature, lighting, noise, or even the test administrator, can influence an individual's test performance.
- *Test form*: Many tests have more than one version or form. Items differ on each form, but each form is supposed to measure the same thing. Different forms of a test are known as parallel forms or alternate forms. These forms are designed to have similar measurement characteristics, but they contain different items. Because the forms are not exactly the same, a test taker might do better on one form than on another.
- *Multiple raters*: In certain tests, scoring is determined by a rater's judgements of the test taker's performance or responses. Differences in training, experience, and frame of reference among raters can produce different test scores for the test taker.

These factors are sources of chance or random measurement error in the assessment process. If there were no random errors of measurement, the individual would get the same test score, the individual's "true" score, each time. The degree to which test scores are unaffected by measurement errors is an indication of the reliability of the test.

Reliable assessment tools produce dependable, repeatable, and consistent information about people. In order to meaningfully interpret test scores and make useful employment or career-related decisions, management needs reliable tools.

Types of Reliability Test

Test-retest reliability

The test-retest method of estimating a test's reliability involves administering the test to the same group of people at least twice. Then the first set of scores is correlated with the second set of scores. The resulting reliability measures the stability of the true score over time. The three main components to this method are as follows:

(i) Implement your measurement instrument at two separate times for each subject;

(ii) Compute the correlation between the two separate measurements; and

(iii) Assume there is no change in the underlying condition (or trait you are trying to measure) between test 1 and test 2.

Alternate forms/parallel forms

Administer Test A to a group and then administer Test B to same group. Correlation between the two scores is the estimate of the test reliability.

Inter-rater reliability

Compare scores given by different raters. e.g., for important work in higher education (e.g., theses), there are multiple markers to help ensure accurate assessment by checking inter-rater reliability.

Internal consistency

Internal consistence is commonly measured as Cronbach's Alpha (based on inter-item correlations)—between 0 (low) and 1 (high). The greater the number of similar items, the greater the internal consistency. That's why you sometimes get very long scales asking a question a myriad of different ways - if you add more items you get a higher Cronbach's. Generally, alpha of .80 is considered as a reasonable benchmark.

Guidelines for test the reliability

.90	high reliability
.80	moderate reliability
.70	low reliability

❖ High reliability is required when (Note: Most standardized tests of intelligence report reliability estimates around .90 (high).

- tests are used to make important decisions.
- individuals are sorted into many different categories based upon relatively small individual differences e.g. intelligence.

❖ Lower reliability is acceptable when (Note: For most testing applications, reliability estimates around .70 are usually regarded as low - i.e., 49% consistent variation (.7 to the power of 2).

- tests are used for preliminary rather than final decisions.
- tests are used to sort people into a small number of groups based on gross individual differences e.g. height or sociability /extraversion.

❖ Reliability estimates of .80 or higher are typically regarded as moderate to high (approx. 16% of the variability in test scores is attributable to error).

- Reliability estimates below .60 are usually regarded as unacceptably low.

19.4 Validity Test

- Validity is the extent to which a test measures what it is supposed to measure. Validity is a subjective judgement made on the basis of experience and empirical indicators. Validity is the most important issue in selecting a test. Validity refers to what characteristic the test measures and how well the test measures that characteristic.
- Validity tells you if the characteristic being measured by a test is related to job qualifications and requirements.
- Validity gives meaning to the test scores. Validity evidence indicates that there is linkage between test performance and job performance. It can tell you what you may conclude or predict about someone from his or her score on the test. If a test has been demonstrated to be a valid predictor of performance on a specific job, you can conclude that persons scoring high on the test are more likely to perform well on the job than persons who score low on the test, all else being equal.
- Validity also describes the degree to which you can make specific conclusions or predictions about people based on their test scores. In other words, it indicates the usefulness of the test.

Types of Validity Tests

The Uniform Guidelines discuss the following three methods of conducting validation studies. The Guidelines describe conditions under which each type of validation strategy is appropriate. They do not express a preference for any one strategy to demonstrate the job-relatedness of a test.

- ***Criterion-related validation*** requires demonstration of a correlation or other statistical relationship between test performance and job performance. In other words, individuals who score high on the test tend to perform better on the job than those who score low on the test. If the criterion is obtained at the same time the test is given, it is called concurrent validity; if the criterion is obtained at a later time, it is called predictive validity.
- ***Content-related validation*** requires a demonstration that the content of the test represents important job-related behaviours. In other words, test items should be relevant to and measure directly important requirements and qualifications for the job.
- ***Construct-related validation*** requires a demonstration that the test measures the construct or characteristic it claims to measure, and that this characteristic is important to successful performance on the job.

Sources of Invalidity

- Unreliability
- *Response Sets*: psychological orientation or bias towards answering in a particular way.
- *Acquiescence*: tendency to agree, i.e. say "Yes". Hence use of half negative and half positive worded items (but there can be semantic difficulties with negatively wording).
- *Social desirability*: tendency to portray self in a positive light. Try to design questions which so that social desirability isn't salient.
- *Faking bad*: Purposely saying 'no' or looking bad if there's a 'reward' (e.g. attention, compensation, social welfare, etc.).

Different Forms of Bias

- *Cultural bias*: does the psychological construct have the same meaning from one culture to another; how are the different items interpreted by people from different cultures; actual content (face) validity may be different for different cultures.
- Gender bias may also be possible.
- Test bias
  - Bias in measurement occurs when the test makes systematic errors in measuring a particular characteristic or attribute e.g. many say that most IQ tests may well be valid for middle-class whites but not for blacks or other minorities. In interviews, which are a type of test, research shows that there is a bias in favour of good-looking applicants.
  - Bias in prediction occurs when the test makes systematic errors in predicting some outcome (or criterion). It is often suggested that tests used in academic admissions and in personnel selection under-predict the performance of minority applicants. Also a test may be useful for predicting the performance of one group e.g. males but be less accurate in predicting the performance of females.

19.5 The Relationship of Reliability and Validity

Test validity is requisite to test reliability. If a test is not valid, then reliability is moot. In other words, if a test is not valid there is no point in discussing reliability because test validity is required before reliability can be considered in any meaningful way. Likewise, if as test is not reliable it is also not valid.

Remember in order to be valid, a test must be reliable; but reliability does not guarantee validity, i.e. it is possible to have a highly reliable test which is meaningless (invalid). It is important to understand the differences between *reliability* and *validity*. Validity will tell you how good a test is for a particular situation; reliability will tell you how trustworthy a score on that test will be. You cannot draw valid conclusions from a test score unless you are sure that the test is reliable. Even when a test is reliable, it may not be valid. You should be careful that any test you select is both reliable and valid for your situation.

❍❍❍

CHAPTER 20

PERFORMANCE MANAGEMENT

20.1 INTRODUCTION

The ultimate goal of any organization is to make profit with taking care of society or nation. And for this reason organization make sure that their employees work hard with perfection for attaining that particular goal. For making employees more productive organization review the performance of their employees and make recommendation for better result. Performance management is the assessment of an employee's effectiveness, usually as undertaken at regular intervals of time for analyzing their work and help in making their bright future. Performance management/appraisal is supposed to be an ongoing process throughout the year. If you as a manager really want your company and your employees to benefit the most from their appraisal, then you have to have regular meetings throughout the year. Those meetings are intended to discuss the employees' performance, achievements, plusses and minuses. In this chapter, we discuss the objectives, process of performance appraisal and different methods of performance appraisal which are suitable of organization.

20.2 CONCEPT AND MEANING

Performance management is the process of obtaining, analyzing and recording information about the relative worth of an employee. The focal point of the performance appraisal is measuring and improving the actual performance of the employee and also the future potential of the employee.

According to Flippo, "Performance appraisal is the systematic, periodic and an impartial rating of an employee's excellence in the matters pertaining to his present job and his potential for a better job." Performance appraisal is a systematic way of reviewing and assessing the performance of an employee during a particular period of time and planning for his future.

Scoot, Clothier and Spriegel have defined merit rating or performance appraisal as the process of evaluating the employee's performance on the job in terms of requirement of the job.[1]

According to Yoder, performance appraisal refers to all formal procedures used in working organizations to evaluate personalities and contributions and potential of group members.[2] An evaluation of how well an employee performs his or her job compared to a set of predetermined standards.[3]

Performance appraisal is a systematic review of a person's work and achievements over a recent period, usually leading to plans for the future.[4]

Process by which a manager or consultant (1) examines and evaluates an employee's work behaviour by comparing it with preset standards, (2) documents the results of the comparison, and (3) uses the results to provide feedback to the employee to show where improvements are needed and why. Performance appraisals are employed to determine who needs what training, and who will be promoted, demoted, retained, or fired.[5]

20.3 Objectives of Performance Management

- It facilitates the relationship and communication between management and employees.
- To assess the performance of the employees over a given period of time.
- To give feedback to the employees about their past performance.
- To find out that any gap between the actual and the desired performance of the employees.
- Provide clarity of the expectations and responsibilities of the functions to be performed by the employees.
- To analyze the strengths and weaknesses of the employees so as to identify the training and development needs of the future.
- To plan career development, human resource planning based on potentialities.
- Performance appraisal can help in development of scientific basis for reward allocation, wage fixation, incentives etc.
- To reduce the grievances of the employees.

20.4 Prerequisites of Effective Performance Management

1. *Purpose should be clear:* Organization must ensure that what are its objectives for performance management. It may be judging employee actual performance or analyzing potential of employee for future purpose.
2. *Known to Appraisee/Empolyee:* The entire process of performance management should be known to empolyee in respect of their goals, targets, parameters and expectation.
3. *Appraiser Training:* Trained appraises should be required for successfully completion of appraisal process. Usually, immediate supervisor play a role of appraiser it will be benefited to employee because their immediate supervisor know each and everything about concerned employee, their attitude towards work or work environment. But some time it may lead biasing towards certain traits about which he himself does not know. To overcome this problem an adequate training is required for appraiser also which ensure uniformity, consistency and reliability in appraisal process.

4. *Frequency of Appraisal process*: Performance appraisal is a continuous process. It should be conducted on regular interval of time. Organizations do their appraisal process either half yearly or annually depending on the requirement for appraisal.
5. *Standardization of Appraisal process*: Standardization of entire process must be done before starting appraisal. Standardization facilitates the appraiser in evaluating performance of their subordinate without any biased behaviour. It may be also help the appraisee as they know in advance expectation and parameter of appraisal process.
6. *Coordinated effort*: Entire appraisal process should be designed by human resource department with the help or consultation from line officers. Because line officers better know their subordinates behaviour and also work related information.

20.5 Process of Performance Management

It is an ongoing process where organization review their employees performance in a particular period of time mainly once in a year. Check their performance and suggest them how to improve their performance against set standards. Performance appraisal process consists of six steps, *first* is, setting standards which are the base of the performance appraisal or simply say that performance will be judged on that standards. The standards set should be clear, easily understandable and in measurable terms for both appraiser and for appraisee. In case the performance of the employee cannot be measured, great care should be taken to describe the standards.

Second, after setting standard now its time to communicate these standards to both appraiser and appraisee. For appraiser it is important because for fulfilling that standards which type of method is used, how the plan is executed, what are the constraint, all these question will be solved easily. For appraisee, they know at what parameter they are going to judge. This will help them to understand their roles and to know what exactly is expected from them. The advantage of this step is, if any modification is recommended by either appraiser or appraisee which is feasible, considered.

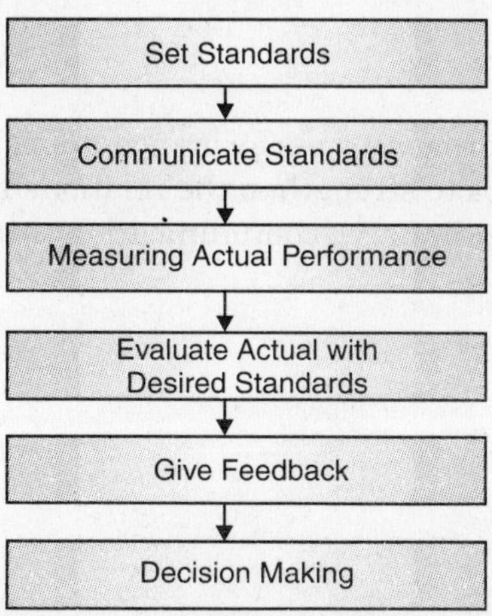

Exhibit 1: Process of Performance Management

Third step, It is a continuous process which involves monitoring the performance throughout the year. This stage requires the cautious while selection of the appropriate method of measurement, taking care that personal bias does not affect the result of the process and providing assistance rather than interfering in an employees work.

Evaluating actual performance with the desired performance standards is the fourth step in performance appraisal process. The comparison tells the deviations in the performance of the employees if any, from the standards set.

At the *next Step*, whatever the result getting from comparing actual with desired performance is communicating to the respective employee and supervisor. The focus of this discussion is on communication and listening. The results, the problems and the possible solutions are discussed with the aim of problem solving and reaching consensus. The feedback should be given with a positive attitude as this can have an effect on the employees' future performance. The purpose of the meeting should be to solve the problems faced and motivate the employees to perform better.

The *final step* is decision-making. Whatever the outcomes from appraisal process should be considered while making organizational plan. Decision related to promotion, rewards, incentives, bonus, transfer, demotion etc. are taken at this step.

20.6 Approaches to Performance Development

Traditional Approach

- This approach was a past oriented approach which focussed only on the past performance of the employees during a past specified period of time.
- This approach did not consider the developmental aspects of the employee performance like his training and development needs or career developmental possibilities.
- The primary concern of the traditional approach is to judge the performance of the organization as a whole by the past performances of its employees.

Modern Approach

- The modern approach to performance appraisals includes a feedback process that helps to strengthen the relationships between superiors and subordinates and improve communication throughout the organization.

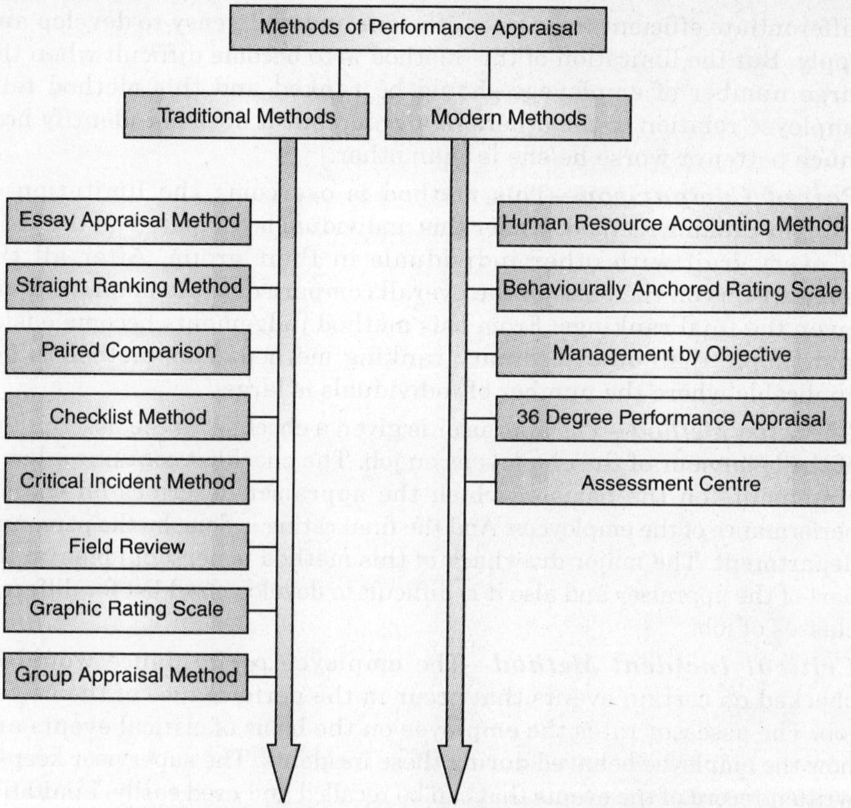

Exhibit 2: Methods of Performance Management

- Appraisals have become ongoing and periodic activity in the organizations.
- The results of performance appraisals are used to take various other HR decisions like promotions, demotions, transfers, training and development, reward outcomes.

20.7 Methods of Performance Management

Traditional Methods

- ***Essay Appraisal Method***—It is also known as "free essay method". Under this method immediate supervisor is playing a role of appraiser and he appraises their subordinates on their past performance. Supervisor writes feedback in their own hand writing. The description is always as realistic and actual as possible. It is easy and can be done without any adequate preparation is the benefit of this method. A major drawback of the method is the inseparability of the bias of the evaluator.
- ***Straight Ranking Method***—In this method an appraiser appraise the appraisee on their whole contribution in the organization. They rank employees from the best to the poorest. It is one of the oldest and simplest methods of performance appraisal. This is the simplest method of

differentiate efficient from least efficient and quite easy to develop and apply. But the limitation of this method is to become difficult when the large number of employees should be ranked and this method tells employee relation to the others in a group but it does not identify how much better or worse he/she is than other.

- ***Paired Comparison***—This method is overcome the limitation of straight ranking method. Under this, individual is compared on the basis of every trait with other individuals in their group. After all the comparisons on the basis of the overall comparisons, the employees are given the final rankings. From this method judgements become easier and simple than other ordinary ranking method. This method is not applicable where the number of individuals is large.
- ***Checklist Method***—The appraiser is given a checklist of the descriptions of the behaviour of the employees on job. The checklist contains a list of statements on the basis of which the appraiser describes on the job performance of the employees. And the final rating is done by the personnel department. The major drawback of this method is personal bias on the part of the appraiser and also it is difficult to develop checklist for different classes of job.
- ***Critical Incident Method***—The employee performance would be checked on certain events that occur in the performance of the ratee's job. The assessor rates the employee on the basis of critical events and how the employee behaved during those incidents. The supervisor keeps a written record of the events that can be recalled and used easily. Limitation of this method is, unfavourable incidents are generally more noticeable, and may supervisor forget to record the concerned employee behaviour.
- ***Field Review***—Under this method, a training officer basically appointed by or even from HR department discusses and interviews the supervisor about how they appraise them respective subordinates. The supervisor is required to give his view about the level of performance, progress, weakness, ability, promotability and others of respective employee. This method reduces the supervisor biasing.
- ***Graphic Rating Scale***—In this method, an employee's quality and quantity of work is assessed in a graphic scale indicating different degrees of a particular trait. The factors taken into consideration include both the personal characteristics (like leadership, co-cooperativeness, loyalty, devotion, attitude, creative ability, initiative etc.) and characteristics related to the on-the-job performance (like responsibility, attendance, quality of work, etc.) of the employees. For example a trait like Job Knowledge may be judged on the range of unsatisfactory, average, above average, outstanding.
- ***Group Appraisal Method***—As a name suggest, the appraisal should be done by the group of assessors. Which consist of their supervisor and few other supervisors who have some knowledge of respective subordinate performance. The immediate supervisor explains to the other assessors of the group the nature of his subordinates duties and responsibilities.

The group then evaluates subordinate actual performance with the standards. If any deviations exist they suggest for future improvement. It is simple and very useful method which remove any biasing but it is very time consuming.

Modern Methods

- ***Human Resource Accounting Method***—Human resources are valuable assets for every organization. Human resource accounting method tries to find the relative worth of these assets in the terms of money. In this method the Performance appraisal of the employees is judged in terms of cost and contribution of the employees. The cost of employees include all the expenses incurred on them like their compensation, recruitment and selection costs, induction and training costs etc. whereas their contribution includes the total value added (in monetary terms). The difference between the cost and the contribution will be the performance of the employees. Ideally, the contribution of the employees should be greater than the cost incurred on them.
- ***Behaviourally Anchored Rating Scales (BARS)***—Under this method firstly critical incidents was set up which is based on some job performance qualities like inter-personal relationship, co-operation, reliability etc. than appraisal should be done on these critical incidents and evaluate on the graphical rating scale. Basically BARS is a relatively new technique which combines the graphic rating scale and critical incidents method. In this method, an employee's actual job behaviour is judged against the desired behaviour by recording and comparing the behaviour with BARS. Developing and practicing BARS requires expert knowledge.
- ***Management By Objectives (MBO)***—The concept of 'Management by Objectives' (MBO) was first given by Peter Drucker in 1954. It can be defined as a process whereby the employees and the superiors come together to identify common goals, the employees set their goals to be achieved, the standards to be taken as the criteria for measurement of their performance and contribution and deciding the course of action to be followed. Management by objectives (MBO) is a systematic and organized approach that allows management to focus on achievable goals and to attain the best possible results from available resources.

  MBO also described as "a process whereby the superior and subordinate managers of an organization jointly identify its common goals, define each individual's major areas of responsibility in term as of result expected of him and use these measures as guides for operating the unit and assessing the contributions of each its members".[6] The main objective of MBO is to participative goal setting, alternatives course of action and decision-making. The performance will be measured on the basis of set standards. The subordinates have been involved with the goal setting and the choosing the course of action to be followed by them, so they are more likely to fulfill their responsibilities. And it also makes sure that everybody within the organization has a clear understanding of the aims, or objectives, of that organization, as well as awareness of their own roles and responsibilities in achieving those aims.

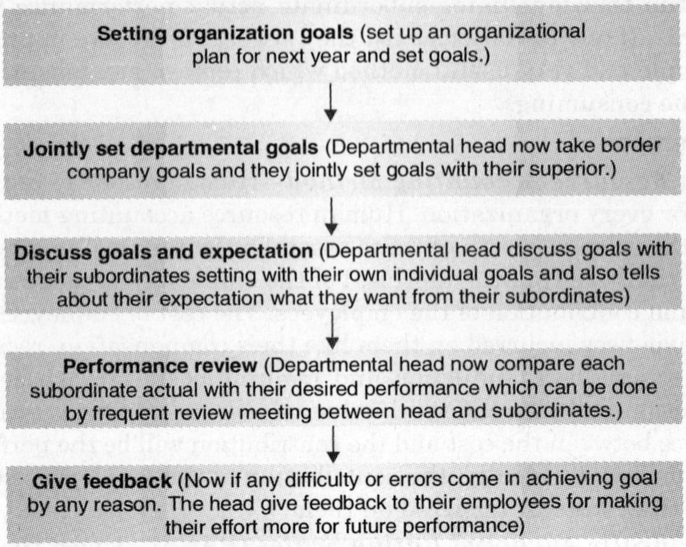

Exhibit 3: MBO Process

- ***360 degree Performance Appraisal System*** — It was developed by the GE Company, USA in 1992. 360° feedback, also known as 'multi-rater feedback', is the most comprehensive appraisal where the feedback about the employees' performance comes from all the sources that come in contact with the employee on his job. It may be their peers, superior, subordinates, team members, customers, suppliers/ vendors—anyone who comes into contact with the employee and can provide valuable insights and information or feedback regarding the "on-the-job" performance of the employee.

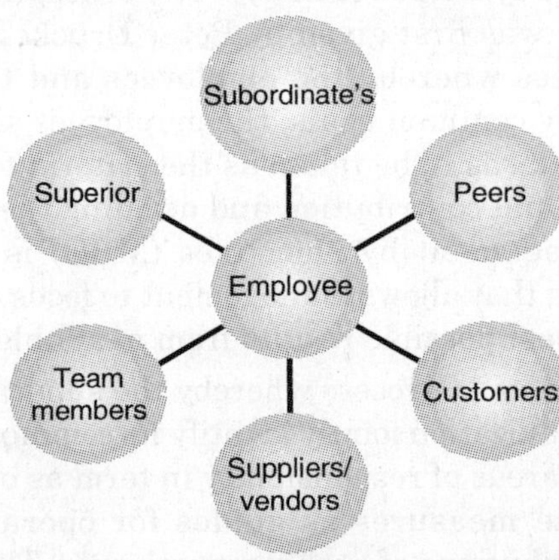

Exhibit 4: 360° Performance Appraisal

360° appraisal has four important elements—self appraisal, superior's appraisal, subordinate's appraisal and peer appraisal. (i) Self appraisal gives a chance to the employee to look at his/her strengths and weaknesses, his achievements, and judge his own performance. (ii) Superior's appraisal forms the traditional part of the 360 degree appraisal where the employees' responsibilities and actual performance is rated by the superior. (iii) Subordinates appraisal gives a chance to judge the employee on the parameters like communication and motivating abilities, superior's ability to delegate the work, leadership qualities etc. (iv) Peers can help to find employees' abilities to work in a team, co-operation and sensitivity towards others. It is also known as internal customer.

- **Assessment Centre**—The basis of this method is to test candidate in a social situation, with the group of assessors and with the variety of procedure. Assessment centres simulate the employee's on-the-job environment and facilitate the assessment of their on-the-job performance. Usually, employees are given an assignment similar to the job they would be expected to perform if promoted. The trained evaluators observe and evaluate employees as they perform the assigned jobs and are evaluated on job related characteristics. The assessment is generally done with the help of paper-pencil test, interview, business games, psychometric tests and simulation exercise.

20.8 The Ethics of Appraisal

M. S. Kellog[8] has suggested the following do's and don'ts:

- Don't appraise without knowing why the appraisal is needed;
- Appraise on the basis of representative information;
- Appraise on the basis of sufficient information;
- Appraise on the basis of relevant information;
- Be honest on your assessment of all the facts you have obtained;
- Don't write one thing and say another;
- In offering an appraisal, make it plan that this only your personal opinion of the facts as you see them;
- Pass on appraisal information only to those who have good reason to want it;
- Don't imply the existence of an appraisal that has not been made:
- Don't accept another's appraisal without knowing the basis on which it was made.

REFERENCES

1. Scott, W.D., Clothier, R.C. and Spriegal, W.R., *Personnel Management*, Tata McGraw-Hill, New Delhi, 1968, p. 160.
2. Yoder, Dale, *Personnel Management and Industrial Relation*, Prentice-Hall, New Delhi, 1976, p. 173.
3. www.pewcenteronthestates.org/template_page.aspx
4. http://wps.prenhall.com/wps/media/objects/213/218150/glossary.html#P
5. http://www.businessdictionary.com/definition/performance-appraisal.html
6. Odiorne, George S., *Management by Objectives*, Pitman, London, 1965, p. 55-56
7. Mamoria, Gankar, *Personnel Management*, Himalaya Publishing House, 2003.
8. Kellog, M.S., *The Ethics of Appraisal*, in Personnel, July-August, 1965, p. 37.

CHAPTER 21

TRAINING AND DEVELOPMENT

21.1 Introduction

Training and development of workers is the crucial task for management. If workers not get proper training about the handling of tools and heavy machinery they not even harm that particular machinery but also themselves which is more valuable for organization. They train and develop their workers by the various means by giving simply demonstration or typically simulator or any other means. In present scenario it becomes more important because of introduction of new technologies. If they not cope with the latest technology than it will resultant into low production. From the workers psychological point of view if they are not getting the proper training and development from their concern according to the need of the worker and requirement of the employer than it will lead dissatisfaction. And it is also required that company must have a systematic programme, otherwise workers will try to lean the job by trial and error which may prove very costly for employers. In this chapter we discuss the training and development in detail like their definitions, objectives, methods, process and their effectiveness.

21.2 Concept and Meaning

Training is a learning process that involves the attainment of knowledge, sharpening of skills, concepts, rules, or changing of attitudes and behaviours to enhance the performance of workers. These are the activities which basically aim at providing the skills, knowledge and aptitudes necessary for employment in a particular occupation (or a group of related occupations) in any field of economic activity.

According to Flippo, "Training is the act of increasing the knowledge and skills of an employee for doing a particular job."[1]

"Training achieves the objectives of redirection or improvement of behaviour so that the performance of the trainees becomes more useful and productive for himself and for the organization of which he is a part," says

Harris. According to Blum and Naylor, "training is a process that develops and improves skills related performance. Effective training programms can result in increased production, reduced labour turnover and greater employee satisfaction".[2]

Training is a process by which a worker learns some new technical or psychological skill. Training leads to improve the performance of the existing workers and prepares them to perform higher specialized and more advance jobs in future.

Training is a process of learning a sequence of programmed behaviour and development cover those activities which improve job performance but also those which bring about overall growth of the personality.[3] Development is broader, more encompassing function than training.

Development is the process of enhancing skills, abilities, knowledge and capacities of the individual of the company. Development not only includes improvement in job performance, it is also including individual growth in the organization. Development aims at making workers not only good performers but also better human being.

Development is an educational process utilizing a systematic and organized procedure by which managerial personnel learn conceptual and theoretical knowledge for general purpose.[4] According to Flippo, "Management development process enables managers and executives to not only acquire skills and competencies but also develop future managerial abilities."

"Management development involves making exercise in manpower flows, future inventories of human skills, abilities to match the demand of expanding and diversifying operations of the organizations," says Madan. It includes all those activities and programmes, when recognized and controlled, have substantial influence on changing the capacity of the individual to perform his present assignment better and in doing so are likely to increase his potential for future management assignments.[5]

21.3 Basic Purposes of Training

- The basic purpose or objective of training is to increase productivity.
- By providing the training to the workers, organizations would improve the quality of work.
- It helps in creating skill inventory by which a company fulfils its future personnel needs.
- To improve organization climate which help in to creating and maintaining congenial working environment.
- To improve health and safety of the workers as well as working conditions.
- Training helps the workers to prevent against accident.
- Last but not the least the one of the most important purpose of training is to improve the personal growth of the workers.

21.4 Basic Purposes of Development

- Improvement in supervision, command, direction and control at each level.
- To create an understanding of the methods and problems of management.
- To develop managers to perform better on their present assignments.
- To prepare them for higher assignments.
- To help them grow fast.
- To create conditions and a climate which contribute to the growth process.
- Inspiring junior executives to do better work.

21.5 Difference between Training and Development

Both terms are used for similar activity i.e. to improve the performance of workers by any means whether it is by giving the knowledge about the new skill or enhance their own capability for task performance. But there is a difference between the training and development as shown in below exhibit 1:

Training	Development
Training is designed for non-managers as well as managers.	It involves only managerial personnel.
It is a short term process.	Long term in nature.
Managerial personnel learn technical knowledge and skills.	Managerial personnel learn conceptual and theoretical knowledge.
The objectives of training are specific job-related purpose.	The objectives have broader overview and consider general knowledge.
Training is concerned with the immediate improvement of the employee, i.e. the ways to make the employee more effective in his current role.	Development is a process to make the employee efficient enough to handle critical situations in the future, i.e. how well he can equip himself for the future demands.
Training means learning new things and refreshing old one.	Development means implementing the learned session and finding new ones.

Exhibit 1: Difference between Training and Development

21.6 Importance of Training and Development

- ***Optimum Utilization of Workforce***—Training and Development helps in optimizing the utilization of workforce that further helps the workers to achieve the organizational goals as well as their individual goals.
- ***Healthy Work-environment***—Training and development helps in creating the healthy working environment. It helps to build good relationship among the workers and supervisors so that individual goals align with organizational goal.
- ***Productivity and Profitability***—Training and development helps in increasing the productivity of the workers as well as the organization.

It also leads to improved profitability and more positive attitudes towards profit orientation.

- ***Team Spirit***—Training and development helps in inculcating the sense of team work, team spirit, and inter-team co-ordination. It helps in inculcating the enthusiasm to learn within the workers.
- ***Quality***—Training and development helps in improving the quality of work and work-life.
- ***Development of Skills of Workers***—Training and development helps in increasing the job knowledge and skills of workers at each level. It helps to enlarge the horizons of human intellect and an overall personality of the workers.
- ***Organization Culture***—Training and development helps to develop and improve the organizational health culture and effectiveness. It helps in creating the learning culture within the organization.
- ***Organization Climate***—Training and development helps building the positive perception and feeling about the organization. The employees get these feelings from leaders, subordinates, and peers.
- ***Morale***—It helps in improving the morale of the work force.
- Training and development helps in developing leadership skills, motivation, loyalty, better attitudes, and other aspects that successful workers and managers usually display.

21.7 Pre-requisites of Effective Training Programme

1. The benefits of training should be clear to the employees, supervisor and to the top management.
2. The objective of training should be outlined on the basis of type of performace is required for the accomplishment of organization goals and commitment.
3. The duration of training programmes varies with the skill to be acquired, the complexity of the subject, a trainee's aptitude and ability to understand and the training media used.
4. Employees at different level require different training.
5. The trainee should be provided with personal assistance when he encounters learning obstacles.
6. Various equipment has been utilized during effective training process it may include audio-visual mode like poster, pictures, movie projectors, slides, tape recorder, booklets etc. Apart from that various management games also included.
7. Adequate training rooms also increase the effectiveness of training programme. It include proper seating facilities, speaker should easily communicate to all, proper ventilation and illumination etc.
8. For conducting fruitful training programme there is an option for collecting trainee's responses or feedback on daily basis or as possible. It may show the need or expectation of trainee towards training programme.

9. There should be flexibility in terms of judging the rate of progress of a trainee in the training programme. It is required because the entire trainee do not progress at the same level due to individual competency.
10. The trainee should get continuous and constructive feedback concerning their progress in training which helps them on acquiring new skills and abilities easily.

21.8 Process of Training

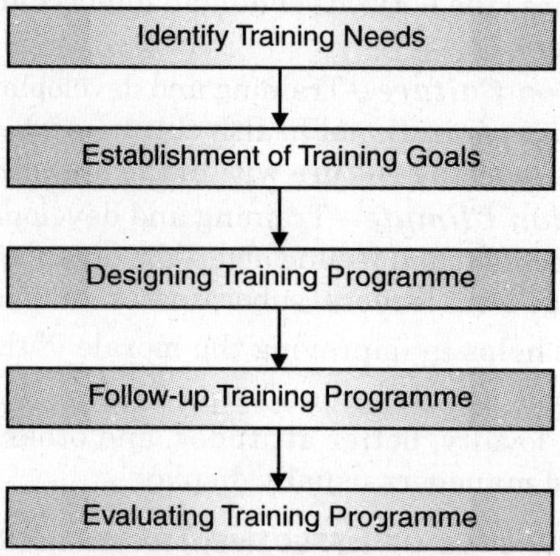

Exhibit 2: Training Process

- ***Identify Training Needs***—The training process started from the identification of the need of the training. Management firstly identify and analysis that their employees actually need any training or not. How these training help the growth of the organization? At what extent it will be beneficial for the workers? By giving particular training they are able to cope with the latest technology or environment? Whether the trained is for skilled, semi-skilled or for unskilled workers? All these questions should be answered at this primary level.
- ***Establishment of Training Goals***—After identifying the need of the training the next step is to establishment of training goals or objective. Management sets a parameter and checks the performance of the workers after introducing training on those parameters.
- ***Designing Training Programme***—This is the most important and critical exercise for the management. Here, management designs the whole training programme. Who are going to be training, who are going to provide training, where the training will executed, what are the methods adopted for training, what are the sequence used for training, how trainee evaluated and many other such types of task should be done at this stage.
- ***Follow-up Training Programme***—Whatever management planned, execution should be done on this stage. If trainee and trainer follow-up

the programme in proper sequence as per the management decided than they get maximum output or better results.

- ***Evaluating Training Programme***—The last step in training process is evaluating the whole training process by the output. This can be done by various methods like reaction of trainees, by questionnaire method, by interviews and others. If any flaws or limitations found than it will be overcome as soon as possible. The evaluating of training process also help in designing future training programme more effective.

21.9 Types of Training

There is lots of method by which management train their employees. They choose methods according to requirement of the training. In general, training is of two types—on-the job training and off-the-job training.

- ***Job Instruction Training* (JIT)**—In this method supervisors train operational workers. It consists of all the necessary steps with proper sequence which was required for a particular task. These steps not only explain what is to be done but also emphasis how it is to be done and why. It involves four steps (i) physically and psychologically prepare the trainees for instruction. (ii) presentation or demonstration of the particular task to the trainees, what are their responsibilities, decription about the job etc. is included in this phase. (iii) at this phase trainees are tried out what they get understand from the instructions. (iv) this is the last phase of JIT where supervisors encourage trainees to solve their queries if any regarding particular task.

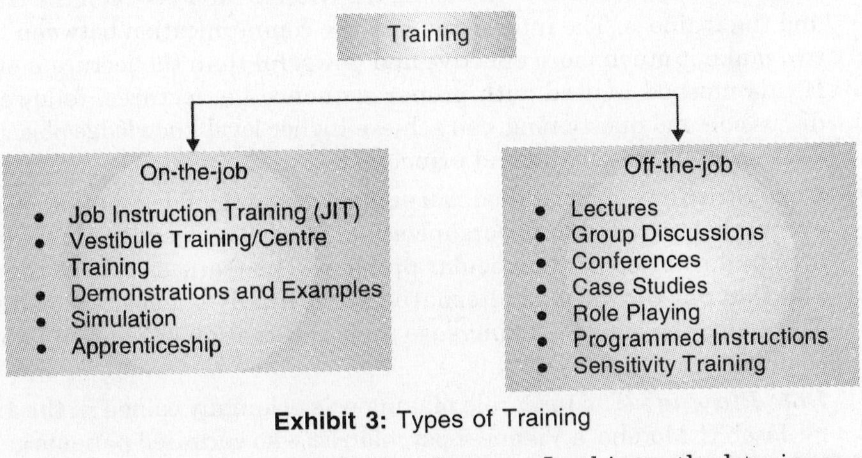

Exhibit 3: Types of Training

- ***Vestibule Training/Training Centre***—In this method trainees are trained in the company classrooms. Where they get theoretical knowledge about the work which they are going to perform. This method is more useful when there is large number of trainees have to be trained for same kind of work at same time.

- ***Demonstrations and Examples***—It is just opposite to classroom or vestibule training methods. Here supervisor describes and display something related to the job and also explains the step-by-step explanations of why and what supervisor or trainer is doing. Supervisor demonstrates to trainees with the help of lectures, picture, text material, power point presentation, discussions.
- ***Simulation***—This method is used for more sophisticated task where errors if not minimized then it leads to heavy losses. It is generally duplicate setup of the workplace, where workers feel and touch the simulated equipments and make practice to use equipment without any problem.
- ***Apprenticeship***—Apprenticeship refers to the period of service as a learner of a trade or handicraft. The apprentice, usually a boy at the beginning of his working life, was bound by a legal agreement to serve an employer for a fixed number of years during which the employer promised to instruct him. Carpenters, a machinist, weavers, jewelers, electricians, a draughtsman, a tool-maker, a printer, a pattern designer, diesinkers etc. are the field in which apprenticeship training is offered.
- ***Lectures***—This method is used to create understanding of a topic or to influence behaviour, attitudes through lecture. A lecture can be in written or oral form. Lecture is telling someone about something. Lecture is given to enhance the knowledge of listener or to give him the theoretical aspect of a topic. Training is basically incomplete without lecture. It is less expensive and can be reached large number of people at same time.
- ***Group Discussions***—This method is more useful than a lecture method. In this method the training is supported, elaborated, explains, or expanded on through interactions both among the trainees and between the trainer and the trainees. The interaction and the communication between these two make it much more effective and powerful than the lecture method. If this method is used with proper sequence i.e. lectures, followed by discussion and questioning, can achieve higher level knowledge objectives, such as problem solving and principle learning.
- ***Case Studies***—This method is usually consisting of description of some events that occurred in the organization. The basic objective of case study is to find solution of a particular problem. The trainees review the case and find out the various alternatives and finally suggest the solution. This helps the learners to increase their observation power and broaden their view.
- ***Role Playing***—The term role playing was originally coined in the 1920s by Jacob L. Moreno, a Viennese psychiatrist who surmised patients gained more from exploring their problems by acting them out than by talking about them.[6] Oxford English Dictionary defines role playing as "the changing of one's behaviour to fulfill a social role". In this method, two or more trainees are assigned parts to play in front of others. These parts do not involve any rehearsals. They are simply informed the situation and the respective roles they have to play. The usual subjects involve in

role playing are grievance handling, hiring, retrenchment, appraisal interview etc.

- ***Programmed Instructions***—Programmed instruction is a computer-based training that comprises of graphics, multimedia, text that is connected to one another and is stored in memory. A programmed instruction involves breaking information down into meaningful units and it provides the trainee with content, information, asks questions, and based on the answer goes to the next level of information i.e. if the trainee gives the correct answer than they forward to the new information. And if the trainee gives the wrong answer then they are revert to their old position and review relevant information in more elaborate manner. This method is very useful because it gives immediate feedback, frequently review the information and it allows the trainee to learn according to their capability.
- ***Sensitivity Training***—This is the method of group therapy in which the members of the group, under the guidance of a leader, seek a deeper understanding of themselves and others, as by the exchange of intimate feelings and experiences, physical contacts, etc. The main objective of sensitivity training is not to make trainees conform to a set of acceptable norms and ideas. It is designed for trainees to confront their own prejudices and biases and broadens their tolerance level. Sensitivity training involves varied methods like case studies, simulated excise, role playing etc.

Tiffin and McCormick (1958) classify training into the following seven categories: [7]

1. Orientation Training–to acquaint new employees with the company.
2. Vestibule Training–simulated on-the-job training.
3. On-the-job Training–actual practice on the job.
4. Apprentice Training–formal apprenticeship for a craft.
5. Technical Training–training in technical aspect of job.
6. Supervisory Training–training in management.
7. Other Training–any unusual situation not included in the above.

21.10 Evaluation of Training Effectiveness

There are various methods by which management check the effectiveness of their training programms. Some are the:

- Reaction of Trainees;
- Learning;
- Behavioural Changes; and
- Impact on Organization Effectiveness and many more.

Reaction of trainee is one of the best methods by which management can evaluate the effectiveness of the training programme. Under this method management tries to collect the response of the trainee. They take help of questionnaire, survey or simple interview by which they are asked certain specific question regarding the training programme and collect the responses.

The learning tendency of worker is more improved after taking training. If they can easily learn the new technologies, cope with surrounding all of this express the effectiveness of the training programme.

One of the ways suggested by Blum & Naylor[8] is by comparing the change in performance of a group receiving training to the change in performance of a comparable group which did not receive the training. If two groups i.e. control group and experimental group are both evaluated before the training introduced. After imposing tests on the experimental group what are the changes seen in the experimental group compare with control group. If any difference is found in the same situation in both comparable groups it leads the importance and effectiveness of training.

The following criteria suggested by Lindahl (1949)[9] for checking the results of training are:

- Better quality of production.
- Increase in the number of operators able to meet job standards.
- Reduction in time required to do a specific job.
- Decrease in breakable supplies or tools.
- Decrease in absenteeism.
- Reduction in separation rate.
- Reduction in operational costs.
- Better performance on personnel tools such as tests, rating scales and attitude surveys.

REFERENCES

1. Edwin B. Flippo, *Personal Management*, McGraw-Hill, Tokyo, 1989, p. 30.
2. Blum & Naylor, *Industrial Psychology: Its Theoretical and Social Foundations*, CBS Publishers, 2002, p. 237.
3. Mammoria, C.B., *Personnel Management*, Himalaya Publishing House, p. 277.
4. A.F. Sikula, *Personnel Administration and Human Resource Management*, 1976, p. 274.
5. National Industrial Conference Board, *The Management Record*, March, 1961, p. 8.
6. Gale, *Encyclopedia of Psychology*, 2nd ed. Gale Group, 2001.
7. Tiffin, J., and E.J. McCormick, *Industrial Psychology*, 4th ed., Prentice-Hall, Englewood Cliffs, N.J., 1958.
8. Blum & Naylor, *Industrial Psychology: Its Theoretical and Social Foundations*, CBS Publishers, 2002, p.266.
9. Lindahl, L.G., *How to Build a Training Program*, Personnel Journal, 1949, 27, 417–419.

❍❍❍

QUESTION BANK

(1) Define industrial psychology. Discuss its characteristics also.

(2) Elaborate the scope of industrial psychology.

(3) Discuss the historical development of industrial psychology.

(4) Discuss the contribution of scientific management to the development of industrial psychology.

(5) Write short notes on:

(i) Contribution of Henry L. Gantt to scientific management.

(ii) Contribution of Gilbreths to scientific management.

(iii) Limitations of scientific management.

(6) Briefly describe the experiments conducted at the Hawthorne plant of General Electric Company, Chicago.

(7) Discuss the implication and limitations of Hawthorne studies.

(8) What do you understand by time and motion study?

(9) "Time study understood as to set up the method to determine the actual time for performing a particular task". Discuss its advantages and disadvantages.

(10) What are the aims and objectives of time study? Explain with the support of time study procedure.

(11) What do you understand by the term 'therblings'?

(12) Elucidate the tools of motion study.

(13) Discuss the advantages and limitations of motion study.

(14) State the difference between the time and motion study.

(15) Discuss the different types of motivation by which supervisor motivate their subordinates.

(16) Define motivation.

(17) "Motivated workers are more productive and work more efficiently". Discuss.

(18) Briefly describe the Maslow's need hierarchy theory.

(19) Write notes on:

(i) ERG theory

(ii) Theory X and Y.

(iii) Acquired need theory.

(20) Discuss the Two factors theory of Herzberg.

(21) Discuss Process theories in detail.

(22) Which motivation theory is based on the relationship between behaviour and its consequences not on need? Explain.

(23) What are the implications of motivation theories on workplace?

(24) Discuss any two studies conducted on workplace motivation.

(25) Give some tips for improving workers motivation.

(26) What do you understand by job satisfaction?

(27) Elaborate the history of job satisfaction.

(28) Discuss the different factors in details which influence job satisfaction.

(29) What are the consequences of satisfaction and dissatisfaction at work place?

(30) Point out some tips which are helpful in minimizing dissatisfaction in workplace.

(31) Define the concept of stress and also discuss the dynamics of stress.

(32) Write short notes on:

(*i*) Eustress

(*ii*) Distress

(*iii*) Hyper stress

(*iv*) Hypo stress

(33) What are the different causes of stress? Explain in detail.

(34) Discuss symptoms or sign of stress.

(35) How do you address the cause of stress? Explain.

(36) Define workplace stress. Explain the different work related stress.

(37) How management manage stress at workplace? What are the steps they have taken to reduce the stress at workplace?

(38) Briefly describe the organizational culture and their importance in organization.

(39) What are the different types of organizational culture?

(40) What are the steps taken by management for changing their organizational culture effectively?

(41) Explain the concept and importance of leadership.

(42) Good leader posses some good qualities. What are these good qualities?

(43) Elucidate the principles of leadership.

(44) How normal leaders become great leader? Explain with the help of process of great leadership.

(45) Discuss any two leadership theories.

(46) Write short notes on:
 (i) Great man theory
 (ii) Trait theory
 (iii) Behavioural theory

(47) Explain participative leadership.

(48) "Best action of the leader depends on a range of situational factors". Explain.

(49) Discuss the different contingency theories.

(50) Compare Bass with Burn's transformational leadership theory.

(51) Elaborate leader-members exchange theory with LMX process.

(52) Define group. And discuss the features of group.

(53) Discuss the concept of group dynamics.

(54) What are the different theories of group formation? Discuss in detail.

(55) Discuss the different phases of group development proposed by Tuckman.

(56) Explain the four stage model of group development.

(57) Discuss the various types of group.

(58) Differentiate between:
 (i) Formal and informal group.
 (ii) Primary and secondary group.
 (iii) Task and command group.

(59) What are the reasons which motivate the individuals to join particular group.

(60) Discuss the reasons proposed by Robbins why individuals join the group.

(61) Write short notes on:
 (i) Group status
 (ii) Group role
 (iii) Group norms
 (iv) Group size
 (v) Group leadership

(62) Discuss the factors which influencing the group cohesiveness.

(63) What do you understand by group cohesiveness? Explain with the help of their advantages.

(64) Examine the importance of atmospheric condition in increasing industrial efficiency. Justify your answer with experimental finding.

(65) Give some tips for reducing adverse effect of atmospheric conditions.

(66) Explain the significance of "Observation" and "Interview" as sources of information for job-analysis.

(67) What do you understand by 'work environment'? Analyze the importance of music in improving the efficiency of workers.

(68) How illuminations affect the efficiency of worker? What are the difficulties comes from illumination and advising tips for reducing that difficulty?

(69) Discuss the influence of long working hours in the efficiency of workers.

(70) Suitable working condition is required for high production. Discuss.

(71) Describe the importance of reducing noise at workplace. Support your answer with experimental studies.

(72) Explain the term Industrial fatigue with example.

(73) What are the different types of Industrial fatigue?

(74) Why do we get fatigued?

(75) What are the basic symptoms of fatigue?

(76) Discuss the causes and remedies of Industrial fatigue.

(77) Describe some experiments which has boned on Industrial fatigue.

(78) What are the effects of fatigue on Industrial workers?

(79) Define Industrial boredom.

(80) Describe the effect of boredom on industrial work.

(81) What are the action taken by the management to reduce the boredom of their workers?

(82) Discuss the different causes and remedies of boredom.

(83) Define the concept of industrial accident.

(84) What are different causes of industrial accident?

(85) What is meant by accident proneness?

(86) 'Accident not only affects the workers but also affect management. Explain.

(87) Write notes on:

(*i*) Accident cost

(*ii*) Accident measurement

(88) How industries prevent accident? Give some safety measure.

(89) Write down some safety measures given by 'US department of Labour' in 1947.

(90) Define the concept of job analysis and also job analysis contents.

(91) Why job analysis is important?

(92) Discuss the different methods of job analysis.

(93) Write short notes on:

(*i*) Work participation method.

(*ii*) Diary method

(*iii*) Group interview

(*iv*) Questionnaire method

(94) How do you define recruitment? Also discuss need of recruitment.

(95) What are the objectives of recruitment?

(96) Discuss the process of recruitment.

(97) What are the factors which influence the recruitment?

(98) Discuss the different sources of recruitment.

(99) How selection is different from recruitment process? What is the objective behind selection?

(100) Discuss selection process in detail.

(101) Figure out the importance of reliability and validity test.

(102) Define reliability test. And also their types.

(103) What do you understand by validity test? Explain with the help of their different types.

(104) Is there any relationship in reliability and validity? Explain.

(105) Define the concept of performance management.

(106) Discuss objectives of performance management.

(107) Explain the process of performance management.

(108) Elaborate the approaches of performance development.

(109) Discuss any two methods of traditional and modern method of performance management.

(110) Write short notes on:

(*i*) Checklist method

(*ii*) Straight ranking method

(*iii*) Critical incident method

(*iv*) Group appraisal method

(111) 'MBO' is the modern method for evaluation of worker performance. Explain MBO with its process.

(112) What do you understand by 360° performance appraisal system?

(113) Write notes on:

(*i*) BARS

(*ii*) Assessment centre

(*iii*) Human resource accounting

(114) Define the concept of training and development.

(115) How training is different from development?

(116) Elaborate the importance of training and development.

(117) Explain the process of training.

(118) Tiffin and McCormick classify training in seven categories, what are these categories?

(119) Discuss the different types of training.

(120) How management evaluate the effectiveness of training program?

❍❍❍

CHAPTERWISE QUESTIONS

CHAPTER 1

(1) Define industrial psychology. Discuss its characteristics also.

(2) Elaborate the scope of industrial psychology.

(3) Discuss the historical development of industrial psychology.

(4) American Psychologist Association, Division of Industrial Psychology, *The psychologist industry*, Washington D.C., 1959 cited seven major areas which comprised the content area of industrial psychology. What are these areas?

(5) Industrial psychology is that branch of applied psychology that is concerned with:

(i) entertainment of workers.

(ii) problems encountered by workers in a mechanized environment.

(iii) relationship with other workers and management.

(iv) none of the above.

(6) Wage are the only factor which directly affect the performance of individuals:

(i) True (ii) False

(iii) None of the above.

(7) Industrial psychology is concerned with people's work-related values, attitudes and behaviours, and how these are influenced by the conditions in which they work.

(8) Industrial psychology is the systematic study of the ....of the people at work.

(i) performance (ii) behaviour

(iii) motivation

(9) According to .... 'Industrial psychology may be defined as the study of people as individuals and in groups and of the relationship between individual and group'.

(i) Thomas W. Harrell (ii) C.S. Myres

(iii) Filipo

(10) 'The Psychology of Industrial Efficiency', book is written by ....

(i) Hugo Munsterberg (ii) Tiffin and Cormick

(iii) Bryan and Harter

CHAPTER 2

(1) Discuss the contribution of scientific management to the development of industrial psychology.

(2) Write short notes on:

(i) Contribution of Henry L. Gantt to scientific management.

(ii) Contribution of Gilbreths to scientific management.

(iii) Limitations of scientific management.

(3) Briefly describe the experiments conducted at the Hawthorne plant of General Electric Company, Chicago.

(4) Discuss the implication and limitations of Hawthorne studies.

(5) Father of scientific management:

(i) Henry Fayol (ii) F.W. Taylor
(iii) Henry Gantt (iv) Lillian Gilbreth

(6) Taylor based his management system on production line ....studies.

(i) time (ii) motion
(iii) both (iv) none of the above

CHAPTER 3

(1) Discuss the contribution of Elton Mayo.

(2) Write notes on:

(i) Experiment on Illumination
(ii) Relay Assembly Test Room Experiment
(iii) Mass Interviewing Programme
(iv) Bank Wiring Observation Room

(3) What are the implications of Hawthorne experiment on Industrial psychology?

(4) Criticise Hawthorne experiment.

(5) According to you which phase is more crucial and why?

(6) Hawthorne plant of the General Electric Company is situated in ....

(i) Canada (ii) Chicago
(iii) New Jersey (iv) Texas

(7) Phase III (1928–30) of Hawthorne experiment was:

(i) Illumination Experiment
(ii) Relay Assembly Test Room Experiment
(iii) Mass Interviewing Programme
(iv) Bank Wiring Observation Room

(8) Relay Assembly Test Room Experiment done in the year.....

(i) 1924–27 (ii) 1931–32
(iii) 1928–30 (iv) None of the above.

(9) The series of Hawthorne studies is conducted to find out the relationship between productivity and ....

(i) performance (ii) incentives
(iii) work conditions (iv) all of the above.

(10) From the mass interview programme, it was discovered that employees' behaviour was being influenced by group behaviour.

(i) True (ii) False

CHAPTER 4

(1) What do you understand by time and motion study?

(2) "Time study understood as to set up the method to determine the actual time for performing a particular task". Discuss its advantages and disadvantages.

(3) What are the aims and objectives of time study? Explain with the support of time study procedure.

(4) What do you understand by the term 'therblings'?

(5) Elucidate the tools of motion study.

(6) Discuss the advantages and limitations of motion study.

(7) State the difference between the time and motion study.

(8) Motion study is a method to establish ....to perform the task.

(i) 'the one best way' (ii) 'the only way'

(iii) 'the difficult way' (iv) 'the shortest way'

(9) Bodily movements called .... are analyzed to find a better method of doing a work.

(i) Gilbreth (ii) Therblings

(iii) Motion (iv) Time

(10) Time study can be made without motion study and vice-versa but it is not possible to fix ideal standards of work without the study of both.

(i) Agree (ii) Disagree

CHAPTER 5

(1) Discuss the different types of motivation by which supervisor motivate their subordinates.

(2) Define motivation.

(3) "Motivated worker are more productive and work more efficiently". Discuss.

(4) Briefly describe the Maslow's need hierarchy theory.

(5) Write notes on:

(i) ERG theory (ii) Theory X and Y.

(iii) Acquired need theory.

(6) Discuss the Two factors theory of Herzberg.

(7) Discuss Process theories in detail.

(8) Which motivation theory is based on the relationship between behaviour and its consequences not on need? Explain.

(9) What are the implications of motivation theories on workplace?

(10) Discuss any two studies conducted on workplace motivation.

(11) Give some tips for improving workers motivation.

(12) Need Hierarchy Theory is given by.......

(i) Herzberg (ii) Maslow

(iii) Edwin Filipo (iv) Clayton Alderfer

(13) Douglas McGregor, a professor at the Massachusetts Institute of Technology and a social psychologist, has given theory of

(i) Two factor theory (ii) ERG theory

(iii) Theory X and Y (iv) Acquired need theory.

(14) Need for achievement, need for affiliation and need for power are the three needs proposed by whom?

(i) Douglas McGregor (ii) David McClelland

(iii) Victor Vroom (iv) J. Stacy Adams

(15) The Expectancy theory of motivation was given by

(i) Douglas McGregor (ii) David McClelland

(iii) Victor Vroom (iv) J. Stacy Adams

CHAPTER 6

(1) What do you understand by job satisfaction?

(2) Elaborate the history of job satisfaction.

(3) Discuss the different factors in detail which influence job satisfaction.

(4) What are the consequences of satisfaction and dissatisfaction at workplace?

(5) Point out some tips which are helpful in minimizing dissatisfaction in workplace.

(6) Salary is the employer related factor which influences the satisfaction of an employee.

(i) agree (ii) disagree

(7) Adequate working condition leads ....level of satisfaction.

(i) lower (ii) high

(iii) moderate

(8) Proper grievance handling machinery reduce conflicts among workers

(i) Agree (ii) Disagree

(9) Job rotation reduces the monotony and leads........

(i) boredom (ii) satisfaction

(iii) dissatisfaction

(10) Dissatisfied workers are more accident prone as compared to satisfied workers.

(i) Agree (ii) Disagree

CHAPTER 7

(1) Define the concept of stress and also discuss the dynamics of stress.

(2) Write short notes on:

(i) Eustress (ii) Distress

(iii) Hyper stress (iv) Hypo stress

(3) What are the different causes of stress? Explain in detail.

(4) Discuss symptoms or sign of stress.

(5) How do you address the cause of stress? Explain.

(6) Define workplace stress. Explain the different work related stress.

(7) How management manage stress at workplace? What are the steps they have taken to reduce the stress at workplace?

(8) Distress is one of the .... types of stress.

(i) Positive (ii) Negative

(9) Increasing self awareness and personal growth is one of the cause of stress lies under:

(i) biological (ii) social

(iii) psychodynamic (iv) spiritual

(10) Some stress is required for performing a job.

(i) Agree (ii) Disagree

CHAPTER 8

(1) Briefly describe the organizational culture and their importance in organization.

(2) What are the different types of organizational culture?

(3) What are the steps taken by management for changing their organizational culture effectively?

(4) 'Changes are good for organization'. Comment.

(5) Beliefs, morals, value systems, behavioural norms are the part of culture:

(i) agree (ii) disagree

(6) Organizational .... is the set of operating principles that determine how people behave within the context of the company.

(i) behaviour (ii) culture

(iii) environment (iv) policy

(7) Culture is "an active living phenomenon through which people jointly create and recreate the world in which they live."

(i) Denison (ii) Gareth Morgan

(iii) None of the above

(8) Leader-centered culture where all the power is concentrated on the leader.

(i) Agree (ii) Disagree

(9) Where core values share by majority of organizational members are termed as....

(i) Dominant culture (ii) Subculture

(iii) Mechanistic culture (iv) Organic culture

(10) Cameron and Quinn suggested four new types of culture, Clan Culture, Hierarchy Culture, Adhocracy Culture and ....

(i) participative culture (ii) dominant culture

(iii) market culture (iv) subculture

CHAPTER 9

(1) Explain the concept and importance of leadership.

(2) Good leader possess some good qualities. What are these good qualities?

(3) Elucidate the principles of leadership.

(4) How normal leaders become great leader? Explain with help of process of great leadership.

(5) Discuss any two leadership theories in detail.

(6) Rensis Likert identified four main styles of leadership. Explain.

(7) Write short notes on:

(i) Great man theory (ii) Trait theory

(iii) Behavioural theory

(8) Explain participative leadership.

(9) "Best action of the leader depends on a range of situational factors". Explain.

(10) Discuss the different contingency theories.

(11) Compare Bass with Burn's transformational leadership theory.

(12) Elaborate Fiedler's Least Preferred Co-worker (LPC) theory.

(13) Elaborate leader-members exchange theory with LMX process.

(14) Leadership is the ability to shape the attitude and beahviour of others, whether in formal or informal situations:

(i) Agree (ii) Disagree

(15) Blake and Mouton managerial grid based on two parameters, one is concern for production other is.......

(i) Concern for task (ii) Concern for management

(iii) Concern for people (iv) None of the above.

(16) Kurt Lewin identified three different styles of leadership, these are autocratic, democratic and.....

(i) Participative (ii) Expert leadership

(iii) Laissez-Faire (iv) None of the above.

(17) LMX theory stands for

(i) Leader-Member Exchange Theory

(ii) Lower-Medium Expert Theory

(iii) Least-Member Exchange Theory

(iv) None of the above.

(18) Least Preferred Co-worker (LPC) theory given by

(i) House and Mitchell (ii) Fiedler

(iii) Kurt Lewin (iv) None of the above.

(19) Hersey and Blanchard's theory of leadership is based on

(i) Trait theory (ii) Situational theory

(iii) Participative theory (iv) None of the above.

(20) Leaders can be made, rather than are born and successful leadership is based in definable, learnable behaviour, these are the assumptions of ....theory.

(i) trait (ii) situational

(iii) participative (iv) behavioural

Chapter 10

(1) Define group. Discuss the features of group.

(2) Discuss the concept of group dynamics.

(3) What are the different theories of group formation? Discuss in detail.

(4) Discuss the different phases of group development proposed by Tuckman.

(5) Explain the four stage model of group development.

(6) Discuss the various types of group.

(7) Differentiate between:

(i) Formal and informal

(ii) Primary and secondary group

(iii) Task and command group.

(8) What are the reasons which motivate the individuals to join particular group.

(9) Discuss the reasons proposed by Robbins why individuals join the group.

(10) Write short notes on:

(a) Group status (b) Group role

(c) Group norms (d) Group size

(e) Group leadership

(11) Discuss the factors which influencing the group cohesiveness.

(12) What do you understand by group cohesiveness? Explain with the help of their advantages.

(13) The word ....means simply that person affiliated with one another because of geographical proximity.

(i) closeness (ii) propinquity

(iii) both (iv) none of the above

(14) The Human's interaction theory based on activities, interactions and ....

(i) Sentiments (ii) Behaviour

(iii) Communication (vi) None of the above

(15) Exchange theory is based upon reward and cost outcomes of ....

(i) sentiments (ii) interaction

(iii) beahviour (iv) none of the above

(16) Four Stage Model of Group Development developed by Hare include latent, adoption, integration and ....

(i) Acceptance (ii) Goal attainment

(iii) Assimilation (iv) None of the above

(17) The third phase of group development process is.......

(i) performing (ii) norming

(iii) storming (iv) none of the above

(18) .... consist of those members who have intimate face-to-face association and co-operations.

(i) Secondary group (ii) Primary group

(iii) Task group (iv) None of the above

(19) ....is defined as a degree to which group members are attracted to each other and are motivated to stay in the group.

(i) Group structure (ii) Group cohesiveness

(ii) Group norms (iv) None of the above

(20) Every group has some acceptable standards behaviour that is shared by the group members. Group norms tell members what they ought and ought not to under certain situations.

(i) Agree (ii) Disagree

CHAPTER 11

(1) Examine the importance of atmospheric condition in increasing industrial efficiency. Justify your answer with experimental finding.

(2) Give some tips for reducing adverse effect of atmospheric conditions.

(3) Explain the significance of "Observation" and "Interview" as sources of information for job-analysis.

(4) What do you understand by 'work environment'? Analyze the importance of music in improving the efficiency of workers.

(5) How illuminations affect the efficiency of worker? What are the difficulties come from illumination and advising tips for reducing that difficulty?

(6) Discuss the influence of long working hours in the efficiency of workers.

(7) Suitable working condition is required for high production. Discuss.

(8) Describe the importance of reducing noise at workplace. Support your answer with experimental studies.

(9) 'The quality of employees will be directly proportional to the quality of life you maintain for them' ....

(i) Pollock and Bartlett (ii) Charles E. Bryan

(iii) Charles E. Domick (iv) None of the above

(10) For making work environment more peaceful and effective introduce music during working hour.

(i) Agree (ii) Disagree

(11) When individual work together they exhale poisonous gas and the air become little bit polluted and unhealthy for the workers.

(i) Agree (ii) Disagree

(12) .... occurs when there is too much direct or reflected light within the field of view.

(i) Glare (ii) Shadow

(iii) Reflectance (iv) Luminance

(13) The reflection of light falling on a coloured surface produces a coloured effect blues and greens are considered ....

(i) aggressive (ii) relaxing or soothing

(iii) hostile (iv) none of the above

(14) The reflection of light falling on a coloured surface produces a coloured effect red and violet is considered ....

(i) aggressive (ii) relaxing or soothing

(iii) comforting (iv) none of the above

(15) There is an association between working long hours and fatigue.

(i) Agree (ii) Disagree

Chapter 12

(1) Elaborate the concept of engineering psychology.

(2) Discuss the need of engineering psychology at workplace.

(3) Disucss various stages of human engineering in detail.

(4) Differentiate between Engineering and Engineering Psychology.

(5) What are the problems have been faced by human engineering?

Chapter 13

(1) Explain the term Industrial fatigue with example.

(2) What are the different types of Industrial fatigue?

(3) Why do we get fatigued?

(4) What are the basic symptoms of fatigue?

(5) Discuss the causes and remedies of Industrial fatigue.

(6) Describe some experiments which has boned on Industrial fatigue.

(7) What are the effects of fatigue on industrial workers?

(8) Fatigue where you may still feel tired even after a night's sleep this comes under .... fatigue.

(i) Acute (ii) Cumulative

(iii) Both (iv) None of the above

(9) Industrial fatigue does not reduce performance and productivity in the workplace.

(i) Agree (ii) Disagree

(10) "Tension, speed, subjection to specification of work and a decrease in the enjoyment of work leads to fatigue"---

(i) Maier (ii) Muscio

(iii) Viteles (iv) None of the above

Chapter 14

(1) Define Industrial boredom.

(2) Describe the effect of boredom on industrial work.

(3) What are the actions taken by the management to reduce the boredom of their workers?

(4) Discuss the different causes and remedies of boredom.

(5) Boredom is considered as one of the most important psychological factor which adversely influence on workplace and also productivity.

(i) Agree (ii) Disagree

(6) Boredom is commonly referred to as .... fatigue which leads to work decrement.

(i) physical (ii) mental
(iii) both (iv) none of the above

(7) Group discussion can be used to reduce boredom.
(i) Agree 2. Disagree

(8) Rest pauses if .... lead to boredom.
(i) Frequent (ii) Lengthy
(iii) Short (iv) None of the above

(9) Boredom is often associated with jobs that are..................
(i) interesting (ii) varied
(iii) repetitive (iv) none of the above

(10) Intelligence caused boredom.
(i) Agree (ii) Disagree

CHAPTER 15

(1) Define the concept of industrial accident.

(2) What are different causes of industrial accident?

(3) What is meant by accident proneness?

(4) 'Accident not only affects the workers but also affect management'. Explain.

(5) Write notes on:
(i) Accident cost (ii) Accident measurement

(6) How industries prevent accident? Give some safety measure.

(7) Write down some safety measures given by 'US Department of Labour' in 1947.

(8) The word accident is derived from the Latin verb ....
(i) Accedere (ii) Accidere
(iii) Acideeree (iv) None of the above

(9) According to the Factories Act, 1948, it is "an occurrence in an industrial establishment causing bodily injury to a person who makes him unfit to resume his duties in the next ...."
(i) 40 hours (ii) 48 hours
(iii) 42 hours (iv) None of the above

(10) Speed of work is one of the ....related cause of accident.
(i) personal (ii) work
(iii) both (iv) none of the above

(11) If work or task is compatible to worker than chance of accident should be minimized
(i) Agree (ii) Disagree

(12) The accident frequency rate is the number of time cost accidents (or injuries which have disabled an employee) per .... man-hours worked.
(i) 1,000 (ii) 1,000,000
(iii) 1,00 (iv) 10,000

(13) The accident ...... is the total number of days charged or lost because of accidents per 1,000,000 man-hours worked.

(i) frequency rate (ii) severity rate
(iii) both (iv) none of the above

(14) Indirect accident cause include:
(i) Loss of production
(ii) Compensation to victim
(iii) Training cost of new workers
(iv) Loss of motivation amongst the workmen.

(15) If two workers are operated on similar machine under identical situation, one may commit more accidents than the other. The first worker will be called an 'accident-prone operator'.
(i) Agree (ii) Disagree

CHAPTER 16

(1) Define the concept of job analysis and also job analysis contents.
(2) Why job analysis is important?
(3) Discuss the different methods of job analysis.
(4) Briefly explain the questionnaire method.
(5) Write short notes on:
(i) Work participation method.
(ii) Diary method
(iii) Group interview
(6) Job analysis includes job description and job ....
(i) rotation (ii) specification
(iii) enlargement (iv) none of the above
(7) Job title, duties, machines, tools and equipment, working conditions and hazards comes under..............
(i) Job specification (ii) Job description
(iii) Both (iv) None of the above
(8) The capabilities that the job holder should possess for doing a particular job from part of ....
(i) job specification (ii) job description
(iii) both (iv) none of the above
(9) Job description includes:
(i) Education (ii) Physical skills
(iii) Training (iv) Job title
(10) There is a list of eleven items of job analysis suggested by............ (1932) known as Guide of Job Analysis.
(i) Lawshe and Satter (ii) Viteles'
(iii) Kurt Lewin (iv) None of the above

CHAPTER 17

(1) How do you define recruitment? Also discuss need of recruitment.
(2) What are the objectives of recruitment?

(3) Discuss the process of recruitment.

(4) What are the factors which influence the recruitment?

(5) Discuss the different sources of recruitment.

(6) How selection is different from recruitment process? What is the objective behind selection?

(7) Discuss selection process in detail.

(8) .... is the process of attracting potential candidates for a particular job vacancy.

(i) Recruitment (ii) Selection
(iii) Both (iv) None of the above

(9) The fourth step in the process of recruitment is..........

(i) identify vacancy (ii) communicating vacancy
(iii) select candidates (iv) managing the responses

(10) Supply and demand of the specific skill in the market place also affect the recruitment process of the organization.

(i) Agree (ii) Disagree

(11) Retired employees is the ....source of recruitment.

(i) Internal (ii) External
(iii) None of the above.

(12) The dependents and relatives of deceased employees and disabled employees are also source of internal recruitment.

(i) Agree (ii) Disagree

(13) .... is a process of selecting most desirable candidates among others for a particular job.

(i) Selection (ii) Recruitment
(iii) None of the above.

(14) The final step in selection process is .... of candidate to their job and workplace.

(i) interview (ii) placement
(iii) application blank (iv) none of the above

(15) External source of recruitment include:

(i) Unsolicited applicant (ii) Retired employees
(iii) Promotion (iv) None of the above

CHAPTER 18

(1) Define the concept of interview.

(2) What is interview? Also discuss its importance.

(3) Discuss various types of interview in detail.

(4) "Exit interview is very helpful type of interview". Discuss.

(5) What kind of preparation should be done before interview?

(6) State the difference between structured and unstructured interview.

(7) Write short notes on:

(i) Stress interview (ii) Exit interview
(iii) Problem interview (iv) Selection interview
(v) Appraisal interview

CHAPTER 19

(1) Figure out the importance of reliability and validity test.
(2) Define reliability test. And also their types.
(3) What do you understand by validity test? Explain with the help of their different types.
(4) Is there any relationship in reliability and validity? Explain.
(5) .... estimates the consistency of test measurement.
(i) Reliability (ii) Validity
(iii) Both (iv) None of the above
(6) ....involves the accuracy of measurement and what management supposed to measure.
(i) Reliability (ii) Validity
(iii) Both (iv) None of the above
(7) Reliability estimates below .... are usually regarded as unacceptably low.
(i) .90 (ii) .60
(iii) .060 (iv) .090
(8) Validity test must be reliable; but reliability does not guarantee validity, i.e. it is possible to have a highly reliable test which is meaningless (invalid).
(i) Agree (ii) Disagree
(9) The test-retest method of estimating a test's .... involves administering the test to the same group of people at least twice.
(i) Reliability (ii) Validity
(iii) None of the above
(10) Construct-related is a type of ....test.
(i) reliability (ii) validity
(iii) none of the above

CHAPTER 20

(1) Define the concept of performance management.
(2) Discuss objectives of performance management.
(3) Explain the process of performance management.
(4) Elaborate the approaches of performance development.
(5) Discuss any two methods of traditional and modern method of performance management.
(6) Write short notes on:
(i) Checklist method (ii) Straight ranking method
(iii) Critical incident method (iv) Group appraisal method
(7) 'MBO' is the modern method for evaluation of worker performance. Explain MBO with its process.

(8) What do you understand by 360° performance appraisal system?

(9) Write notes on:

(i) BARS (ii) Assessment centre

(iii) Human resource accounting

(10) ....review of a person's work is termed as performance management.

(i) Occasionally (ii) Systematic

(iii) Irregular (iv) None of the above

(11) ....is the third step of performance management process.

(i) Give feedback

(ii) Measuring actual performance

(iii) Decision making

(iv) None of the above

(12) ....approach focused only on the past performance of the employees during a past specified period of time.

(i) Modern (ii) Traditional

(13) Appraisals have become ongoing and periodic activity in the organizations is the ....approach.

(i) Modern (ii) Traditional

(14) Under this, individual is compared on the basis of every trait with other individuals in their group.

(i) Checklist method (ii) Essay method

(iii) Straight ranking method (iv) Paired comparison method

(15) Under this method, a training officer basically appointed by or even from HR department discusses and interviews the supervisor about how they appraise them respective subordinates.

(i) Critical Incident Method (ii) Graphical Rating Scale

(iii) Field Review (iv) Paired Comparison Method

(16) BARS stands for:

(i) Base assessment rating scales

(ii) Broader appraisal rating scales

(iii) Behaviourally anchored random scales

(iv) Behaviourally anchored rating scales

(17) The concept of 'Management by Objectives' (MBO) was first given by

(i) Peter Ronald (ii) Peter Drucker

(iii) S.P. Robbins (iv) P.S. Robbins

(18) "A process whereby the superior and subordinate managers of an organization jointly identify its common goals, define each individual's major areas of responsibility in term as of result expected of him and use these measures as guides for operating the unit and assessing the contributions of each its members"

(i) MBO (ii) BARS

(iii) Human Resource Accounting (iv) 360 degree

(19) 360° feedback, also known as 'multi-rater feedback'

(i) Feedback only from supervisor (ii) Multi-rater feedback

(iii) Feedback only from colleagues (iv) None of the above

(20) 360°appraisal has four important elements are.................., superior's appraisal, subordinate's appraisal and peer appraisal.

(i) Self appraisal (ii) Customer appraisal

(iii) Trade union appraisal (iv) None of the above

CHAPTER 21

(1) Define the concept of training and development.

(2) How training is different from development?

(3) Elaborate the importance of training and development.

(4) Explain the process of training.

(5) Explain simulation test with the help of example.

(6) Write short notes on:

(i) Sensitivity training (ii) Role playing

(iii) Case studies method

(7) Tiffin and McCormick classify training in seven categories, what are these categories?

(8) Discuss the different types of training.

(9) Briefly describe the JIT.

(10) How management evaluate the effectiveness of training program?

(11) Training is a ....term process where development is a ....term process.

(i) long and short (ii) short and long

(iii) none of the above

(12) Under .... managerial personnel learn technical knowledge and skills.

(i) Training (ii) Development

(iii) None of the above

(13) ....refers to the period of service as a learner of a trade or handicraft

(i) Simulation (ii) Apprenticeship

(iii) Vestibule training/Training centre

(iv) None of the above

(14) A .... involve breaking information down into meaningful units and it provides the trainee with content, information, asks questions, and based on the answer goes to the next level of information.

(i) Programmed instruction (ii) Sensitivity training

(iii) Role playing (iv) Vestibule training/Training centre

(15) In ....method supervisor describes and display something related to the job and also explains the step-by-step explanations of why and what supervisor or trainer is doing.

(i) group discussions (ii) lecture

(iii) role playing (iv) demonstration

❍❍❍

SOLVED EXAMINATION PAPER

B.TECH
(SEM IV)THEORY EXAMINATION 2013-14
INDUSTRIAL PSYCHOLOGY

Time: 2 Hours ***Total Marks: 50***

Note: Attempts all questions.

1. Attempt any four parts of the following: (4×3.5=14)

(*a*) *Define Industrial Psychology and discuss its scope.*

Ans. Industrial psychology is concerned with people's work-related values, attitudes and behaviours, and how these are influenced by the conditions in which they work. Industrial psychology is the systematic study of the behaviour of the people at work. It studies how the social, industrial, economic, political and other factors affect the behaviour of the people at work.

C.S.Myres, 'The aim of industrial psychology is primarily not to obtain greater production or output but to give the worker greater ease at his work'.

According to Thomas W. Harrell 'Industrial psychology may be defined as the study of people as individuals and in groups and of the relationship between individual and group'.

Scopes of Industrial Psychology

- *Scientific selection of workers*: Industrial psychology offers a whole arrangement of tests such as systematic depth interviews and psychological tests of intelligence, aptitude, skills, abilities and interest and the personnel characteristics etc,.
- *Proper division of work*: One of the scopes of industrial psychology is the work should be properly divided according to the abilities, skills and aptitude of the workers so they may feel comfortable and satisfied.
- *Minimizing the wastage of human efforts*: Industrial psychology tires to minimize the wastage of human power.

- Promoting Labour welfare: It promotes the welfare of the labour by introducing adequate working environment.
- Developing industrial relations: Industrial psychology studies the attitude of the employer and employees. This will help in developing industrial relationship among workers and management.
- Increase production: It helps in attaining the major objective of the organization that to get the best output from the existing resources.

(b) *Enumerate the contribution of scientific management.*

Ans. Scientific management (also called Taylorism or the Taylor system) is a theory of management that analyzes and synthesizes workflows, with the objective of improving labour productivity. **Taylor** (1985–1915) rested his philosophy on four basic principles:

(i) The development of a true science of management instead of rule of thumb so that the best method for performing each task could be determined.

(ii) Scientific selection of workers so that each worker would be given responsibility for the task for which he or she is best suited.

(iii) The scientific education and development of workers.

(iv) Intimate friendly cooperation between management and labour.

Henry L.Gannt(1861–1919) came up with new idea.

- Every worker who finishes day's assigned work load win 50 per cent bonus.
- Then he added a second motivation, the supervisor would earn a bonus for each worker who reaches a daily standard.
- Plus an extra bonus if all the workers reaches it.
- This great reason would spur supervisors to train their workers to do a better job.
- Every worker's progress will be rated publicly and recorded individualy by bar charts. On the basis of this chart they will be rewarded.

(c) *Discuss the implication and limitation of Hawthorne studies.*

Ans. Implications of Hawthorne studies are as follows:

- It is now clear that factory is a social system and informal group in a plant; equally affect human behaviour as formal group.
- A worker is not merely an 'economic man' who is motivated only by the monetary benefits. Non-monetary incentives are sometime more important in influencing workers' attitude to their work.
- There is a possibility of conflict between company and informal group. It may be because of incompatible objectives of the both.

- Sometimes, informal leaders are more important and impressive than formal in directing group behaviour because he identifies group attitude, opinion, and objective more efficiently than formal leader.

Limitations

- Behavioural scientists believe that in this series of experiment whatever conclusion were drawn it lacks scientific objectivity.
- Some felt that there was bias and preconception on the part of the Harvard researcher.
- The study has ignored the existence of trade unions.

Apart from these criticisms, the Hawthorne studies comes with the outcome of human relation is an important part of company. And it drew attention to the social needs as an additional source of motivation.

(d) *Figure out the importance of reliability and validity of test.*

Ans. Importance of reliability and validity test on recruitment.

Reliability and validity are two technical properties of a test that indicates the quality and usefulness of the test. These are the two most important features of a test. Management should examine these features when evaluating the suitability of the test for organization use. Reliability estimates the consistency of test measurement, or more simply the degree to which an instrument measures the same way each time it is used under the same conditions with the same subjects. Validity, on the other hand, involves the accuracy of measurement and what management supposed to measure. An employment test is considered "good" if the following can be said about it:

- The test measures what it claims to measure consistently or reliably. This means that if a person were to take the test again, the person would get a similar test score.
- The test measures what it claims to measure. For example, a test of mental ability does in fact measure mental ability, and not some other characteristic.
- The test is job-relevant. In other words, the test measures one or more characteristics that are important to the job.
- By using the test, more effective employment decisions can be made about individuals. For example, an arithmetic test may help you to select qualified workers for a job that requires knowledge of arithmetic operations.

The degree to which a test has these qualities is indicated by two technical properties: reliability and validity

(e) *Explain the different work related stress.*

Ans. The word 'stress' is defined by the Oxford Dictionary as 'a state of affair involving demand of physical or mental energy'. According to

McGrath, 'A person experience stress when a situation is perceived as presenting a demand which threatens to exceed the person's capabilities and resources for meeting it'.

Stress is a condition of strain on one's emotions, thought processes and physical conditions that seem to threaten one's ability to cope with the environment.

The common causes of workplace stress are:

- The fear of losing one's job.
- Unreasonable demands for performance.
- Lack of interpersonal relationship among the employees.
- Lack of interpersonal communication between the employer and the employees.
- Long working hours.
- Less time to spend with the family.
- Under utilization of skills.
- Underpaid jobs.
- A promotion that did not materialize.

Unlike stress in general, the work related stress affects men and women equally. Older employees are affected more than their younger counterparts. Stress at workplace could be due to:

- External causes like dangerous working condition or poor interpersonal relationship with the colleagues.
- Internal causes like physical or psychological illness.
- Acute causes.
- Long term causes.

(f) Suitable working condition is required for high production. Discuss.

Ans. *'The quality of employees will be directly proportional to the quality of life you maintain for them'* – **Charles E. Bryan.**

In the factories like low illuminations which result into eye strain, headache, fatigue, increased number of accidents, low quality of work, low output which also create low morale and satisfaction among the workers. These changes also affect the social climate of the factory. With better working conditions workers' feel that something is being done for them. This providés psychological satisfaction which helps in to maintain congenial environment with increased efficiency. Therefore, suitable working condition is required for high production.

In short,

- For higher production.
- For higher efficiency of workers.
- Increased morale and satisfaction.

- Reduce boredom and monotony.
- Reduce fatigue
- Better communication between the workers' itself and with the management.
- Encourage innovations.
- Reduce absenteeism and turnover.
- Reduce accident proneness.
- Provide healthy environment and many more.

2. Attempt any two parts of the following: (2×6=12)

(*a*) *Describe any two theories of motivation in detail.*

Ans. A simple definition of *motivation* is the ability to change behaviour. It is a drive that compels one to act because human behaviour is directed towards some goal. Motivation has been defined as: the psychological process that gives behaviour purpose and direction. It is also defined as a predisposition to behave in a purposive manner to achieve specific, unmet needs. Motivation is an internal drive to satisfy an unsatisfied need.

Maslow's hierarchy of needs is a theory in psychology, proposed by Abraham Maslow, (a professor at Brandeis University and a practicing psychologist) in his 1943 paper *A Theory of Human Motivation*,which he subsequently extended to include his observations of humans' innate curiosity.

The five levels of needs are the following:

- *Physiological*: These are basic physical comfort or bodily needs: food, sex, drink, and sleep. In the workplace, these needs translate into a safe, ergonomically designed work environment with appropriate base salary compensation.
- *Security/safety*: People want to feel safe, secure, and free from fear. They need stability, structure, and order. In the workplace, job security and fringe benefits, along with an environment free of violence, fills these needs.
- *Belongingness and love*: This is a need for friends, family, and intimacy—for social acceptance and affection from one's peers. In the workplace, this need is satisfied by participation in work groups with good relationships among co-workers and between workers and managers.
- *Esteem*: People want the esteem of others and they want to be regarded as useful, competent, and important. People also desire self-esteem and need a good self image. In the workplace, increased responsibility, high status, and recognition for contributions satisfy these needs.

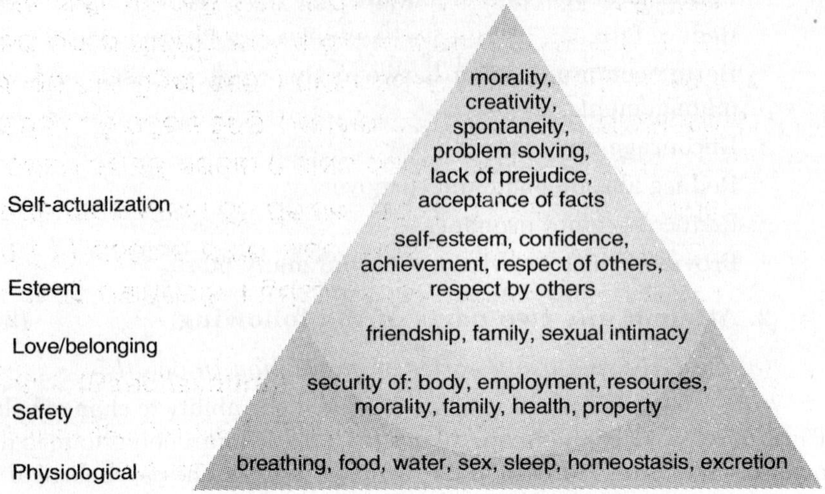

Exhibit 1

- *Self-actualization*: This highest motivation level involves people striving to actualize their full potential, to become more of what they are capable of being. They seek to attain self-fulfillment. In the workplace, people satisfy this need by being creative, receiving training, or accepting challenging assignments.

Focusing on the needs of retraining for growth and challenge as well as rewards and recognition is important to the quality of work life. Managers can affect the physical, social, and psychological environment in the workplace, and they have a responsibility to help employees fulfill their needs.

ERG Theory

In his work, Clayton Alderfer expanded on Maslow's hierarchical theory. He proposed three need categories and suggested that movement between the need levels is not necessarily straightforward. Failure to meet a higher-order need could cause an individual to regress to a lower-order need. These *ERG theory* categories are:

- *Existence needs*: Needs for physical well-being.
- *Relatedness needs*: Needs for satisfactory relationships with others.
- *Growth needs*: The development of human potential and the desire for personal growth and increased competence.

(*b*) *what are the consequences of satisfaction and dissatisfaction at workplace?*

Ans. Job satisfaction occurs when an employee feels he has accomplished something having importance and value; worthy of recognition; sense of joy. Satisfaction creates confidence, loyalty and ultimately improved quality in the performance of the workers. Job satisfaction describes how content an individual is with his or her job. According to Robbins, job satisfaction is "a positive feeling about one's job resulting from an evaluation of its characteristics". Job satisfaction has been defined as a pleasurable emotional state resulting from the appraisal of one's job.

Consequences of Job Satisfaction/ Dissatisfaction

- *Work Performance*–Work environment, relationship with co-workers, superior and management help to make workers more efficient and by this they get satisfied more easily as compared to others. All their satisfaction is reflected in their better work performance.
- *Absenteeism / Turnover* – There is a positive relation between the absenteeism/ turnover and satisfaction. If workers are satisfied than the rate of absenteeism/turnover reduced.
- *Motivation* –If workers are satisfied from their job than he/she is easily motivated to do the job.
- *Conflicts* – Worker who are psychologically satisfied reduces the chance of conflicts with management, co-workers and their own intra conflicts/ inner conflicts.
- *Attitude* – Satisfied workers have positive attitude towards work. They are more committed to management and their own work. They help to maintain healthy environment in the workplace.
- *Health Problem* – It includes not only physical but mental health also. Dissatisfied workers have the problem of anxiety, headache, muscular pain, low concentration, sleeping disorder and many more problems.
- *Accident Proneness* – Dissatisfied workers are more accident prone as compared to satisfied workers. There are many reasons which increase the frequency of accidents due to lack of concentration, poor health, stress etc.

Tips for Reducing Dissatisfaction

- Provide adequate working environment.
- Promotion as par the capability and efficiency of individual.
- Salary should be equal and justice.
- Provide guidance or counseling for dissatisfied workers.
- Workers view are taken into consideration in decision making. (Workers Participation in Management)
- Provide safety measure to reduce accidents.
- Unbiased behaviour of superior should be avoided.
- Proper grievance handling machinery to reduce conflicts.
- Impose flexible work system/work hour.
- Increased autonomy.

- Emphasis on team work by which if team has not accomplished there objective within prescribed time than it will not lead dissatisfaction for individual.
- Job rotation reduces the monotony.
- Proper communication system between co-workers and management.
- Equal chance of training and development or required workers.

(c) *What are the reasons which motivate the individual to join a particular group?*

Ans. Groups exist in every organization and they affect the behaviour of their members. They not only affect the behaviour of individuals but also influence the work performed by them which ultimately affect the organization. Such groups are created by the organization as well as by organization members for their own satisfaction.

A group is defined as 'two or more individuals, interacting and mutually dependent on each other, who have come together to achieve particular objectives' or 'group are consisting two or more persons who are interacting with one another in such a way that each person is influenced by each other. In simple words, group means two or more individuals who share common values, norms and interest.

Why Individuals Join the Group?

Most of the individuals join the informal groups because some of their needs will be satisfied. They work in vocational groups because they must make a living, they join social groups because they need the companionship of others and they join clubs for reason of prestige. E.V. Schneider holds that informal groups are meant to afford the workers:

(i) Relief from monotony, boredom and fatigue.

(ii) Opportunity to acquire status.

(iii) An increased flow of emotional responses.

(iv) Opportunity for independence.

(v) Increased security.

Beach lists five reasons which he claims, are responsible for the formation of groups:

(i) *Companionship and Friendship* – A group gives a person a feeling of belonging and makes it possible for him to socialize with his/her friends.

(ii) *Security and Protection* – A group can be a source of security and protection against management, especially if a member of the group has made mistake and need to keep the foreman from discovering them.

(iii) *Advance their own Interest* – They may try to secure benefits such as better and higher piece rate or in the case of office workers, large desks, longer lunch hours or other symbols of status including favourable working conditions.

(iv) *Need for Assistance/Advice on one's job* – Some times individual wants or need some sort of advice or assistance for their betterment.

(v) *Communicating Information* – Group serves as a means of communicating information about the company or organization which does not come through official channels or comes faster on the grapevine/informal communication.

Stephen P. Robbins gives six reasons of why people join groups:

(i) *Security* – By joining a group, individuals can reduce the insecurity of "standing alone". People feel stronger, have fewer self doubts and are more resistant to threats when they are a part of a group.

(ii) *Status* – Inclusion in a group that is viewed as important by others provides recognition and status for its members.

(iii) *Self Esteem* – Groups can provide people with a feeling of self worth. That is, in addition to conveying status to those outside the group, membership can also give increased feelings of worth to the group members themselves.

(iv) *Affiliation* – Groups can fulfill social needs. People enjoy the regular interaction that comes with group membership. For many people, these on-the-job interactions are their primary source for fulfilling their needs for affiliation.

(v) *Power* – What cannot be achieved individually often becomes possible through group action. There is power in numbers.

(vi) *Goal Attainment* – There are times when it takes more than one person to accomplish a particular task—there is a need to pool talents, knowledge or power in order to complete a job. In such instances, management relies on the use of a formal group.

3. Attempt any two of the following: (2×6=12)

(*a*) *What are the actions taken by the management to reduce the boredom of their workers?*

Ans. Boredom is commonly referred to as mental fatigue or psychological fatigue which leads to work decrement. Boredom is often associated with jobs that are repetitive. It is usually associated with work that is basically uninteresting to the workers who perform that particular task.

According to Maier (1970), "It is claimed that repetitive work makes robots of men and that it destroys such human values as pride in workmanship and individuality".

Boredom has been defined by C. D. Fisher in terms of its central-psychological processes: "an unpleasant, transient affective state in which the individual feels a pervasive lack of interest in and difficulty concentrating on the current activity."[2]

M. R. Leary and others describe boredom as "an affective experience associated with cognitive attention processes."[3]

These definitions make it clear that boredom arises not from lack of things to do but from the inability to latch onto any specific activity.

Causes and Remedies of Boredom

- *Repetitive Nature of Work*

  Boredom caused by repetitive work. When workers do the same job over prolonged period of time, then the chance of being bored from that particular work is on high. It is true fact that, when the work is repeated it becomes like machine and require no logical work, attention, concentration on the part of the worker which results into boredom.

  The best method to overcome the boredom at this stage is 'job rotation' or exchange of jobs. By this, worker becomes more attentive, they concentrate on new task which automatically encourage them to do work.

- *Rest Pause*

  If rest pauses becomes if lengthy it leads to boredom. A long rest pause usually creates disturbance in different type of mental work because the worker loses the continuity and interest of work.

  The remedy is to introduce frequent and short rest pauses seem to be more effective. The amount of rest pause varies with the nature of work because manual work require more frequent rest pause as against mental work.

- *Ambience*

  Unfavorable ambience also creates boredom. When an employee dislike his/her workplace then after some time they automatically get bored.

  One of the remedy to overcome this problem is introduction of music. Music at workplace helps in reducing boredom, improving the mental state of workers and raising the level of production and efficiency.

- *Intelligence*

  One of the causes of boredom is intelligence. It seemed quite unusual that the most important asset of the workers' leads to boredom. The reason behind is that worker with low intelligence may be satisfied with the job like floor cleaning but under such situations an intelligent worker will not find any interest and job satisfaction.

How to overcome this problem is one of the major concerns for employer. Here, employers try to designate the work based on employee's capability and interest and of course their personal profile definitely minimizes the chance of being bored.

- *Incomplete Task*

  If work is not completed at time, worker develops a sense of dissatisfaction which sometime creates boredom. If management divides the task into different sub-parts and when a part is completed, the employee experiences a feeling of completion.

Other ways to reduce Boredom

- Psychological guidance and counseling should be given to neurotic workers. Because neurotic workers lose interest in the job and get bored very quickly.
- If repetitive work is made entirely automatic or semi-automatic, the feeling of boredom can be reduced to a considerable extent.
- Group discussion can be used to reduce boredom.
- When feeling of progress is introduced amongst the worker's at workplace, it avoids boredom.
- Introduction of social events also reduce the work boredom like picnic, formal get-together etc.
- Encouraging informal group in workplace will differently reduce the boredom.
- Boredom reduces by giving employees a responsibility and opportunities of judgments.

(*b*) *Define the concept of job analysis and also explain job analysis contents.*

Ans. A job is a bundle of tasks that is performed by the workers' in an organization. A job analysis involves an systematic collection of information about a job. It is an accurate study of the various components of a job. It is not only concerned with the analysis of duties and conditions of work but also with the individual qualification and experience of the workers.

Definition

Job analysis is the process of gathering and organizing detailed information about various jobs within the organization so that managers can better understand the process through which they are performed most effectively.

Job analysis includes job description and job specification. Job description includes tasks and responsibilities of a job. Job title, duties, machines, tools and equipments, working conditions and hazards comes under job description.

The capabilities that the job holder should possess for doing a particular job forms a part of job specification. Education, experience, training, skills, communication are a part of job specification. Whatever the particular job demands, there are certain abilities required to discharge the task. Job analysis is important if an organization is to fully understand the skills and competencies required to perform a particular job.

Contents of Job Analysis

Job description is written record of duties, responsibilities and requirement of a particular job. It is concerned with the job itself and not with the work. It is a statement describing the job in such terms as its title, location, duties, working condition etc. In other words, it tells us "what to be done and how it is to be done and why". It is a standard of function, in which it defines an appropriate and authorized content of a job.

Job specification is a standard of personnel qualifications and designates the qualities required for an acceptable performance. It is a written record of the requirements sought in an individual worker for a given job. In other words, it refers to a summary of the personnel characteristics required for a job. It is a statement of the minimum acceptable human qualities necessary for the proper performance of a job.

Job Analysis

Job Description

A statement containing items such as:
- Job title
- Location
- Job summary
- Duties
- Machines, tools and equipment
- Materials
  Supervision given or received
- Working condition
- Hazards

Job Specification

A statement of human qualification necessary to do the job. Usually contains such items as:
- Education
- Experience
- Training
- Judgement
- Initiative
- Physical effort
- Physical skills
- Responsibilities
- Communication skills
- Emotional characteristics
- Unusual sensory demands such as sight, smell, hearing.

(c) *Discuss selection process in detail with the help of suitable example.*

Ans. Selection is a process of selecting most desirable candidates among others for a particular job. Picking those candidates who have relevant qualification to fill jobs in an organization. Selection process is to determine whether an applicant meets the qualification for a specific job and to choose the applicant who is most likely to perform well in that job. In other words, to find out which job applicant will be successful, if hired.

Process of Selection

Selection is generally a series of hurdles or steps. Each one must be successfully cleared before the applicant proceeds to the next.

1. **Invite application:** For successfully complete the process of selection it is required that number of applicants should be large. At the time of receiving application, office manager or even receptionist entertain the candidate thus to make good image of the organization in the mind of applicants.
2. **Screening of application :** Whatever the application received by organization is now screened with certain criteria like education, experience, age and other related information for a particular job. From here the rejection will be started, applicant who is desirable comes to next stage and who are not will be rejected at this initial stage.
3. **Preliminary interview:** When the large number of applicants are available, the preliminary interview is desirable of both the applicant seeking employment and of the company also.
4. **Application Blank:** Application blank is one of the easiest and common method by which company gets the maximum information on various aspects of the candidate's academic, social, demographic, working experience and references should be in their own hand-writing.
5. **Psychological Test:** The next step in the process of selection is very important because from here the main and critical test of candidature begins. What kind of psychological test is used for judging the candidate is another important decision? A test is standardized, having objective to measure of a candidates' behaviour, performance or attitude by the attitude test, intelligence test, personality test, achievement test, simulation test etc.
6. **Interview:** When the candidates pass their psychological tests then the next step is to face interview. Interview is a face to face interaction between interviewer and interviewee. The interviewer checks that the particular candidature is suitable for specified job or not and interviewee gets maximum information about their job profile, salary, etc.
7. **Reference Checking:** The use of references is common in most selection procedure. It helps in checking out the candidate' character, their qualification what they have, their experience is appropriate or not, other related data should be authenticated or not.

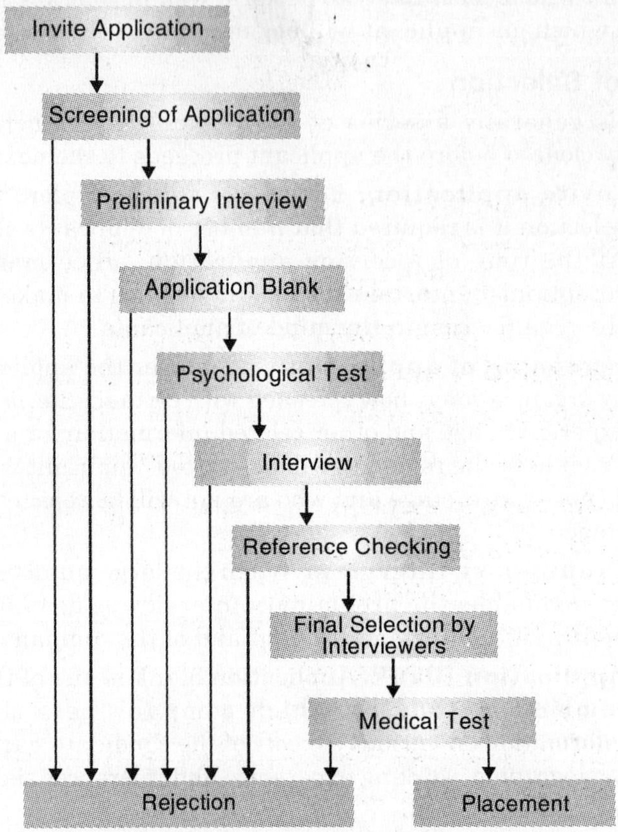

Exhibit 2: Selection Process

8. **Final Selection by Interviewers:** After completing entire above steps final selection should now be done by the interviewers.
9. **Medical Test/ Physical Examination:** Physical or medical examination reveals whether or not a candidate possess physical qualities like acute hearing, clear vision, high stamina, clear tone of voice.
10. **Placement:** The final step in selection process is placement of candidate to their job and work place.

4. Attempt any two parts of the following:

(a) What do you mean by performance appraisal? Discuss its objectives.

Ans. Performance appraisal is the process of obtaining, analyzing and recording information about the relative worth of an employee. The focal point of the performance appraisal is measuring and improving the actual performance of the employee and also the future potential of the employee.

According to Flippo, "Performance appraisal is the systematic, periodic and an impartial rating of an employee's excellence in the matters pertaining to his present job and his potential for a better job." Performance appraisal is a systematic way of reviewing and assessing the performance of an employee during a particular period of time and planning for his future.

Scoot, Clothier and Spriegel have defined merit rating or performance appraisal as the process of evaluating the employee's performance on the job in terms of requirement of the job.

According to Yoder, performance appraisal refers to all formal procedures used in working organizations to evaluate personalities and contributions and potential of group members. An evaluation of how well an employee performs his or her job compared to a set of predetermined standards.

Performance appraisal is a systematic review of a person's work and achievements over a recent period, usually leading to plans for the future.

Process by which a manager or consultant (1) examines and evaluates an employee's work behaviour by comparing it with preset standards, (2) documents the results of the comparison, and (3) uses the results to provide feedback to the employee to show where improvements are needed and why. Performance appraisals are employed to determine who needs what training, and who will be promoted, demoted, retained, or fired.

Objectives of Performance Management

- It facilitates the relationship and communication between management and employees.
- To assess the performance of the employees over a given period of time.
- To give feedback to the employees about their past performance.
- To find out any gap between the actual and the desired performance of the employees.
- Provide clarity of the expectations and responsibilities of the functions to be performed by the employees.
- To analyze the strengths and weaknesses of the employees so as to identify the training and development needs of the future.
- To plan career development, human resource planning based on potentialities.
- Performance appraisal can help in the development of scientific basis for reward allocation, wage fixation, incentives etc.
- To reduce the grievances of the employees.

(b) Discuss the different types of training methods.

Ans. There are lots of methods by which management train there employees. They choose methods according to the requirement of the training. In general, training is of two types: on the job training and off-the-job training.

- *Job Instruction Training (JIT)* – In this method supervisors train operational workers. It consists of all the necessary steps with proper sequence which is required for a particular task. These steps not only explain what is to be done but also emphasis how it is to be done and why. It involves four steps (i) physically and psychologically prepare the trainees for instruction. (ii) presentation or demonstration of the particular task to the trainees, what are their responsibility, description about the job etc. is included in this phase. (iii) at this phase trainees are tired out of what they understand from the instructions. (iv) this is the last phase of JIT where supervisors encourage trainees to solve their queries if any, regarding particular task.
- *Vestibule Training/Training Centre* – In this method trainees are trained in the company classrooms. Where they get theoretical knowledge about the work which they are going to perform. This method is more useful when there are large number of trainees, have to be trained for same kind of work at same time.

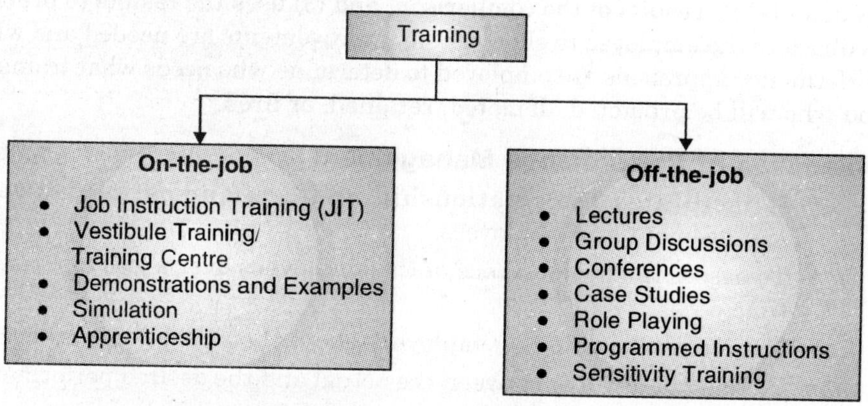

Exhibit 3: Types of Training

- *Demonstrations and Examples* – It is just opposite to classroom or vestibule training methods. Here supervisor describes and display something related to the job and also explains the step-by-step explanations of why and what supervisor or trainer is doing.
- *Simulation* – It is generally duplicate setup of the workplace, where workers feel and touch the simulated equipments and make practice to use equipment without any problem.
- *Apprenticeship* – Apprenticeship refers to the period of service as a learner of a trade or handicraft. The apprentice, usually a boy at the beginning of his working life, was bound by a legal agreement to serve an employer for a fixed number of years during which the employer promises to instruct him. Example are carpenters, a

machinist, weavers, jewellers, electricians, a draughtsman, a tool-maker, a printer, a pattern designer, diesinkers etc

- *Lectures* – This method is used to create understanding of a topic or to influence behaviour, attitudes through lecture. A lecture can be in written or oral form. Lecture is, telling someone about something. It is less expensive and can be reached to large number of people at same time.
- *Group Discussions* – In this method the training is supported, elaborated, explained, or expanded on through interactions both among the trainees and between the trainer and the trainees. The interaction and the communication between these two make it much more effective and powerful than the lecture method.
- *Case Studies* – This method usually consists of description of some events that have occurred in the organization. The basic objective of case study is to find solution of a particular problem. The trainees review the case and find out the various alternatives and finally suggest the solution.
- *Role Playing* – In this method two or more trainees are assigned parts to play in front of others. These parts do not involve any rehearsals. They are simply informed about the situation and the respective roles they have to play. The usual subjects involve in role playing are grievance handling, hiring, retrenchment, appraisal interview etc.
- *Programmed Instructions* – Programmed instruction is a Computer-based training that comprises of graphics, multimedia, text that is connected to one another and is stored in memory. A programmed instruction involves breaking information down into meaningful units and it provides the trainee with content, information, asks questions, and based on the answer goes to the next level of information *i.e.*, if the trainee gives the correct answer than they forward to the new information. And if the trainee gives the wrong answer then they revert to their old position and review relevant information in more elaborate manner. This method is very useful because it gives immediate feedback, frequently review the information and it allows the trainee to learn according to their capability.
- *Sensitivity Training* – This is the method of group therapy in which the members of the group, under the guidance of a leader, seek a deeper understanding of themselves and others, as by the exchange of intimate feelings and experiences, physical contacts, etc. The main objective of sensitivity training is not to make trainees conform to a set of acceptable norms and ideas. Sensitivity training involves varied methods like case studies, simulated exercise, role playing etc.

(c) *How can the effectiveness of training programme be evaluated?*

Ans. There are various methods by which management check the effectiveness of their training programmes, some are:

- Reaction of Trainees;
- Learning;
- Behavioural Changes; and
- Impact on Organization Effectiveness and many more.

Reaction of trainee is one of the best methods by which management can evaluate the effectiveness of the training programme. Under this method management tries to collect the response of the trainee. They take help of questionnaire, survey or simple interview by which they asks certain specific questions regarding the training programme and collect the responses.

The learning tendency of worker is more improved after training. If they can easily learn the new technologies, cope with surroundings all this express the effectiveness of the training programme.

One of the ways suggested by Blum and Naylor[8] is by comparing the change in performance of a group receiving training to the change in performance of a comparable group which did not receive the training. If two groups *i.e.*, control group and experimental group are both evaluated before the training introduced after imposing tests on the experimental group what are the changes seen in the experimental group is compared with control group. If any difference is found in the same situation in both comparable groups it leads to the importance and the effectiveness of training.

The following criteria are suggested by Lindahl (1949)[9] for checking the results of training:

- Better quality of production.
- Increase in the number of operators able to meet job standards.
- Reduction in time required to do a specific job.
- Decrease in breakable supplies or tools.
- Decrease in absenteeism.
- Reduction in separation rate.
- Reduction in operational costs.
- Better performance on personnel tools such as tests, rating scales and attitude surveys.

❍❍❍